DREAM POWER

IT CAN CHANGE YOUR LIFE.

"I can almost guarantee that your whole life will be different if you read and study DREAM POWER. Why do I recommend it as one of the most important self-help books ever written? DREAM POWER changed my life." **Barbara Seaman**
author of FREE AND FEMALE

"Ann Faraday looks through eclectic glasses at the phenomenon of dreaming. Faraday's background fits the topic admirably... She believes that we should not leave dream research to the therapist but that each of us should deepen his self-knowledge by analyzing his own dreams ... Helpful ..." *Psychology Today*

"A book for dream fanciers and fancy dreamers. DREAM POWER offers a controversial cook's tour of the night life of the mind." **Alvin Toffler**
author of FUTURE SHOCK

IT CAN CHANGE YOUR LIFE.

"Stimulating and provocative, an encouragement to probe into our dreams and our personalities. One of the first stages in an exciting exploration—and a simple do-it-yourself dream interpretation kit." *Washington Post*

"Intelligently analyzed, our dreams can give us significant insights into our relationships with others . . . DREAM POWER spells out a three-stage process by which any dreamer can examine his dreams for different kinds of meaning . . . Tremendously important messages can come on this objective level . . . spectacular examples." *Reader's Digest*

"An accessible method of tapping the 'dream power' within us all. Admirably readable, often charming—with remarkably candid references to her own life. Her theory is a discriminating mixture of Jung, Calvin Hall, and the Gestalt master Freederick Perls." **Theodore Roszak**

IT CAN CHANGE YOUR LIFE.

DREAM POWER

DR. ANN FARADAY

BERKLEY BOOKS, NEW YORK

I should like to thank Dr. Calvin Hall for having read and approved the chapter on himself and John O. Stevens of the Real People Press for allowing me to quote extensively from the works of Frederick Peris.

Copyrights from which permission to quote has been granted: Eliot, T. S. "Little Gidding" in *Four Quartets*. Copyright 1943 T. S. Eliot. Reprinted by permission of Harcourt Brace Jovanovich, Inc.
Gibran, Kahlil. *The Prophet*. Copyright 1923 Kahlil Gibran; renewed 1951 Administrators C.I.T. of Kahlil Gibran Estate. Reprinted by permission of Alfred A. Knopf, Inc.
Laing, R. D. *Knots*. Copyright © 1970 the R. D. Laing Trust. Reprinted by permission of Pantheon Books, a division of Random House, Inc.

This Berkley book contains the complete
text of the original hardcover edition.
It has been completely reset in a typeface
designed for easy reading, and was printed
from new film.

DREAM POWER

A Berkley Book / published by arrangement with
Coward, McCann and Geoghegan, Inc.

PRINTING HISTORY
Coward, McCann and Geoghegan edition published 1972
Berkley Medallion edition / February 1973
Berkley edition / May 1980

ISBN: 0-425-09498-7

A BERKLEY BOOK ® TM 757,375
Berkley Books are published by The Berkley Publishing Group,
200 Madison Avenue, New York, New York 10016.
The name "BERKLEY" and the "B" logo
are trademarks belonging to Berkley Publishing Corporation.

PRINTED IN THE UNITED STATES OF AMERICA

30   29   28   27   26   25

We begin life with the world presenting itself to us as it is. Someone—our parents, teachers, analysts—hypnotise us to "see" the world and construe it in the "right" way. These others label the world, attach names and give voices to the beings and events in it, so that thereafter, we cannot read the world in any other language or hear it saying other things to us.

The task is to break the hypnotic spell, so that we become undeaf, unblind and multilingual, thereby letting the world speak to us in new voices and write all its possible meanings in the book of our existence.

Be careful in your choice of hypnotists.

SIDNEY JOURARD

This book is dedicated to my hypnotists for showing me the error of their ways.

Respect your brothers' dreams.
　　　　　　　　　　—American Indian proverb

CONTENTS

INTRODUCTION

When I was a small child, I used to have recurring dreams of being pursued by "Creamers"—men wearing long white coats and tall white hats—whose leader was named Beasley. I remember asking my mother what Creamers were, and she replied, "I think they're chocolates, darling." But I knew they weren't—they were men dressed in white who chased me throughout the night. I knew Beasley was the little caretaker of the tennis club across the road, but his apparent insignificance and harmlessness bore no resemblance to the Creamer leader. I also had another recurring dream around the same time. The "Candy Man"—a man dressed in clown's garb and with a skin disease down one side of his face—would wait in shop doorways or behind hedges and try to kiss me when I came by. Neither my parents nor teachers could throw any light on the Creamers, Beasley, or the Candy Man and passed them off as "nothing but bad dreams," exhorting me to put the whole thing out of my head.

After a year or two, these dreams stopped, but I had

others just as incomprehensible and worrying, and no one was able to help me with them. Many years later, I took a psychology degree in the hope of learning about the unconscious aspects of experience, including dreams, but again was disappointed. I learned much about rats, reaction time, and statistics, but nothing about myself. After graduation, I went on to do research but soon found that no funds would be forthcoming for any study of the *meaning* of dreams, a subject the academic establishment deemed far too unscientific. So I plunged into experimental research on the dreaming process and obtained my PhD for a thesis on "Factors Affecting the Experimental Recall of Dreams." It was my hope that something of human interest might come out as a by-product of this research, and indeed it did, although the most interesting feature of the work never found its way into my reports.

My experiments involved volunteer subjects coming to my home or the hospital, being wired up to recording apparatus and awakened several times during the night to report their dreams. They were all firmly informed in advance that they would receive no dream interpretation and no help with their problems, since my concern was solely to measure their recall of dreams. They all accepted this condition without demur, saying they were delighted to offer their nocturnal adventures to science. Their dreams, however, told me a different story. Time and time again, my subjects would dream of me as a psychotherapist, doctor, mother, or teacher to whom they brought their dreams in the hope of help with their problems. It became clear that, almost without exception, every subject at a deep level expected some personal help from revealing his dreams.

This did not really surprise me, as man has always sought significance in his dreams. In earlier ages, people consulted shamans, priests, or other wise men for interpretations. More recently, this role has passed to psychotherapists with each particular school of therapy having its own theory about the meaning of dreams. But the subjects who brought their dreams to me were not "sick," any more than I had been as a child. They were merely curious

14

and a little troubled about their dreams which they felt might help them solve some of their life problems, but had no reason whatever to seek professional psychotherapeutic help. Meanwhile, I had myself embarked on a Freudian training analysis but found this so dogmatic that it gave me little more help in understanding my own dreams than my research work did. In fact, I soon came to the conclusion that I could interpret my dreams better than my analyst. So I began to wonder whether, just as modern experimental dream research has shown that we all dream regularly, it might be possible to take this process one stage further by showing how any reasonably intelligent person could learn to recall, interpret, and use his dreams for greater self-knowledge without expert help. So my studies leading to this book began.

The book is divided into four parts. Part I, "The Stuff of Dreams," gives a general review of the more important aspects of modern experimental dream research which I feel are essential for a comprehensive approach to dream interpretation. While some of this work has been widely publicized during the past few years and many readers will already be familiar with it, I have found from personal experience that many old myths about dreams still persist and have indeed been joined by new ones. People have a tendency to pick out the results of modern research that fit their own particular view of dreams and to forget all those that contradict it. I have also found that many of the more exciting speculations arising out of the early dream experiments during the 1950's have been accepted as facts although subsequent research has failed to verify them.

The literature on dreaming is now so vast that it has been impossible for me to cover all aspects of it, and I give suggestions for further reading at the end of the book. Chapter 1 gives a very general background and may be skipped by those who are familiar with it. The following four chapters incorporate some material not previously published, including results from my own experimental dream research. My findings are based on five years of research carried out at London University on approximately one hundred long-suffering subjects, who I hope will now receive the help they were denied at the time. Chapter 3, on the forgetting of dreams, is particularly relevant to the practical use of dreams for self-understanding, and Chapter 5 presents my conclusions about the nature of the dreaming process. These conclusions, together with the facts about dreaming presented in Part 1 of the book, are based on present knowledge and may well have to be revised later in the light of new findings.

Part II reviews the dream interpretation theories and methods of four major "Explorers of the Dream" in the light of modern experimental findings. This review is not purely theoretical but draws on my personal experience of all of them. For example, I describe a number of incidents from my Freudian training analysis, consisting of both individual and group work, and I spell out how the dogmatism of the Freudian approach led me to abandon it after a period of some three years. I also draw on my experience of a shorter period of Jungian analysis and on my subsequent training and practice in the Gestalt therapy of Frederick Perls, which I now use with both individuals and in groups. And for the past fifteen years I have been collecting my own dreams at home and interpreting them along the lines suggested by Calvin Hall in his pioneer work *The Meaning of Dreams,* published in 1953.

Part III presents my own comprehensive and simplified approach to the use of dreams at home, drawing upon all four methods in the light of modern knowledge. I call it "The Three Faces of Dreaming," since in my view dreams should always be considered in three aspects. Looking outward, they often bring to our attention things we have failed to notice in waking life. Second, we may use them as mirrors that reflect our attitudes and prejudices, and finally, by looking inward and treating the dream as an existential message about the state of our inner world, we can often discover the hidden source of our problems and regain long-buried aspects of the personality. Once such knowledge has been made available to us through dreams, it is then up to us to change irrational and destructive patterns of behavior which may previously have been impairing our capacity for happiness and fulfillment in everyday

16

life, and I suggest ways in which this may be done.

Part IV is called "Looking Forward" and expresses some of my hopes and speculations about the future possiblities of dream power. Chapter 11 considers ways in which the use of dreams for greater self-knowledge could become a growing feature of life throughout our society, in families, churches, education, and even business and government, as well as in many new forms of professional psychotherapy. It is a commonplace that mankind stands on the brink of disaster if technological progress is not soon matched by some comparable psychological or spiritual growth, and I am convinced that dream power offers a royal road to such growth. In this, I may appear somewhat visionary, but I feel that without enthusiasm and vision no new project ever gets off the ground. In my final chapter, I consider dreams that hint at some of the strange new mental powers that become available to us if we learn to remove some of the emotional blocks that at present bedevil ordinary life.

In my view, psychoanalysts have done us a disservice by associating dream interpretation with psychological illness and spreading the idea that any form of self-therapy which involves "probing the depths" is a dangerous business. While it is true that there are disturbed people who cannot cope with life without expert therapeutic help, there are also millions of other intelligent and basically "normal" people who are perfectly capable of exploring their own dreams for greater self-knowledge. Those who experiment with dream power and find it unduly disturbing should of course seek professional help, but in my experience, very few people fall into this category. Even those who do will profit by having their need for help brought to their notice. Anyone who becomes really disturbed by the experiment suggested in this book is in fact stirring up not "monsters of the deep," but conflicts already hovering just below the surface of conscious awareness which are likely to break out and cause trouble at any moment. If these conflicts come to light during the course of do-it-yourself dream interpretation, they are thereby forestalled from breaking out under more dangerous circumstances.

I believe we have entered a new age of self-reliance and personal responsibility in which former reticence about the inner life is being abandoned and the demand for external conformity is being relaxed. The need in this new age is for more deliberate inquiry into the hidden forces of the personality which shape our waking behavior and for communication of our insights for public discussion. The main theme of this book is that much of man's unhappiness is caused, first, by self-ignorance and, second, by self-concealment. It is for this reason that I have exposed much of my inner life by describing my personal adventures and experiments with dreams. In this, I believe I am breaking new ground. There are many books in which psychotherapists have described their patients' dreams and case histories, but most have remained silent about their own or else used a pseudonym in reporting them. This reticence probably springs from a fear that frankness about their personal lives will detract from their authority as therapists, but I am convinced that reliance on this kind of authority is entirely misplaced in the modern world. The day of the guru is over. I hope that my attempts at self-disclosure will encourage others to share their own experiences of dream power in a similar spirit of openness and honesty.

It is probably now too late for me to solve the mystery of the Creamers, Beasley, and the Candy Man. My psychotherapist friends to whom I have related them have been prolific with suggestions, but none of them has resonated at a feeling level in my own mind. The only sure way of penetrating the meaning of a dream is for the dreamer to explore it as soon as possible after experiencing it. As parents and teachers learn the art of dream power in their own lives, they will find they are able to help their children understand the mysteries of the night, and perhaps my greatest hope for this book is that it may play a part in helping the next generation to grow up in a world where this extra dimension of human experience is accepted as everyone's birthright.

PART I

THE STUFF OF DREAMS

CHAPTER 1

THE THIRD STATE OF EXISTENCE

The year 1953 was a fatal one for many long-cherished myths about dreams. Until this time, it was generally believed that a dream was a random, fleeting, and probably instantaneous experience, dependent for its occurrence on such stimuli as indigestion, a full bladder, worry, or creaking doors. A night of deep, dreamless sleep, started well before midnight, was a well-known prescription for health and happiness, believed even by those who speculated that dreams might have a psychological or possibly prophetic meaning. The scientific literature on the subject contained nothing to contradict such views, nor was it able to throw light on the puzzling phenomenon of why some people recall a dream almost every night, while others deny all knowledge of the experience.

The discovery which marked the turning point in the history of dream research, and replaced fantasy with fact, took place in the Department of Physiology at the University of Chicago and, like so many other scientific discoveries, was made quite by accident. Professor Nathaniel Kleitman, the world-famous expert on sleep, was conducting a series of experiments on the sleep of babies when one of his students, Eugene Aserinsky, noted that an infant's eyes moved rapidly and jerkily under the closed lids for short periods during sleep. He reported this finding to Kleitman, and together they decided to extend their study to the sleep of adults to discover whether or not similar rapid eye movements would be observed, and if so, what might be their significance.

While it is possible to observe eye movements directly during sleep by standing over the sleeper and watching the eyeballs move under the closed lids, this is a wearisome if not impossible task for an experimenter to undertake for any length of time. So Aserinsky and Kleitman improved on this method by monitoring the eye movements of sleeping subjects by means of an electroencephalograph, commonly known as an EEG machine. This is a device normally used to make recordings of the electrical activity of the brain by means of electrodes, tiny metal disks attached to the scalp of the subject. These electrodes transmit signals from the brain to the EEG machine, which amplifies them a million times so that they are translated into a written record that can be read by the human eye. The record is made on long rolls of paper and is known as the electroencephalogram, or EEG for short, and it represents a picture of the person's brain waves. In a similar way, electrodes placed around the eyes detect the electrical activity that occurs when the eyes move, thus producing a record of eye movements—known to researchers as the electro-oculogram, or EOG.

The Chicago pioneers made a breakthrough, not only by monitoring eye movements concurrently with brain waves, but also by making *night-long* EEG and EOG recordings, an operation never previously attempted. They observed four distinct kinds of brain wave spanning the entire sleep period, which are now known as Stages 1, 2, 3, and 4 EEG. Stage 1 is considered to be the lightest stage of sleep because it corresponds most closely to the kind of record obtained from people who are awake, while Stage 4 is considered the deepest stage of sleep because its record closely resembles that of coma.

Until this time, it had been supposed that sleep consisted of a gradual transition from waking to drowsiness, followed by an increase in depth from Stage 1 through to Stage 4, and then a gradual return to Stage 1 and wakefulness at the end of the sleep period. By carrying out all-night recordings, Aserinsky and Kleitman made the striking discovery that during the course of seven or eight hours of normal sleep, there were *four or five* periods of "emergence" from the deeper stages of sleep back to Stage 1. They found that as the subject falls asleep, he passes quickly through "descending" Stage 1, spending perhaps five minutes in this stage, before progressing rapidly through Stages 2, 3, and 4 to deepest sleep. He may spend half an hour or more in Stage 4 before ascending through Stages 3 and 2 to his first period of "ascending" or "emergent" Stage 1 sleep. Usually, he spends no more than a few minutes in this stage before once again descending to deeper sleep.

During this second cycle, he may not even reach Stage 4, but if he does, he spends much less time here than he did during the first cycle. He then ascends once more to Stage 1, this time spending perhaps twenty minutes or so in this stage before once again descending into deeper sleep. This cycle of descent and ascent is repeated throughout the night in cycles lasting approximately ninety minutes. The periods of Stage 1 sleep become progressively longer, and Stages 3 and 4 become shorter as morning approaches. Indeed, toward the end of the sleep period, a person is spending most of his time in Stages 1 and 2.

It must be emphasized that the above is an idealized picture of the sleep cycle. Actual sleep patterns vary somewhat from one individual to another, or for the same person from night to night. But the fact remains that the cyclic nature of sleep generally has never failed to appear in all the thousands of subjects who have taken part in sleep experiments throughout the world during the past two decades. It seems to be an in-built mechanism dependent

21

on some biological rhythm within the body.

The sleep cycle is not affected by our bedtime if this remains more or less constant from night to night. (If we go to bed much later than usual on a particular night, we may have our first emergent Stage 1 period sooner after sleep onset than we normally do). So, whether we follow the advice of the health pundits and settle down before midnight, or whether we normally retire several hours later, the sleep cycle follows its inexorable pattern, in which almost all our deep sleep takes place during the first few hours, and most of our light sleep toward morning. The motto "early to bed" may be a very good one for many reasons, but we do not increase our normal quota of deep sleep by obeying it. During a night of seven or eight hours' sleep, we spend approximately 12 percent of this time in Stage 4 sleep and 25 percent in Stage 1 sleep.

The cyclic nature of sleep was not the only dramatic discovery made by the Chicago pioneers. When they came to look at the eye-movement record, they found that Stages 2, 3, and 4 were normally accompanied by slow eye movements or ocular quiescence, while the periods of *emergent* Stage 1 were almost invariably associated with rapid, jerky eye movements which often appeared in clusters. (They did not appear in "descending" Stage 1 at sleep onset.) The researchers also noted that these rapid eye movements—or REM's, as they are now called for short—were binocularly synchronous, that is, both eyes moved in the same direction as though the sleeper were watching a play, in contrast to the slow eye movements of the non rapid eye movement (NREM) periods, Stages 2, 3, and 4, in which the eyes no longer moved in unison. And a very exciting play it must be, mused the researchers as they watched the sometimes frantic flickings of the pen over the paper during Stage 1 REM periods.

Increased activity in other parts of the body was also noted during REM periods. The autonomic nervous system showed great irregularities in pulse and respiration rates, and in blood pressure. There was a higher rate of oxygen consumption in the brain, and males displayed full or partial penile erections. Most muscles became quite flaccid

22

and lost their reflexes although very small movements such as twitching or grimacing were sometimes observed. The researchers also noted with some puzzlement that while major body movements, such as turning over in bed or stretching, generally increased immediately prior to and just after REM periods, they decreased to almost total stillness during these periods of heightened cerebral, ocular, and autonomic excitement.

One of the researchers likened the sleeper, as he is about to enter a REM period, to a spectator at the theater. Before the curtain rises, he shuffles and fidgets in his seat. As the curtain goes up, he becomes still and attentive. The play begins and he follows the action with his eyes: he becomes excited as the plot unfolds, his breathing speeds up, and his heart thumps. As long as the play continues, he is wholly immersed in it, unmoving and unspeaking (sleep-walking and -talking normally take place in Stage 2 sleep). When the curtain falls, he moves and stretches, and his former bodily composure is regained. To the early investigators, the analogy seemed almost too good to be true: the sleeper could indeed be watching a play during his periods of REM sleep, but a play of his own making in which he himself was the director, producer, stage manager, principal actor, and audience all at the same time. He must, it seemed obvious, be dreaming.

The hypothesis was tested in the only way possible, by waking subjects during REM periods and asking them whether or not they were dreaming. The historic results were reported in the journal *Science* in 1953: 80 percent of awakenings from REM periods yielded vivid, detailed dream recall, against only 7 percent from the NREM periods of sleep. The excitement was enormous because until that time there had been absolutely no way of knowing exactly *when* a sleeping person was dreaming, a handicap which had virtually brought the whole area of dream research to a halt. Now, through the EEG and EOG records of sleeping subjects, it became possible for the first time in history to answer with any degree of certainty such questions as how often we dream, how long a dream lasts, whether or not there really are people who never dream, and a thousand other intriguing issues about dreams which had mystified mankind, throughout the ages.

THE D-STATE

Since the first experiment, Kleitman's results have been confirmed by many independent studies, all of them demonstrating quite clearly that the REM period is the time during which an awakening is likely to elicit the report of what we normally call a dream. It is for this reason that the REM period is often referred to as the *D-state*. Many researchers go even further in calling it the "third state of existence," a state in many ways as different from ordinary sleep (the S-state) as it is from waking.

REM sleep is also sometimes called "paradoxical" sleep for several reasons. In the first place, it appears to be a very relaxed state from the point of view of muscle tone and movement, and yet is tremendously active in so many other ways. Secondly, while its EEG is one of light sleep akin to that of waking, subjects in Stage 1 sleep are not aroused as easily by a stimulus, such as a noise or touch, as they are from all but the deepest stage (Stage 4) of NREM sleep. The high waking threshold of REM sleep thus indicates that, in one way at least, it is a state of deep sleep. It has been suggested that the sleeper is so engrossed in his dream in REM sleep that only a very strong stimulus reaches him.

NREM sleep, by contrast, is sometimes referred to as "orthodox" sleep. While awakenings from it do not normally result in vivid, detailed dream reports, the mind is far from blank at these times. NREM dream reports tend to be shorter, less visual, and less vivid than those reported from REM periods, and subjects often feel themselves to have been thinking rather than dreaming. For this reason, many investigators refer to mental content reported from NREM periods as "thinking" to distinguish it from the real "dreams" of the REM period. However, this is a moot point, and there are those who argue that *any* mental activity reported on waking from sleep merits the label "dreaming." This point is discussed fully in the next chapter.

If the overt activity of the sleeper is any indication of his internal experience, this discovery—that NREM content is usually less visual in nature than REM content—is not surprising, for NREM sleep is not associated with the rapid, directed eye movements which accompany REM dreaming. The Chicago workers were so impressed by the apparent scanning activity of the REM period that they wondered whether the sleeper was actually following the dream pictures and events with his eyes. Some of the early experiments seemed to corroborate this hypothesis, but it is generally agreed now that there is no one-to-one association between dream action and eye movement, although clues about the *general* nature of the dream we are having can often be ascertained by a look at the REM record. For example, if the eye movements are small and sparse, we are probably having a peaceful, rather passive dream, whereas larger and more continuous REM's suggest a more active and emotional dream. (Recent research indicates that movements of the inner ear also occur during sleep and may be generally correlated with auditory content in dreams.)

REM's appear to be a fundamentally biological activity, part of an overall pattern of body functioning occurring at regular intervals during the sleep. They are found in newborn babies and the congenitally blind, although in the latter case they usually decrease with growth. It is generally considered among dream researchers that the subjective experience of dreaming is somehow superimposed on this basic biological process and modifies what would otherwise be an entirely random pattern of eye movements.

POPULAR MYTHS ABOUT DREAMING

Many people are convinced they never dream in color, but modern research can prove them wrong. Experiments have shown that if subjects are questioned about color immediately on waking from a REM period, they report colored dreams on over 80 percent of occasions. The trees are green, the sky gray, the front door blue—the dreams are just as colored as any normal, everyday experience. Color in dreams, however, is forgotten very rapidly unless something specifically catches our attention, so unless we are questioned immediately on waking, it is likely to be lost. Similar results have been obtained from the more visual NREM dreams.

One of the surprising facts to come to light as a result of the early studies is the vast amount of dreaming taking place in each one of us every single night of normal sleep. The average adult will have at least three REM periods a night and probably more, which suggests that he is producing something like one thousand dreams a year (excluding all his NREM dreams), of which only a tiny fraction are ever recalled. The forgetting of dreams has always been a great puzzle to man, and now, for the first time in history, we have the answer, which is given in Chapter 3. It is sufficient to emphasize at this point that people who never or rarely recall dreams under normal conditions are able to do so on a high proportion of occasions when awakened directly from REM periods in the laboratory.

Along with the I-never-dream notion, many other popular myths about dreaming have been exploded in the light of the new research. For example, it is still widely believed that dreams take place in a flash. This idea is commonly associated with the famous guillotine dream of a Frenchman, Alfred Maury, in the 1890's, in which he was brought before the tribunal during the French Revolution, questioned by Robespierre and Marat, condemned to death, and led through the streets to the scaffold. His head was laid upon the block and the blade fell. He felt his head separate from his body and awoke in great anxiety, only to find that the top of the bed had fallen down and had struck the base of his neck. Maury reasoned that the blow must have initiated the dream and that all the dream imagery was compressed into the short interval between the initial perception of the stimulus and the awakening.

Neat as this reasoning seems, modern evidence casts doubt on the conclusion, since repeated measurements normally show a close relation between the length of the dream report and the length of the REM period before the dreamer wakes. Sometimes when the dream describes a simple action like a game of tennis, there is a direct relation between the time taken by the game and the time of the REM period. On other occasions, the dream story may seem to cover hours, days, or years, but here too there seems to be a correlation between the duration of the REM period and the time it takes the dreamer, when awake, to imagine the action as a film scenario. There is very little evidence of telescoped dreams occurring in the kind of split second proposed by Maury. Modern researchers suggest that Maury's guillotine experience was not a real dream at all, but a fantasy which had lain dormant in his mind until brought to conscious awareness in a single revealing flash by the blow on his neck (an idea originally put forward by Freud in 1900).

Whatever the true explanation, Maury was certainly wrong in thinking that the blow *initiated* the dream. All the evidence suggests that in normal adults dreaming begins automatically when the REM period begins and ends when the REM period ends. External stimuli, like the proverbial creaking door, may find their way into an *ongoing* dream and become part of the dream story, but they are in no sense responsible for it. External stimuli are incorporated into a REM dream on about half the occasions they are presented.

The following example from my own studies is typical of the way in which a stimulus is incorporated into a dream. Thirty seconds before waking the subject from a REM period, I had sprinkled cold water on her hand, which was lying on the bed covers. When awakened and asked to report what had been passing through her mind just prior to waking, she reported:

I had just jumped on a train as it started to move off, and was feeling very relieved I had managed to catch it. I was just lighting a cigarette when I felt water on my

27

hand and saw that the rain was coming in through the window. I got up to shut it, when I heard the carriage door open from the other end, and a man in a chef's hat came in and sat down. He pretended to read his paper, but I could feel him looking at me out of the corner of his eye. I muttered something about the weather but he didn't answer. I got panicky and edged my way to the door. I could do it only when he wasn't looking. I kept sitting down and standing up, trying to get out, when you woke me up.

Stimuli applied during NREM periods may sometimes be incorporated into the ongoing mental activity. For example, one of my subjects did not respond to the waking buzzer during a NREM period, so I rang again. He woke up and reported, "I was worrying about my exams, not being prepared and wondering whether I could get out of them, when the telephone rang. I thought it must be Dr. X. asking for my essay and decided not to answer it. I'm glad you woke me up."

The new findings about dreaming also explode the common myth that cheese and pickles eaten late at night increase our dream ration. Like illness or worry, indigestion may tend to make us restless so that we awaken more often during the night than we normally do, with the result that we catch more dreams than usual. What may seem like a night of constant dreaming is really only increased dream *recall*. In fact, on restless or disturbed nights our REM time may be decreased, since once a REM period has been interrupted, it is not normally continued on our falling asleep again.

This last finding led research workers to speculate about the possible consequences of depriving subjects completely of their REM sleep. This strange state of "aroused sleep," they argued, which appears so unremittingly night after night from birth onward, must surely have some unique function necessary for health and well-being. So despite the extraordinary ethical problems involved, a dramatic series of "REM deprivation" experiments was carried out on both human beings and animals, with some remarkable results.

THE FUNCTION OF REM SLEEP

The first famous "dream deprivation" experiments, as they were called in the early days, were carried out at Mount Sinai Hospital in New York in 1960 by Dr. William Dement, who had helped to pioneer the new dream research at Chicago. His method was to awaken subjects on several consecutive nights every time they entered a REM period, thus depriving them of approximately 90 percent of their REM sleep. Two very significant results were noted.

In the first place, subjects invariably had more REM periods than usual, so that by the fifth deprivation night some of them had to be awakened twenty or thirty times. After ten days it became impossible to continue the experiments, as the subjects fell back into REM sleep every time they were awakened. Second, on the "recovery" nights after the experiment, when the subjects were allowed to sleep undisturbed, their REM time was markedly increased, sometimes taking up 40 percent of total sleep time (although there are great individual differences here). It seemed as though the subjects were trying to make up their lost REM sleep.

Dement and his colleagues also noted that subjects deprived of REM sleep tended to become tense and anxious as the experiment continued. They had difficulty in concentrating the following day and showed signs of fatigue, increased irritability, and slight memory loss. These symptoms, Dement reasoned, could not be attributed to mere sleep disturbance, since a control group of subjects who had been awakened just as many times during NREM sleep showed perfectly normal behavior. All symptoms disappeared when subjects were allowed to sleep

29

normally again. Dement believed that longer and more severe deprivation would result in "a serious disruption of the personality."

This first experiment led to the excited speculation by many people in the early 1960's that perhaps the human being has a psychological need to dream, a need for a nightly voyage of fantasy to compensate for the dull routines of the day, or perhaps a descent into the creative depths of spiritual refreshment. Psychoanalysts seized on this research as a possible corroboration of Freud's theory of the dream as a safety valve, harmlessly discharging repressed sexual and aggressive impulses denied expression in waking life Alas, subsequent REM deprivation experiments have failed to come up with any significant support for such intriguing theories.

When Dement later increased the REM deprivation period to over fifteen nights by the use of certain drugs, his three subjects showed only relatively minor psychological disturbances: one became suspicious and aggressive, while another became giddy, light-hearted, and irresponsible in a very atypical manner, but these effects could have been attributable to the drugs. In any case, both subjects regained their normal equanimity after the first recovery night. Similar deprivation experiments by other investigators have consistently failed to demonstrate any really serious disruption of the personality after REM deprivation.

As further periods of REM deprivation on human beings would have presented ethical problems, Dement turned his attention to cats. (The REM state has been observed in all mammals studied.) His cats were placed on a small platform just above the surface of a pool of water. Each time the cat began a REM period, its neck muscles relaxed, its head dropped into the water, and it woke with a start. After a while, the cats learned to wake up before they even touched the water. The swimming-pool technique produces almost complete REM deprivation, but even seventy days of such torture did not succeed in producing observable impairment of behavior. There were certain noticeable *changes*, such as increased food seeking and sexual activity, but Dement was compelled to admit that such changes would actually be improvements from the point of view of a cat that had to survive in the wild.

Of course, it can be argued that since a certain amount of mental activity takes place outside REM periods in NREM sleep, REM deprivation does not necessarily result in total dream deprivation. Some support for this argument comes from experiments in which subjects have been totally sleep-deprived—in which case, no dreaming at all could take place—with disastrous effects. After as little as three days' total sleep-deprivation, hallucinations, persecutory delusions, memory loss, and even delirium may occur.

It is unlikely, however, that these effects are attributable solely or even mainly to lack of dreaming in the psychological sense of creative fantasy, since premature babies need sleep, and animals whose higher brain centers have been removed show increased REM sleep after having been deprived of it. And when adult volunteers who allowed themselves to be totally sleep-deprived embarked on their recovery periods, it was found that the first kind of sleep to be recovered was the very deep sleep of Stage 4, which in all other research appears to be least associated with mental activity of any kind. The recovery of lost REM sleep, which in normal adults seems most closely associated with fantasy life, takes second place and is not made up until subsequent recovery nights.

In fact, the unremitting character of the whole sleep cycle strongly suggests that common opinion has been correct in assuming that it has something to do with the fundamental physical re-creation of the total bodily organism, rather than with psychological processes. Modern research has recently found a good deal of direct support for this view. For example, one experiment showed that athletes who had exercised in the afternoon had more Stage 3 and 4 sleep than usual the following night. Another experiment has shown that people lacking the thyroid hormone (this hormone has the same effect as exercise in burning up body tissues) had no Stage 3 and 4 sleep, but regained it when the hormone was administered to them. And Dr. Ian Oswald and his colleagues at Edinburgh University have found that when the thyroid hormone is present in excess, the proportion of Stage 3 and 4 sleep is enormously increased. Oswald concludes that when body tissue has been burned up by exercise or other means, NREM sleep helps to restore it to normal.

Further corroboration of this theory comes from the observation that during NREM sleep there is an outpouring of growth hormone from the glandular system into the blood, especially during Stages 3 and 4. Growth hormone increases the synthesis of protein and assists body growth, maintenance, and repair. If we are deprived of sleep, the amount of growth hormone decreases, so that cell repair and renewal are impaired. This could account for many of the deleterious effects of total sleep loss and is consistent with the fact that the absolute amount of time spent in NREM sleep each night by the average person is at its highest in childhood and adolescence, when the body is growing and highly active. The common view that lack of proper sleep may stunt a child's growth would seem, on these findings, to be well founded.

What then is the function of REM sleep, which periodically interrupts the output of the growth hormone? Oswald puts forward convincing evidence that just as NREM sleep serves to renew general bodily tissues, so REM sleep is important for *brain* growth and renewal. Studies of premature babies have shown that in the month or two before the time for birth, up to 80 percent of total sleep time may be spent in REM sleep. It is just before birth that the brain is growing most rapidly—in fact, the gray matter of the cortex doubles in thickness and folds into crowded convolutions in the month before birth. Senile people have very little REM sleep, and it has been shown that their brains literally shrivel up as the normal processes of braincell renewal fail. This finding has the interesting implication that senility might be abolished by the administration of certain drugs which increase REM time, though this is pure speculation at the moment.

Mental defectives also have little REM sleep, which suggests that it is somehow crucial for keeping brain tissue in good working order so that the higher functions, such as thinking, learning, and remembering can be carried out efficiently. Experiments have shown that drugs which prevent the synthesis of brain protein can prevent the formation of permanent memories. And at Colorado, Dr. J. Stoyva and his colleagues, whose subjects wore special glasses which made the world look upside down, found the proportion of REM sleep was greatly increased while they were learning to adjust to the new state of affairs. So it appears that REM sleep has an important part to play in learning and remembering.

Further corroboration of the hypothesis that REM sleep is somehow crucial for keeping the brain tissue in good working order, probably by the synthesis of brain protein, comes from Oswald himself, who found large rebounds in the amount of REM sleep in patients after suicide attempts in which they had taken single large doses of sleeping pills. Superficially they looked fully recovered from the drug within a few days, but for the first month there was very little Stage 3 and 4 sleep and an enormous amount of REM sleep—an amount far exceeding the loss during the three or four days of recovery. Thus, after the brain has suffered chemical injury by drugs, REM sleep has a high priority over NREM sleep. Oswald says he is reminded of a kick on the shins, where temporary incapacity may be followed by a day or two of limping yet the bruise takes a couple of months to disappear.

Whatever the evolutionary origin of the REM cycle, there is little doubt that in human and probably in other mammalian life, its relation to the processes of chemical synthesis needed to keep the brain in fully efficient order is now one of its main functions, with survival value in its own right. There is no contradiction between this view and the fact that no immediate behavioral defects follow from REM deprivation. It is a well-known fact that the brain can continue to function more or less normally after quite extensive brain damage. My own conclusion is that many different cells have the job of carrying out the same function, so that if one particular group is unable to work at any given time, another group can do the job. Electronic computers are constructed nowadays on the same principle, so that faulty parts can be replaced without interference with the ongoing work.

So if one function of REM sleep is to provide opportunities for the brain to carry out complicated chemical syntheses connected with the duplication of memories and "programs," REM deprivation would not be expected to cause impaired behavior—at least, not for a very long time. The brain would still continue to perform its functions, such as the consolidation of memory traces during waking life, but would be operating without some of its usual safety margins. In the recovery period after REM deprivation, we should expect the brain to work some overtime to carry out this duplication and restore itself to full efficiency.

Again, a severe shock, such as an overdose of drugs, might damage a large part of the brain yet still not destroy its overall capacity to function. However, extended periods of REM sleep would be expected to occur for weeks afterward in order to restore the extra copies of memories and programs in the damaged cells, and only at the end of this time would the brain be restored to full efficiency and strength. If a severe task of relearning is imposed on the brain, as with subjects who had to learn from scratch to adapt to upside-down vision, we should again expect increased REM sleep, in order to deal with the complete program change. Similarly, newborn babies would need very large amounts of REM sleep to cope with the almost overwhelming amount of new stimulation from the environment.

Mechanisms that work on the multiplication-of-function principle are generally able to carry out all their tasks even if much of their machinery is out of action, but they do not carry them out quite so well. The final action, in other words, is a cooperative effort of several parts pulling together. In the case of the brain, we should expect that interference with the task of laying down "multiple copies" of newly learned information would not result in total forgetting, but rather less perfect memory than under normal conditions.

CÓNCLUSION

Whatever the functions of REM and NREM sleep—which despite all our theorizing still remain a mystery—it is likely that the subjective experience we call dreaming is merely a by-product of an essentially physiological process somehow connected with learning and remembering. This does not mean that dreams have no value or that we should ignore them. On the contrary, they could well have survival value to the human species at its present stage of social evolution by providing man with information about himself which normally remains hidden. Just as the chemical components of urine are of great diagnostic importance to a doctor, even though they are simply breakdown products of the body with no function of their own at all, so dreams can bring to our notice the many basic irrationalities and inconsistencies in the personality which constantly threaten to spoil our lives. Moreover, as I shall show later, dreams bring us face to face with all kinds of hidden talents and potentialities we never knew we possessed. In forming a bridge between body and mind, dreams may be used as a springboard from which man can leap to new realms of experience lying outside his normal state of consciousness and enlarge his vision not only of himself, but also of the universe in which he lives.

CHAPTER 2

WHAT IS A DREAM?

It is an astonishing fact that although modern dream research is now almost twenty years old, there is still no standardized definition of a dream. If we accept the *Oxford English Dictionary*'s definition of a dream as "a vision, series of pictures or *events,* presented to a sleeping person" (italics mine), it is clear that any mental activity experienced during sleep must be considered a dream. Similarly, Webster's *New World Dictionary* defines a dream as "a sequence of sensations, images, thoughts, etc., passing through a sleeping person's mind." On the other hand, Professor Calvin Hall, an American dream expert, prefers to be more specific. According to him, "a dream is a succession of images, predominantly visual in quality, which are experienced during sleep. A dream commonly has one or more scenes, several characters in addition to the dreamer, and a sequence of actions and interactions usually involving the dreamer. It resembles a motion picture or dramatic production in which the dreamer is both a participant and an observer. Although a dream is a hallucination, since the events of a dream do not actually take place, the dreamer experiences it as though he were seeing something real." On this definition, only our longer, more visual, vivid, and active sleep experiences would merit the label "dreaming."

The distinction is important because if we accept the first definition of a dream as *any mental activity* experienced during sleep, then we have to reject the famous discovery of modern dream research—that of the REM period as an "objective indicator" of dreaming. Experiments have shown that the mind seems to be continually active during sleep and that a person awakened from NREM periods often recalls images or thoughts, sometimes superficially indistinguishable from those reported from REM periods.

For example, in the early experiments, Dement and Kleitman considered their subjects to have been dreaming only if they could relate a coherent, fairly detailed description of dream content: in other words, they were using a definition of dreaming similar to that used by Hall. It was not surprising, therefore, that 80 percent of REM period awakenings resulted in "dream" reports, while only 7 percent of NREM reports were of this nature. In another experiment in which the definition of dreaming was "any item of specific mental content," similar to that of the *Oxford English Dictionary,* 80 percent of REM period awakenings still produced "dream" reports, while the figure for NREM awakenings jumped to 54 percent. In the latter case, the NREM period could hardly be called a "nondreaming" period. The issue was confused even further when the definition of dreaming was "anything passing through the mind" on being awakened: in this case, 74 percent of NREM awakenings resulted in "dream" reports.

Apparently, the investigators were not the only ones to be confused about what exactly constituted a dream. Dr. Donald Goodenough, who joined the Chicago dream team in 1956, discovered quite by accident that some of his subjects had similar difficulties. In his experiment, subjects were instructed before going to sleep that they would be awakened by a bell which they could turn off by lifting the bedside telephone from its cradle: they were then to report immediately whether or not they had been dreaming, and the detailed content of any dream recalled. Goodenough was surprised when one subject, having received his presleep instructions asked, "How will I know whether I have had a dream or not?" On consideration, he concluded that the question was not an unreasonable one if the subject had never previously recalled a dream.

He also found that many subjects, notably those who rarely recalled dreams spontaneously at home, seemed to mislabel their dream experiences. One sleeper, aroused during an unmistakable REM period, reported that he had been "asleep and thinking," while others were not sure whether they had been "asleep and dreaming" or "awake and thinking." The difficulty of distinguishing between "dreaming" and "thinking" was a real one for many subjects. One man said he felt he was riding down an avenue and was conscious of the houses and buildings passing by. He stated, "I may have thought that or dreamed it." Another subject, with a similar difficulty, concluded he must have been dreaming, not thinking, as the events of the "dream" were unreal and inconsistent with the facts of everyday life.

It appears that there is considerable opportunity for the word "dream" to acquire a highly individualized meaning. Accordingly, to ask a subject about his "dream" can hardly be considered a scientific procedure. Dement remarked in 1965, "It is somewhat startling, in view of all this, that no one has thought to ask a group of volunteers to define a dream or to question them about what they would call a dream before using them as subjects."

Dr. David Foulkes of Wyoming University hoped to bypass the problem of dream definition by changing the interview techniques. His subject was first asked whether or not he had been dreaming prior to the awakening stimulus: if so, he was to report his dream. If he was unable to recall a dream, he was then asked whether anything had been passing through his mind. Foulkes found that "something" was passing through his subjects' minds on 87 percent of awakenings from REM sleep and on 74 percent of awakenings from NREM sleep. Recall was almost equally distributed through Stages 2, 3, and 4 sleep, indicating that the entire NREM period was capable of sustaining mental activity. The typical NREM report seemed to be somewhat dreamlike, merely less so than the typical REM report.

These results led Foulkes to attempt an analysis of REM and NREM reports. He found that the latter were less emotional and involved less physical action than REM reports: they were also less elaborated, and the narrative contained fewer scenes and was usually less dramatic in character. NREM reports showed a greater correspondence to recent events in the subjects' waking life than did REM reports, and were much less distorted. So many of them resembled thinking rather than dreaming in the usual sense that Foulkes was tempted to refer to REM reports as "dreams" and NREM reports as "thoughts." He concluded, "Dream reports were elicited with some success in all categories of awakening. Dreaming or some form of cognitive and perceptual activity might conceivably occur continually in the sleeping human being, and REM periods might be useful only in differentiating different kinds of dreams, rather than as signs of dreaming and nondreaming."

Personally, I prefer to use the terms "REM dream" and "NREM dream" to distinguish these two kinds of mental activity during sleep. NREM content is often sufficiently dreamlike to make nonsense of the notion that it is either "nondreaming" or "thinking." And yet it is sufficiently different from REM content that anyone can learn, with a little practice, to distinguish correctly between the two most of the time. The task is even simpler when it comes to recognizing *our own* REM and NREM dreams.

As an example, I should like you to try the following experiment. Bearing in mind the general rules that on the whole NREM dreams are . . .

Shorter
Less vivid
Less visual
Less dramatic
Less elaborated
Less emotional

Less active
More plausible
More concerned with current problems
More purely conversational
More thoughtlike

. . . than REM dreams,
I want you to read through the following six dreams of my
subject, Dr. Y., and try to decide which three came from
REM periods and which three from NREM periods. On
each awakening, Dr. Y. was asked to report anything that
was passing through his mind prior to the waking stimulus.

THE DREAMS OF DR. Y.

Dream 1

I was thinking that perhaps something had gone
wrong with your machine and that you were not going to
wake me . . . then just before that I was seeing some patients for Dr. B. in his surgery. Dr. H. was sitting outside
and he said the whole set-up was ridiculous. I said,
"Jealousy gets you nowhere." I think you were one of
the patients.

Dream 2

It was all very vague. I was in a street with two
shadowy figures, and we were talking about something. I
think one of them was a woman, the other male, but I
couldn't see their faces and have no idea who they were.
I was saying, "Go here, go there" or something. I was
telling them where to go.

Dream 3

I was standing outside a posh hotel when two Indians
drew up in a big car. One looked very ill. He tried to get
up, looking agonized, and I was afraid he would hurt
himself. They were dressed in white and I had seen them
driving somewhere before.

And before that, I dreamed I was at the M. Hospital. Someone said to me, "This used to be near St. B.'s," and I replied, "Yes, that's feasible." He said, "What do they do there?" and I replied, "It was a big neurosurgery unit and there were some psychiatric beds." Then we went for a walk after lunch.

Then there was another dream. It took place here in this house. I was here in bed and there was a detective looking for something under my door. It was something to do with the experiment. He was eavesdropping, or spying on me, or something.

Deam 4

I was drinking a cup of milk in bed here. And I was talking to somebody but I don't know who it was. That's all.

Dream 5

I was just getting up, stepping out of bed as the buzzer went. I heard the buzzer in the dream as I was getting out of bed. It was morning, the end of the experiment, and I was sitting up in bed about to get out. Jones was supposed to be there—he does the sports ground, you know.

Dream 6

I was in a hospital talking to two people I know. I asked one chap whom he was working for. I thought he was working for S. but he said not. I asked if he were working for D. He replied, "No, he went long ago. That dates you!" Then I walked down a road looking at nameplates. This was a bit muddled.

Before that, there was a red Mini, and the man driving it didn't have a license. I was very worried about this. The car started to go and I ran after it to stop it. I held onto the window trying to keep it back. I thought I'd better try and turn it on its side. This would cause damage

41

but it seemed to me less troublesome than if this fellow was caught driving without a license. I thought I had better run round to the driver's side and knock on the window. but I knew if I did I should lose my hold on the car and it would go. I was frantically trying to keep the car back but wasn't succeeding.

Dreams 3 and 6 can be identified immediately as REM dreams on account of their length, vividness, visual and dramatic quality, and amount of activity. Dream 2 is certainly a NREM dream on account of its vagueness. Dream 4 is also a typical NREM dream, mainly on account of its brevity and vague conversational quality, devoid of any visual components: subjects often describe such dreams as "interludes" rather than dreams proper.

This leaves only Dreams 1 and 5 for classification, one of which is a REM dream, the other a NREM dream. Both are short and express an undisguised concern about the ongoing experiment, qualities which would tend to place them in the NREM category. But Dream 1 slips from mere "thinking" in the experimental setting to a fantasy of taking surgery and engaging in a brief drama with identifiable people. Dream 5 never gets off the ground, as it were—the dreamer remains in his bedroom thinking of Jones. For this reason, a practiced observer would diagnose Dream 1 as the REM dream and Dream 5 as the NREM dream, which is in fact the case.

Length of dream report is another important criterion in the classification of dreams, the majority of REM reports being much longer than NREM reports. In my own studies, I found that the average length of a REM report was 253 words compared with an average of 59 words for a NREM report. Dr. Y.'s averages are 134 and 48 respectively, and all three of his REM reports are longer than his NREM reports.

Dr. Y.'s dreams illustrate another important difference between REM and NREM dreams in that all his REM dreams consist of more than one episode. For example, in Dream 1 he finds himself thinking about the experiment and then switches abruptly to the fantasy of being in a doctor's office; Dream 3 contains three separate episodes concerning the Indians, the hospital scene, and the drama of the detective. In all cases, he appears to report his dream episodes in reverse order—that is, his first report consists of the episode he was experiencing just before the buzzer went, and he gradually works his way back over prior dream experiences of that particular REM period.

If he could have been observed directly during sleep, we should almost certainly have noticed large body movements, such as turning over in bed, occurring between each episode. The research indicates that these body movements are responsible for breaking an ongoing dream and starting a new one within the same REM period, in much the same way as a sudden disturbance in everyday life brings us out of one reverie, either into another or back to reality. Some of my subjects' REM periods, particularly those occurring just before waking, produced up to six separate dream episodes. NREM dreams, on the other hand, rarely seem to be recalled in episodes as such, although they may consist of several apparently isolated thoughts. For example, Dream 5 suddenly switches from Dr. Y. getting out of bed to "Jones, who does the sports ground." As large body movements occur quite frequently during Stage 2 and to a lesser extent during Stage 3 sleep, it is certainly possible that ongoing NREM mental activity is divided into episodes which are less well recalled than their REM counterparts. As we shall see in the next chapter, NREM sleep seems to inhibit the formation of memory traces in the brain so that we tend to forget what has been taking place during it.

The inability of NREM sleep to form stable memory-traces may also account for the vagueness of many NREM dreams. Dr. Y.'s dreams illustrate this point clearly. For example, even in Dream 1, which is vague by most REM dream standards, he is able to identify his colleague as Dr. H. and the setting as Dr. B.'s surgery, whereas in Dream 2 he is unable to recognize either the street or the people in it. Nor is he sure of the ongoing conversation. The whole experience is more like an impression, or a feeling, than a proper dream.

43

This vague kind of NREM dream in which the dreamer wanders through gray streets conversing with strangers is so often elicited from laboratory awakenings that it deserves further comment, particularly as such dreams are not often recalled under normal circumstances at home. They came as a complete surprise to many of my subjects. "They are like verbal thoughts," said one subject. "Is it possible to have dreams like that?" "It's like wandering in no-man's-land," said another, "conversing with ghosts and feeling quite lost." Some subjects were frankly worried by the amorphous nature of these dreams, in which they often felt disorientated and even disembodied. One subject said on being awakened from an NREM period,

> I was walking, or rather floating, along a street, and there was someone floating toward me. I don't know who it was or where I was. I think I asked the person where I was. Gosh, it reminds me of T. S. Eliot's "Little Gidding"—you remember those lines—

> > In the uncertain hour before the morning
> > Near the ending of interminable night . . .
> > Between three districts whence the smoke arose
> > I met one walking . . .
> > As if blown towards me. . . .

I've forgotten the rest, but I think he asked the ghost a question—yes—

> > So I assumed a double part, and cried
> > And heard another's voice cry: "What! are *you* there?"
> > Although we were not. I was still the same,
> > Knowing myself yet being someone other—
> > And he a face still forming. . . .

My dream was like that. Now I know what Eliot was talking about in so many of his poems.

As dreams are believed to be one of the major sources of artistic expression, it is not unreasonable to suppose that Eliot was, in fact, describing one of his own NREM experiences, perhaps without knowing it. This particular type of dream may also be responsible for the age-old notion of ghostly, twilight worlds, haunted by spirits of the dead seeking a resting place. Indeed, the analogy to the concept of purgatory seems almost too good to be true, particularly as some of my subjects added that they felt they were trying to atone for something. "I was out in the street again," said one, "trying to put something right that was wrong." "Wandering around," said another, "and the feeling of having to explain or atone for something." How many ancient ideas, I wonder, spring from dreams?

Certainly, Jean Cocteau's vision of the other world through the mirror in his film *Orphée* was exactly like a NREM dream—a strange, gray, shadowy land where people walk as if in slow motion, or glide slowly along with weird chants, as though lost in eerie mists.

In many NREM dreams, the dreamer does not even take the trouble to leave the comfort of his own bed in order to think, feel, converse, and even act. In Dream 4, for example, Dr. Y. drinks a cup of milk in bed and converses with someone, and in Dream 5, he feels it is morning and time to get up. It is not surprising, therefore, that many subjects awakened during NREM periods felt they were awake and thinking at the time, even though the EEG machine showed they were fast asleep. In NREM periods, the mind usually remains in fairly close contact with reality, in contrast to REM periods, when the dreamer is drawn further and further inward toward a world of complete fantasy. Subjects awakened from REM periods often report a feeling of having been "called back" from some faraway place—from deep, deep sleep—and it is possible that this illusion of distance accounts for the fact that it is more difficult to awaken a subject from a REM than from a Stage 2 or 3 NREM period.

NREM sleep seems to lack those special qualities of REM sleep which are necessary for converting thoughts into clear pictures. Subjects awakened from REM periods usually report dreams of considerable visual intensity, whereas NREM periods often elicit reports of mere thinking or worrying, usually about some current problem. This is the only reason why NREM experiences have sometimes been labeled "thoughts" rather than dreams by some investigators. This is not to imply that thinking does not take place in REM dreams, for clearly it does, but it is usually concerned with, and obscured by, the surrounding dream fantasy. In Dream 6, for example, Dr. Y. is preoccupied throughout with the problem of what to do about the runaway Mini, and several possible solutions pass through his mind. The NREM counterpart of this dream would perhaps be one in which he merely worried from his bed about the fact that his driving license was out of date.

In a similar way, NREM dreams often consist almost solely of vague conversations (see Dr. Y.'s Dreams 2 and 4) or spoken words, whereas these appear in REM dreams as part of the ongoing drama. For example, one of my subjects, on being awakened from an NREM period, stated that she just heard a voice out of the blue say very clearly, "You must not allow your dog to foul the footpath." Another subject heard a voice proclaim, "We must have a symbol for the New Age." It is probably from such dreams that we awaken with the feeling that we have just received the great secret of the universe. One of my subjects struggled very hard for several moments to bring back some communication of the utmost importance. It was "Readers who are opposed to a more exact coddling of the band than the situation warrants should fill in this form!" And another subject who was looking for a striking title for his new book on organic chemistry triumphantly awoke with the solution: it was *Twelve Bedsteads in Search of an Answer!*

Dreams of reading in which words and letters (often nonsense) float around in the mind's eye are usually the product of NREM sleep. One subject reported that her dream was "like reading a book or thinking while asleep."

Another subject said, "There was a conversation going on but I don't know why I was there or whether I was in it. It was rather like reading a very dull book, you know: when you wake up it's so irrelevant that it just goes automatically."

And this is exactly what *does* happen to most NREM dreams. Normally, we sleep right through them, as we do not often awaken spontaneously from NREM sleep, but even if we should chance to catch a NREM dream, it is usually so pale, colorless, and apparently irrelevant that it quickly passes into oblivion. As I shall show later, this is no great loss to us, as the majority of NREM dreams seem to yield little that can be interpreted for any useful purpose. But it is essential for the reader to know about these strange "wasteland" dreams before starting an investigation into his own dream life.

Of course, the best way to get a full feeling for their nature is by personal experience, and so for the reader who has not actually met a typical NREM dream in the course of ordinary life, I suggest the following experiment. Wake yourself up by means of an alarm clock at intervals of approximately ninety minutes throughout the night and write down immediately on waking whatever was going through your mind just prior to the waking stimulus. In this way, because you are interrupting the sleep cycle at different points, you have a good chance of collecting several REM and NREM dreams, though this cannot be guaranteed, of course. In the morning, examine them all carefully and see whether you can pick out the typical kind of NREM dream which has been described in this chapter. Without an EEG machine, there is, of course, no way of checking up objectively. It cannot be done purely on timing because there is no way of controlling how long you will take to fall asleep after each awakening. After a few trials, however, the difference between REM and NREM dreams will usually be so marked as to leave little doubt in most cases.

Just one warning. People can vary quite considerably in their dreaming habits, and you may find that your dreams are nothing like those reported by Dr. Y., who was chosen because he seemed to represent the "norm." If you are what I call a big dreamer, you will have longer, more vivid, and more dramatic REM dreams than Dr. Y., with the result that your NREM dreams will also be much more "dreamlike" than those discussed in this chapter. While your NREM dreams may be easily distinguished from your own, even more dreamlike REM experiences, they may not appear so different from the REM dreams of a "small dreamer," whose sleep experiences generally are less intense than average. Those who normally recall many dreams spontantaneously in everyday life tend to be "big dreamers," whereas those who rarely or never spontaneously remember a dream tend to be small dreamers.

Another difficulty is that both REM and NREM experiences tend to be longer and to have more dreamlike properties toward the end of the sleep period, so that although one of your own late NREM reports may be very different from one of your own late REM reports, it may not be so easy to distinguish it from your initial REM report. Hence our difficulty in deciding to which category Dr. Y.'s first REM dream and his last NREM dream belonged.

Even more confusing is the fact that light sleepers— those who are awakened easily by external stimuli such as noises—often report quite dreamlike material from their NREM periods, while deep sleepers seem to limit their dreaming proper to REM periods. But even if you are a light sleeper, you should still be able to distinguish between your own REM and NREM dreams.

In the end of the day, the question "What is a dream?" must be answered by the dreamer himself. My own conclusion is that, on the whole, it makes sense to talk of two typical kinds of dream: the REM dream, which is usually vivid and predominantly visual in nature, and its blander, more thoughtlike counterpart, the NREM dream. This issue has been discussed at some length because it is one which pervades the entire literature on dreaming and may confuse the uninformed reader. More important, however, is the fact that those who wish to probe more deeply into their hidden dream life should be able to recognize these two kinds of dream when they meet them.

"DREAMLETS"

Before closing this chapter, brief mention should be made of a third kind of dream, which occurs at sleep onset, the borderland between wakefulness and deep sleep. It is known as the "hypnagogic" dream, and often takes the form of unusual kinds of bodily sensation, strange conversations, and hallucinations, such as disembodied faces passing before the mind's eye. These may give way to dreams very similar to those experienced during REM periods, even though the sleep onset period is not accompanied by rapid eye movements themselves. On the whole, however, hypnagogic dreams tend to be shorter and less dramatic than REM period dreams, and for this reason are sometimes referred to as "dreamlets."

The reader who is interested in catching these dreamlets may try the following experiment. Lie flat on your back in bed, but keep your arm in a vertical position, balanced on the elbow, so that it stays up with a minimum of effort. You can slip fairly easily and deeply into the hypnagogic state this way, but at a certain point, muscle tonus decreases, your arm falls down and wakes you up. Write down immediately whatever was going through your mind just prior to waking. The results can be amusing and may even provide some useful material for interpretation along the lines I shall be discussing in later chapters.

CHAPTER 3

WHY WE FORGET OUR DREAMS

Why is it that some people wake up with a dream in mind almost every morning while others claim to dream no more than once a month, once a year, or never? We know that people do not differ in the number of REM periods they experience each night of normal sleep, and that "nondreamers" report almost as many dreams on experimental awakenings as "dreamers." This led investigators to conclude that the apparent widespread differences in dreaming activity must be variations in the *memory* of dreams rather than differences of dream frequency, and they now refer to those who recall a dream less than once a month as nonrecallers and to all others as recallers.

It has often been suggested that those who awaken slowly have a better chance of recalling dreams than those who are normally awakened by a sudden stimulus, like an alarm clock. This is not so. In fact, the contrary is the case: abrupt awakenings following a loud noise result in much more recall than gradual awakenings produced by means of a soft whisper, which suggests that the dream dissipates rapidly in the time between sleep and full awakening. For this reason, fairly loud buzzers or telephone bells are usually used in dream collection experiments. In my own work, the awakening stimulus was a buzzer which sounded rather like an angry bull. This sometimes upset my subjects, who would declare plaintively, "I'm sure I'd remember more if you used a softer buzzer." In the end, I was persuaded to try this, but with negative results.

The extent to which individuals habitually experience one or the other kind of awakening in their normal sleeping environment, such as always being awakened in the morning by an alarm clock instead of coming to gradually, may account for a small portion of individual differences found in everyday dream recall. As the last REM period of the night is sometimes an hour in length, we all have a good chance of awakening from it, but those who are suddenly awakened will have more chance of catching the dream than others who take their time to wake up.

Other experiments have shown that habitual nonrecallers normally need a stronger stimulus to wake them up than recallers, which suggests that the former are deeper sleepers than the latter. This could mean that one reason some people are recallers is that they wake up more often during the night and catch more dreams than their deeper-sleeping brethren.

DREAM FORGETTING AND PERSONALITY

However, the general weight of evidence points to the fact that the difference between recallers and nonrecallers is more a matter of the psychological characteristics of their personalities than their depth of sleep or the way they wake themselves up. Several years ago investigators observed to their surprise that nonrecallers showed more actual rapid eye movements per second on their REM/EOG records than recallers, which suggested that they experienced more active dreams. Why then did the nonrecallers usually report shorter, blander, and less vivid dreams than recallers?

51

This paradox was answered when it was discovered that in waking life more eye movements are executed in *looking away* from an object or scene than in *looking at* it. When pictures were shown to a group of subjects whose waking eye movements were being recorded, it was observed that more eye movements appeared on their records when they glanced away from some of the more distressing and threatening aspects of the pictures than when they looked straight at them. In a further study, when subjects were asked to imagine a particular event, few eye movements were present, but many more appeared on the records when they were asked to try and suppress it. Some subjects looked aimlessly around the room as if trying to distract attention from their fantasies.

The investigators reasoned that it was possible for nonrecallers to behave in a similar shifty-eyed way toward their dreams, particularly if they are unpleasant. This would explain why the nonrecallers usually experience less exciting dreams than recallers. Of course, it could be argued that because the dreams of nonrecallers are rather dull, they are harder to remember than the more interesting dreams of recallers. The bulk of the evidence, however, suggests that nonrecallers are decidedly reluctant to remember their dreams, just as they tend to avoid or deny unpleasant experiences and anxieties in everyday life. In fact, nonrecallers have been shown by means of psychological tests to be more inhibited, more conformist, and more self-controlled on the whole than recallers, who tend to be more overtly anxious about life and more willing to admit common emotional disturbances, such as anxiety and insecurity. The willingness to confront this dimension of experience—some have called it self-awareness—which manifests a close interest in the inner, subjective side of life, is probably the crucial difference between recallers and nonrecallers.

I cannot help being reminded here of Jung's famous classification of people into two types: extroverts, who are more concerned with their relation to the external world than with their inner life, and introverts, whose energies are mainly directed inward. Future research may well show low and high dream-recall to be closely correlated with the personality measures of extroversion and introversion, respectively.

THE REPRESSION OF DREAMS

Psychoanalysts would say that nonrecallers "repress" their dreams—that is, they "deliberately" banish all memory of them from conscious awareness because they contain distressing ideas and wishes. Analysts believe that we all harbor infantile sexual and aggressive wishes which, denied expression in waking life because they are incompatible with the high moral code we impose upon ourselves, find a kind of vicarious gratification in dreams. In one way, the analysts argue, we are all repressors of dreams, in that the repressive mechanism functions universally and automatically to disguise these unacceptable wishes in dreams so that we never become aware of them. However, sometimes the disguise is very flimsy, in which case we would then use repression to dissipate all memory of the dream. It is in this sense that nonrecallers can be said to be *more* repressive than recallers—they condemn more of their anxiety-provoking dream life to oblivion than their more courageous brethren, who use it for further growth and self-knowledge.

The alleged disguise function of the dream is discussed fully in a later chapter, so we will not pursue it further at this point. It is enough to mention here that many analysts are convinced that their nonrecalling patients fail to remember even their disguised dreams because they are afraid that underlying horrors will be revealed by means of interpretation. A nonrecalling friend of mine became very upset when her analyst kept accusing her of being out of touch with her unconscious mind for this reason. I offered her an experimental session in which we would conspire to take the unconscious by force by waking her from REM periods and obtaining immediate dream reports. The experiment was a failure in that her record showed the presence of three distinct REM periods during the course of the night, yet she was unable to report a single dream when awakened from them, although each time she felt she had been dreaming. She admitted sadly to her analyst that he was right, and became resigned to her "dreamless" existence. Some time later, however, I discovered that she had taken her usual sleeping pill before going to sleep on the experimental night. Suspecting this might have something to do with the failure of the experiment, I asked her if she would be willing to return for a second session, this time without her pill.

Although she was convinced she would never fall asleep without it, she eventually agreed, and the night resulted in three "big" dream reports which she presented triumphantly to her analyst the following day, saying, "Out of touch with my unconscious, indeed! It's just those wretched sleeping pills I've been taking." In her case, the pills probably had the effect of deepening her sleep in some way so that the memory of dreams was lost between the time of the buzzer and full wakefulness. On the other hand, barbiturates have been known to reduce the number of rapid eye movements in REM periods, which may result in more passive and therefore less memorable dreams. On the rare occasions when I take a sleeping pill, I have noticed that I rarely remember a dream.

However, as I said earlier, it does appear that some people really are "out of touch with their unconscious minds" (implying that they are completely unaware of the hidden parts of their personality), and that lack of dream recall is symptomatic of this. I am sometimes approached by psychoanalysts and psychotherapists who ask if I will give their nonrecalling patients a going-over in the laboratory, in order to capture a few dreams for the purpose of analysis. While psychoanalysts can manage to work without a patient's dreams, it makes life a lot easier if they are produced from time to time. While the laboratory methods have been successful in eliciting dreams from chronic nonrecallers, it must not be forgotten that if a patient is really resistant to getting in touch with the hidden part of himself, merely waking him from REM periods and asking him for dream reports is not necessarily going to solve the problem automatically.

For example, it is not unusual for a subject who has been referred to the laboratory because he fails to recall dreams spontaneously at home to produce a dream on the first couple of awakenings and then have nothing more to report for the rest of the night. Or he may be quite successful on the first experimental night and fail to produce anything on subsequent nights, often reporting that he knew he was dreaming but that the dream seemed to slip away as he woke up. One subject became very cross, and said, "Everytime you've woken me up, I know I've been dreaming, but I just can't get them back. Is it a defense, do you suppose? I really am interested to know what I'm dreaming about." There is no doubt she was speaking the truth, and I think a psychoanalyst would be correct in assuming that her unconscious mind, having been taken unawares on the first few awakenings and burgled of dreams, became wise to the trick played upon it and was fighting back by causing the dreams to be repressed.

The repression of a dream probably takes place just before waking or even at the moment of waking, so that either the dream is forgotten completely or only innocuous fragments remain. The theory of dream repression is an attractive one for those of us who have witnessed countless unsuccessful struggles on the part of our subjects to hang onto a dream as it is literally being sucked under. But this is not the whole story in dream forgetting, as we shall see later.

Even normal volunteer subjects who are in the habit of regularly remembering their dreams at home often show (unconscious) resistance to remembering their dreams in the laboratory. One apparently keen and willing subject, who said she was really looking forward to the experiment, produced several bland, unexciting dream reports from the first few REM awakenings of the night. On the last awakening, she was unable to remember anything except that she felt she had been in the middle of a long, dramatic dream when I woke her. She expressed considerable impatience that she was unable to remember any of it. She telephoned me the following afternoon to say that the dream had just come back to her but it was too personal to tell. "Even if I'd remembered it at the time," she said, "I doubt whether I should have told it to you. After all, dreams are very private things, aren't they?" They are indeed, and many an enthusiastic volunteer takes part in dream experiments quite unaware of his underlying anxiety about revealing too much either to himself or to the experimenter.

Other subjects sometimes express their unconscious fears and resentments about the experiment in the dreams, themselves. One overtly cooperative subject made it clear after the very first dream report that we were in for a trying time. He dreamed he saw a doctor on the landing between the experimental room in which he was sleeping and my room, where I sat recording his dreams on a tape recorder. This doctor, who had a sinister appearance, was apparently trying to cut the wires between the two rooms or in some way stop the experiment. My subject was just going to warn me about this, he said, when he was awakened by the buzzer. As he himself was a doctor, I had little doubt about the real identity of the saboteur, and my fears were realized when, halfway through the night, he developed a migraine and the experiment had to be terminated.

So the psychotherapist looking for dreams to interpret will not find the new laboratory techniques a panacea. Nevertheless, they can be very useful in helping chronic nonrecallers to begin to become aware of their dream life, and this is of value not only to those who are having professional psychotherapy, but to all of us, as the later chapters of this book are designed to show.

For recallers, on the other hand, the new methods may have little to offer, as only a limited number of dreams can be dealt with in the course of therapy—normally two or three a week at the most. Indeed, in professional psychotherapy even this number can be embarrassing. When I first began analysis, I kept a dream diary in which I recorded over 200 dreams during the first year. In the end, I stopped doing this, as neither I nor my analyst could cope with so much material. I later read with interest that Freud had eventually destroyed his own dream diary: his reason—"The stuff simply enveloped me as the sand does the Sphinx."

Also, as every psychotherapist knows, too many dreams can be as symptomatic of resistance to therapy as too few. I am reminded of a weekly psychoanalytic group I used to attend in which one of the members would invariably pull out a thick wad of dream reports halfway through the session and proceed to bore us to death with them for the following hour. These were his dreams of the previous week, and very long and complex some of them were, too. In the end, the group leader did not even bother to interpret the dreams but interpreted the member's preoccupation with them instead, saying that this was his method of avoiding the deeper issues which he was unwilling to face!

I do not mean to imply that laboratory methods of dream catching have nothing to offer the psychotherapist. On the contrary, many therapists have used them to advantage, particularly in attempts to discover how far repression plays a part in the forgetting of a *once-remembered dream*. As far back as 1900, Freud wrote:

It not infrequently happens to me, as well as to other analysts and to patients under treatment, that, having been woken up, as one might say, by a dream, I immediately afterwards, and in full possession of my intellectual powers, set about interpreting it. In such cases, I have often refused to rest till I have arrived at a complete understanding of the dream: yet it has sometimes been my experience that after finally waking up in the morning, I have entirely forgotten both my interpretive activity and the content of the dream, though knowing that I have had a dream and interpreted it. It happens far more often that the dream draws the findings of my interpretive activity back with it into oblivion than that my intellectual activity succeeds in preserving the dream in my memory.

Freud also noted that many of his patients, while recounting a dream in the consulting room, would suddenly pause and recall a part of the dream they had previously forgotten. He considered that these forgotten fragments were of more importance than the remembered parts of the dream. "Often when a patient relates a dream," he wrote, "some fragment is entirely forgotten. The forgotten part provides the best and readiest approach to the understanding of the dream. Probably that is why it sinks into oblivion."

Professor Roy Whitman and his colleagues at the University of Cincinnati College of Medicine, Ohio, have recently produced evidence that Freud might be correct in his view that the dream or part of the dream which is *not* remembered is of more significance than that which is recalled. Two subjects who were undergoing psychotherapy were awakened from REM periods on several nights and asked to report their dreams to the experimenter. The following day, they both had therapy sessions with a psychoanalyst. From the early sessions, the female subject reported most of her sex dreams to the experimenter but not to the analyst, while dreams containing sexual and aggressive material directed toward the experimenter were told only to the analyst. Dreams in which she expressed her fears of analysis and denied any need for treatment were reported to the experimenter but not to the analyst. The male subject retold to the analyst all dreams which highlighted his capabilities as a man, but omitted to relate those dreams in which he expressed homosexual tendencies. As the meanings of these dreams were not always immediately apparent, Whitman inferred that the subjects understood at least subconsciously the meaning of their dreams, and therefore kept them from anyone who was likely to see through them. This the subjects did by means of conscious suppression of the dreams or by unconscious repression along the lines we have been discussing.

Whitman writes that "it is usually taken for granted that the dream reported in the therapeutic session contains one of the major conflicts with which the patient is struggling at the time. These findings suggest that therapists should maintain a degree of suspicion, for one or more of the major interpersonal conflicts of the patient may well be contained in the dream that is *not* told." He believes that modern techniques of dream detection could be clinically useful if used along the lines of his experiment in making *forgotten* dreams available to the analyst in order to increase his knowledge of the subject's deepest fears and resistances. However, I have a feeling that a really repressive patient would soon learn to "forget" his dreams at source, as it were, by using some of the methods observed in my own subjects.

While I have no doubt that a certain amount of repression is responsible for the forgetting of dreams, this cannot be the whole story, as Freud believed, since even extremely open and self-aware people find it difficult and often impossible to counteract the almost overwhelming tendency to forget dreams. Even if dreams are remembered briefly on waking, they are gone the moment we allow ourselves to doze. And even the most prolific dreamers do not recall four or five dreams every morning, although the evidence of REM periods suggests that we all experience something like this number during a night of seven or eight hours' sleep. In fact, the evidence suggests that the great majority of dreams are never remembered at all, while others are retained only as fragments. How and why do we forget so many of our dreams?

THE UNIVERSAL TENDENCY TO FORGET DREAMS

Kleitman has suggested that the poor recall of dreaming may be attributable to the impaired efficiency of the brain during sleep, and he likens the sleeper's condition to that of the very young, the very old, and the very drunk! Oswald agrees with him: "The forgetting of dreams is extremely rapid, and it is not necessary to invoke repression to account for the failure of recall of most dream material, any more than it would be in the case of post-traumatic amnesia, amnesia after drunkenness, electroplexy or other states in which cerebral vigilance is impaired for a time." In other words, the condition of the brain during sleep is probably quite inadequate for the laying down of memory traces.

At first sight, this seems to contradict our earlier view, discussed in Chapter 1, that the conditions of REM sleep are actually *optimal* for the consolidation of existing memory traces in the brain. But it is one thing to say that REM sleep completes the consolidation of *already-existing* memory traces formed during the course of the day, and quite another to say that it is also capable of laying down *new* traces of the *dream itself* as it occurs during the REM period. The evidence suggests that REM activity does not continue long enough at any one time to allow the formation of a dream trace strong enough to sustain itself beyond the end of a REM period.

Experiments have shown how the dream swirls away from memory, first fragmenting and then completely evaporating. When a subject is awakened from a REM period, he nearly always reports a vivid dream. If he is awakened five minutes after the end of a REM period, he can catch only fragments of it: and if the awakening takes place ten minutes after the end of a REM period, the dream is almost completely lost. Just on the basis of the number of words used to report a dream, there is a straight and dramatic decline.

It is obvious then that unless a subject is awakened during a REM period, he is likely to forget the mental content experienced during it. Much of everyday recall probably arises from spontaneous awakenings from the last long REM period of the night: since we normally do not awaken for any length of time during the night, a natural process of forgetting occurs. One of the great values of the new experimental techniques in dream research is that many of these early dreams, which would otherwise be lost, can be caught and their content recorded.

Further experiments suggest that the chief culprit responsible for the forgetting of dreams is the relatively passive and inactive state of NREM sleep. Subjects awakened at hourly intervals throughout the night and shown a word on a screen above the bed were usually able to remember the word in the morning only if they were kept awake for ten minutes or so after seeing it. If they were allowed to drift back to sleep immediately after identifying it, it tended to be quite forgotten. As a person almost invariably falls into Stage 2 NREM sleep after an awakening, it seems likely that any experience—including a dream—followed by NREM sleep passes rapidly into oblivion. On the other hand, the act of keeping the person awake for ten minutes or more seems to have the effect of strengthening a memory trace so that the incident will be remembered at some future date.

Normally, then, the only dreams we are likely to remember are those from which we awaken directly and stay awake, either in the middle of the night or in the morning. In the ordinary course of events, a sleeper awakens for only very brief periods during a normal night's sleep, and therefore never remembers most of his dreams. We have all probably experienced the strange, uncomfortable feeling of being in touch with two worlds at the same time on restless, disturbed nights after overeating or during fever, our constant brief awakenings resulting in snatches of dream recall, most of which appears meaningless and trivial and is quite forgotten by morning. In these cases, our awakenings are probably not long enough for memory traces of the dreams to be formed so that we remember them only briefly and then they are gone forever. Incidentally, this is one reason why many people think they dream more when they are restless: what really happens is that wakefulness results in more dream recall than normal, but never in extra dreams.

Most of us, like Freud, have also had the experience of waking from a vivid dream in the middle of the night and thinking we must remember it in the morning. We may turn it over in our minds several times and even attempt some kind of interpretation, as he did, but if we doze back to sleep within about ten minutes of waking, the whole lot will probably be gone by morning. I don't believe Freud was repressing the memory of his dreams and their interpretations—at least not on all occasions. I suspect rather that he did not allow a long enough interval between waking and

61

falling back into NREM sleep for the formation of an adequate memory trace of the whole experience.

For this reason, I advise those who are intent on catching their dreams to write them down as soon as they wake up, even if this is in the middle of the night. The effort involved in sitting up, putting on the light, and writing down the dream all help to bring about a state of wakefulness which is necessary if we are to catch most of the details. Incidentally, Freud advised his patients not to write down their dreams, as he believed that this increased the chances of their repression. Dreams, he thought, resist all efforts at capture and the intention to write them down is a sure way of frightening them off. However, as we have been led to conclude that dreams disappear more on account of weakness of memory trace than of wickedness of content, we shall have no hesitation in ignoring Freud's advice on this point.

Most of our spontaneously recalled dreams probably come from the last long REM period just before waking in the morning. The best way to catch these dreams is, once again, to sit up immediately and write them down, instead of either continuing to doze or leaping out of bed and hurrying off to work.

It is reasonable to assume that there is always a better chance of recalling an emotional dream than a bland one, a long one than a short one, and a vivid one than a vague one, just as we tend to remember our more exciting and dramatic experiences in waking life. There is, however, no way of testing this assumption, as we have no access to the original dream material. The most we can do is to collect dream reports from awakenings during the night and compare them with a second recall the following morning. In my own studies I found that REM dreams reported from nocturnal awakenings were better recalled the following morning than NREM dreams reported during the night. Further analysis showed that this was mainly on account of their tendency to be longer, more vivid, and more emotionally intense than NREM dreams. Emotional intensity, irrespective of whether it was pleasant or unpleasant, was a particularly strong factor in determining whether or not the memory of a dream reported during the night would survive until morning.

In a further experiment, I tested the hypothesis that subjects who were set or motivated to recall their dreams would do better than those with no motivation. Two groups of subjects slept in the laboratory, believing that the purpose of the experiment was merely to monitor their eye movements during sleep. Before going to sleep, one group was requested to try and remember their dreams the following morning, while the other group received no such instructions. The former group remembered far more dreams than the latter, indicating that we tend to recall more dreams when we are in some way set to catch them than when we take a more casual attitude toward them.

How the mechanism of "set to recall" works is uncertain. It may cause more frequent awakenings during the course of the night; it may cause us to awaken specifically from REM periods; or it may operate directly on the dream itself, making the content more vivid and intense, and so more memorable. One thing is certain—suggestions put to the mind before one goes to sleep are often carried out in some mysterious way. For example, I can almost always wake up at a certain hour without the aid of an alarm clock once I have given myself instructions to do so. And in a broader setting, anyone who has undergone psychotherapy knows that dream recall increases markedly if it becomes apparent that the analyst welcomes dreams in his work with a patient. Such experiences as psychotherapy, participation in dream experiments (many of my subjects reported increased dream recall at home after taking part in experiments), and even listening to lectures or reading books on the subject, all stimulate dream recall by combating the natural physiological processes which seem inevitably to lead to dream forgetting.

This is not to imply, however, that the psychological process of repression plays no part in dream forgetting, although this has not yet received much experimental support. Psychotherapists are only too well aware of the incompatibility of conscious and unconscious desires, the patient's consciously wishing to rid himself of the neurotic tendencies which are spoiling his life, at the same time unconsciously striving to maintain the status quo within the personality. The experiences mentioned above which sensitize one to awareness—psychotherapy, dream experiments and so on—probably assist in combating not only the physiological processes which cause dream forgetting, but also the unconscious psychological forces responsible for repression.

THE SPONTANEOUS RECALL OF DREAMS: A SUMMARY

1. The major factor in the spontaneous recall of dreams appears to be the fortuitous awakening directly from a dream, either during the course of the night or just prior to rising in the morning. Usually a sleeper does not awaken often during the course of a normal night's sleep, which means that most dreams, are never brought into waking consciousness and, therefore, are never remembered.

2. Given, however, that an awakening does occur, what determines the quantity and quality of dream recall? In the first place, there is always a better chance of detailed recall if we happen to awaken from a REM period rather than an NREM period.

3. Secondly, if we do happen to awaken from a REM period, several factors contribute to what is finally recalled:

    a. Long, vivid, emotionally intense dreams have more chance of being recalled than short, vague, bland dreams.

    b. A sudden awakening normally results in more recall than a gradual awakening.

    c. Self-aware people are likely to produce more striking dreams than repressors.

    d. Those who are set to recall dreams will probably collect more details than those without such motivation.

4. Assuming that some content is remembered on waking during the night, what determines whether or not it will survive until morning? The crucial factor here seems to be the opportunity for memory trace formation. The person must stay awake long enough with his dream in mind for consolidation of the trace to take place (at least ten minutes), otherwise NREM sleep will intervene and wipe out all memory of the dream.

5. Given a trace that is adequately formed during the night, what determines the quantity and quality of morning recall? My own studies suggest that the longer, more vivid, and more emotional dreams have a better chance of survival than their shorter, vaguer, and blander counterparts.

As my own studies have also shown that approximately half the content of each dream reported after nocturnal awakenings has disappeared by morning, readers who are really serious about confronting their dreams are advised to keep pencil and paper by the bedside and to write down their dreams immediately on waking from them. Further detailed instructions on how to catch dreams are given in Appendix A.

CHAPTER 4

A ROYAL ROAD
TO THE UNCONSCIOUS

The idea that dreams may have useful information to give us about the conduct of our lives goes back to prehistoric times. For most of human history it was taken for granted that the sleeping mind was in touch with the supernatural world and that dreams could be interpreted as messages from the gods, with prophetic or healing functions. The great surge forward of science in the nineteenth century led to a considerable reaction against this way of thinking, however, and dreams were widely dismissed as mere jumbles of fantasy resulting from indigestion, creaking doors, or memories of the previous day. Although something of the older view survived among people who looked to dreams as sources of creative inspiration, educated opinion generally took it for granted that dreams were meaningless.

This was the position at the turn of the century, when a Viennese neurologist, Sigmund Freud, pointed out that two people who experience similar events during the day or are subjected to the same stimulus during sleep weave two entirely different dream stories around them. Why, for example, does one person hearing a noise during sleep dream that a roaring lion is about to attack him, while another person dreams he is sunbathing by the Mediterranean, listening to the sound of waves upon the shore? Noise and other stimuli received by the sleeping brain, together with events of the previous day, are mere hooks upon which we hang our innermost wishes and feelings, said Freud, and we weave around them fantasies which spring from the depths of the unconscious mind.

So he set out to develop a theory of the dream process which would enable him to interpret dreams as clues to the problems and conflicts taking place within the personality. It would be no exaggeration to say that the theory he developed has been one of the major formative influences in Western culture over the past half century, and almost all modern thought about dreams derives something from it, even when in conflict with it. It is for this reason that the development of his dream theory is traced in detail here—and also because it is one of the most entertaining and dramatic stories in the history of psychological discoveries.

FREUD'S DISCOVERY OF "THE SECRET OF DREAMS"

In the early days of his clinical practice, Freud observed that many of his patients suffered from symptoms for which there appeared to be no underlying physical cause. These were sometimes manifested physically as headaches, rashes, blindness, or paralysis, and sometimes mentally as phobias, obsessions, delusions, and hallucinations. He concluded that they must all be emotional in origin, and he found that when he allowed his patients to talk freely about their problems, the symptoms often disappeared. This seemed to occur whenever a particularly painful forgotten memory was brought to light, along with its attendant feelings.

As these memories were often concerned with sexual

and aggressive acts and wishes originating in childhood, Freud concluded that they had been thrust out of conscious awareness, or repressed as he called it, because they were too painful and shameful to think about. These repressed wishes, he believed, were far from dormant in the mind and, being denied direct expression in overt behavior, found an outlet for their energy in the form of symptoms.

Freud observed that as his patients talked freely while lying on a couch—a technique known as free association—they sometimes recalled a dream which proved to be the starting point of a new and fruitful chain of memories and ideas. Many of these dreams led right back to the same repressed urges and wishes responsible for the neurotic symptoms. By examining his own dreams and those of his patients more thoroughly, Freud was slowly led to consider that repressed wishes in the unconscious mind found substitute gratification during waking life in the form of symptoms and during sleep in the form of dreams. For this reason, he never wholly abandoned the idea that the dream is a kind of neurotic symptom in its own right.

All through the 1890's, Freud pressed on with his self-analysis, exploring his innermost thoughts and feelings, until in 1895 he hit on what he believed to be the secret of dreams. He was sitting on the terrace of the Bellevue hotel in Vienna pondering a dream of the previous night in which a hysterical patient of his, Irma, told him she still had pains and was far from cured. She looked so ill in the dream that Freud became alarmed and thought he must have overlooked some organic sickness. His colleagues in the dream reached the same conclusion and said she was suffering from an infection as a result of an injection administered by Freud's friend Otto with a dirty syringe.

The dream had obviously been sparked off by the fact that on the evening before the dream, Otto had actually visited Freud and told him that he had seen Irma on holiday and that she looked better but not well. Freud thought he detected a note of reproach in Otto's voice and carried over his anxieties into sleep.

This famous Irma dream, which now has a prominent place in the history of great discoveries, was actually more complicated than I have related it here, and Freud spent much time over it, exploring various aspects of it at great length. But the major revelation which hit him in a blinding flash of insight as he sat on the terrace, and which has since become the foundation of psychoanalytic practice and theory, was that *the motive for the dream was a wish and its content was the fulfillment of that wish.* "The dream," he wrote, "fulfilled certain wishes which were started in me by the events of the previous evening. . . . The conclusion of the dream . . . was that I was not responsible for the persistence of Irma's pains, but that Otto was. Otto had in fact annoyed me by his remarks about Irma's incomplete cure, and the dream gave me my revenge by throwing back the reproach on him. The dream acquitted me of the responsibility for Irma's condition by showing that it was due to other factors. . . . The dream represented a particular state of affairs as I should have wished it to be." It was as though an unconscious wish had conspired with the sleeping brain to remold reality nearer to the heart's desire in the form of a dream.

The Irma dream seems relatively straightforward compared with many of our own more complicated and apparently incomprehensible dream fantasies. Nor does the underlying wish seem, at first sight, particularly horrifying in a sexual or aggressive way. Freud cannot be blamed for wanting to clear himself of the charge of professional negligence. However, the dream indicates that he achieved this by placing the blame on his friend Otto, a mean, aggressive action which he would not have "dreamed" of doing in waking life. Even worse is the possibility that Freud, being a very ambitious man, unconsciously wished to destroy any successful colleagues and rivals anyway. Examples like this led Freud to suspect that the unconscious mind was capable of committing any crime in fantasy in order to fulfill some hidden wish.

Most dreams, like the Irma dream, can be interpreted on many levels and contain many different wishes. For example, at one point in the dream, Freud was somehow able to see right through Irma's dress, noting that she had something wrong with her chest. In discussing this later in his book *The Interpretation of Dreams,* Freud wrote, "Frankly, I had no desire to penetrate further at this point," probably on account of the sexual implications. Although Freud does not go into detail here, it is highly likely that, according to his theory of the infantile origin of unconscious wishes, this part of the dream revealed not only a present wish to indulge in sexual relations with Irma, forbidden by professional ethics, but also, at a deeper level, a repressed infantile wish to do the same with his own mother. Such a wish, thought Freud, would be so overwhelmingly horrifying to the conscious mind that it must be heavily disguised and distorted before it dared appear in a dream.

It was this special kind of wish fulfillment in dreams which came to interest Freud most as he worked on his theory, and this was why, when he came to publish his work right at the end of the nineteenth century, he called his book *The Interpretation of Dreams.* He freely admitted that many dreams need no interpretation since they embody a wish openly and directly. Children in particular are well known for continuing the pleasures of the day in dreams: my small daughter often reports a night spent on the swings or at the zoo. Freud was even prepared to believe that animals might have wish-fulfillment dreams of this type. The twitching and sniffing of a sleeping dog, he suggested, probably represents a reliving of the day's pleasant experiences, and he quotes a Hungarian proverb which states that "Pigs dream of acorns and geese dream of maize." He also mentions an old Jewish proverb which asks, "What do hens dream of?"—the answer being "Millet"!

Other examples of simple, direct wish fulfillments are often found in the dreams of the recently handicapped and in those whose lives are in some way unsatisfactory or unpleasant. For example, a friend of mine who became permanently blind three years ago at the age of sixty tells me that for the first few months of his blindness he dreamed night after night that he was still able to see, until the despair of waking up every morning to the dark reality almost drove him to suicide. He still has visual dreams, but has come to terms with his handicap so that he no longer dreads waking up. At a particularly gray period of my own life I had recurrent dreams of glorious landscapes in vivid technicolor: and once when I was in hospital the ward orderly, a colored immigrant, told me of a dream in which her husband, a manual laborer, placed a beautiful gold necklace around her neck. An army psychiatrist once told me that during World War I his soldiers used to dream regularly about being back home with their families. Indeed, if they started dreaming regularly about the war, they were often sent home, as this was considered symptomatic of lowered defenses and likely to be followed by a breakdown.

Freud's observations of children led him to the conclusion that their dreams rapidly became more complex than this simple, direct kind of wish fulfillment, and at quite an early age it seems as though something lies hidden under the obvious content of the dream. For example, my three-year-old daughter is beginning to report dreams in which Leo, her toy lion, bites me, or in which she throws her doll out of the window because it has done something to upset her. Freud believed that dreams of this kind represent disguised fulfillments of wishes that are too "naughty" to be admitted directly—in my daughter's case, he would say, Leo is a disguise for herself in the first dream, the doll a disguise for me in the second, because she feels cross with me but knows that to bite or hurt me is naughty. As she grows older, Freud would predict that her dreams will become increasingly disguised until expert interpretation is required to expose the unconscious wishes underlying them.

Freud called the dream as it is remembered the manifest dream to distinguish it from its underlying wishes and impulses, which he called the latent content. His method of interpretation, which is discussed in detail in Chapter 6, was to associate to every element in the manifest dream, a process which gradually led back to the latent content which he believed instigated it. Working hard on his own dreams in this way, Freud was led back to many childhood memories and feelings of which he had hitherto been unaware. He found many of them painful and shocking. "Being entirely honest with oneself," he wrote, "is a good exercise. Some sad secrets of life are being traced back to their first roots, the humble origins of much pride and precedence are being laid bare." To Freud, this latent dream material was always of much more importance than the manifest dream, which he believed served merely as a cover for it. He insisted firmly throughout life that this distinction between manifest and latent dream content should be made, and many psychoanalysts today still remain unsatisfied with a dream interpretation until they have discovered its source in some repressed childhood conflict.

The disguise function of dreams, thought Freud, serves a dual purpose. Not only does it allow the harmless discharge of repressed energy in the forbidden wishes, but by concealing the true nature of these wishes allows the dreamer to sleep on undisturbed. For example, he argued, if some of our more primitive sexual and aggressive urges found direct expression in a dream, we would surely awaken in anxiety. Thus the dream acts not only as a safety valve for the fantasied expression of pent-up emotions, but also as the guardian of sleep. Sometimes, however, the disguise fails and the dreamer awakens—the victim of a nightmare. For this reason, Freud modified his theory to read that every dream represents an *attempted* wish fulfillment. The various ways in which the "dream work," as Freud called it, is supposed to bring about the disguise of repressed wishes is discussed fully in Chapter 6.

The Interpretation of Dreams remained Freud's favorite book throughout life. It contained, he wrote, "the most valuable of all discoveries it has been my good fortune to make. Insight such as this falls to one's lot but once in a lifetime." Dreams, he believed, represented a "royal road" to the unconscious parts of the mind which had hitherto been inaccessible in man's search for self-knowledge. In a letter to his friend Fliess, Freud described a return visit to the Bellevue hotel, where he had had his famous Irma dream, asking, "Do you suppose that some day a marble tablet will be placed on the house, inscribed with the words?—'In This House on July 24th, 1895, the Secret of

Dreams was revealed to Dr. Sigmund Freud,' " adding "at the moment there seems little prospect of it."

He was right about the last point. Although his publisher was so impressed with the book's epoch-making character that he postdated it *1900* so that it bore the date of the new century, it took eight years to exhaust the first small edition of 600 copies. Freud's ideas were in fact actively opposed by many of his psychiatric colleagues, who, like the public, particularly resented the implication that we are all basically nasty sexual and aggressive creatures. Since then, however, the book has gone through many editions and has been translated into most languages, now occupying a place of honor among the great classics of the world.

But if ever a plaque were to have been placed at Bellevue, it would by now have been modified to read, "In this house on July 24, 1895, *several important insights on the nature of dreams* were revealed to Dr. Sigmund Freud," for modern research shows that while some of his ideas were indeed epoch-making, others were in fact quite wide of the mark.

THE DREAM AS THE GUARDIAN OF SLEEP

In the first place, Freud's theory that the function of dreaming is to preserve sleep must be revised in the light of modern research. That dreams *can* act in this way, by incorporating bladder pressure, stomach ache, or external noises into the dream story when they might otherwise wake us up, seems in little doubt. Indeed, modern research has provided added evidence of the dream's power to do this, in the sense that we now have cases of dreams incorporating artificial stimuli like sprinkled water which then becomes a dream of rain, a smell of burning which gives rise to a dream of a forest fire, and so on. But in Freud's view this kind of guardianship of sleep was only secondary. In fact, he actually anticipated one aspect of modern research-findings by saying that while external stimuli might be incorporated into an ongoing dream, they could never in themselves initiate one.

In Freud's view dreams were always initiated by the energy of repressed wishes striving for discharge and could not be formed without it. While these wishes could be activated by the events or thoughts of the day. he believed that they were prevented from entering consciousness during waking life by means of what he called the repression barrier. During sleep, he thought, this barrier is lowered and the wishes surge forward in the direction of consciousness. However, because the body is paralyzed during sleep, they cannot achieve gratification in the external world (which is just as well, since he believed most of them to be lustful, murderous, and incestuous!) and so they settle for fantasy gratification in the form of a dream. But, said Freud, if they appeared overtly in all their horror in a dream, the dreamer would be so upset that he would awaken in distress. So before entering the sleeper's mind, they assume a guise of respectability by attaching themselves to innocuous "day residues"—Freud's term for the thoughts and memories of the previous day—which chaperone them into the dream, and then clothe themselves with symbols and other protective devices so that they become totally unrecognizable. The dreamer is then able to get the sleep his body needs by having a dream whose true meaning remains hidden from the sleeping mind and continues to remain hidden even in waking life until a psychoanalyst comes along to interpret it.

Freud assumed that the repressed wishes usually made themselves felt when arousal was imminent—that is, in light sleep—and it is clear from his writing that he thought this occurred under ordinary circumstances close to the time of awakening. He did say, however, that if a wish were really frantic for discharge a dream could occur in deep sleep. In all cases, he remained adamant that no dream could ever be formed without the energy of repressed wishes.

We now know, however, that REM periods—the times during which the type of dream described by Freud usually occur—are not dependent on repressed wishes at all, but take place several times a night in a regular, unremitting cycle which modern research suggests is triggered off at definite intervals by a physiological clock mechanism in the brain. It is just not feasible to suppose that naughty wishes arise from the unconscious approximately every ninety minutes and instigate a dream. What is reasonable, however, is that if such a wish happens to be around at the time of a REM period, it may invade a dream in exactly the same way as other mental contents, most of which are likely to be innocuous thoughts or trivial concerns (or, on special occasions, external stimuli and bodily discomforts). Modern research corroborates this view, as it has shown that the majority of our dreams are indeed rather dull, bland, and trivial, even those occurring during REM periods.

Of course, a psychoanalyst could try to argue that even the dullest dreams are still repressed infantile wishes which happen to have found a very effective disguise, but there seems to be no good reason to try to fit the facts to the theory in this way. As I shall be showing later, psychoanalytic attempts to interpret straightforward dreams can lead to some very farfetched conclusions, and often cause the dreamer to overlook some quite real worry about his present daily affairs.

Moreover, modern experimental work has shown that very often we sleep quite happily through some of our most shocking dreams, when, according to Freud, we should be leaping out of bed in horror because the disguise function has failed. In my own work, for example, I have frequently had the experience of waking subjects up during quite overt dreams of incest, murder, and all kinds of other forbidden activites which, in Freud's view, should certainly have been disguised. Sometimes the dreamer was pleased to have been awakened, and sometimes angry with me for spoiling his fun. On one occasion a girl who was awakened from a long REM period which I felt must be nearing its end reported that she had been wandering endlessly around a hospital in great distress, trying to find a doctor who would give her an abortion because she was pregnant by an animal. No one took any notice of her or gave her help.

When I woke her, she was sobbing in the dream with frustration and despair, having reconciled herself to her condition and wondering what animal it was going to be. She remembered having once taken her pet rat to bed with her as a child and she had on various occasions slept in stables. "What a relief to wake up," she said, "and find that it's not true." I have no doubt that had I not awakened her, she would have slept right through this dream and not even remembered it.

On another occasion, a male student dreamed he was in bed with his mother, who was stroking and cuddling him: he became very excited and was most indignant at my interrupting him. I remember, too, when I first became interested in the new dream-catching techniques and carried out experiments on myself, I had several lovely dreams of my brother making love to me from behind, and was very cross to be awakened from them by the alarm clock. As I had never spontaneously remembered dreams of this nature previously, I can only suppose that normally I sleep right through them. In all these cases, the disguise function had obviously failed, according to Freud, but we slept on and in some cases thoroughly enjoyed the forbidden activities!

As I have said, there is no reason to deny that dreams can express wishes, and it is also quite likely that some may express them obliquely. For example, my daughter might well have fantasied her toy lion's biting me in waking life (because lions are more effective biters than little girls), so it would not be surprising for this fantasy to find its way into her dream. Far from being disguised, this dream is only too blatant in its intent: in fact, she reported it to me with a big grin on her face, not with signs of distress.

In many ways, the true relation between sleep and dreams would seem to be the reverse of Freud's theory. Modern evidence has shown that whenever sleep occurs in normal human beings, if it lasts long enough, dreams will always accompany it: sleep, in fact, is the guardian of the dream.

THE DREAM AS A SAFETY VALVE

Nor does the idea of the dream as a safety valve for repressed wishes stand up very well in the light of modern findings. In the first place, as we have seen, the majority of our dreams are so trivial and lacking in energy that it seems quite unreasonable to insist that they are all bursting beneath their disguise for fantasy gratification. Secondly, the whole concept of drive discharge during sleep needs to be questioned as it is doubtful whether fantasy is able to achieve any lasting satisfaction for the organism. True, one American researcher claims to have discovered that thirsty subjects who dreamed of drinking actually drank less on waking the following morning than those whose attempts to relieve their thirst in a dream had failed. I am very skeptical about drawing any general conclusion from this, however, since it is difficult to see how the principle could apply in most cases. For example, it is a common dream experience to find ourselves frantically searching for a lavatory when bladder pressure becomes acute during sleep, but those who succeed in relieving themselves in a dream surely cannot urinate any less the following morning than those whose dream efforts to do so were frustrated!

As far as sexual and aggressive drives are concerned, there is no really convincing evidence that they find release in dreams, and my own personal experience suggests that the reverse may be the case. There have undoubtedly been occasions on which dreams of sexual or aggressive activity were followed by temporary cathartic feelings of well-being the next morning, but far from making me feel less sexually or aggressively inclined toward my dream victim in waking life, the fantasy has often had the reverse effect of stimulating feelings which were exerting little or no conscious pressure before the fantasy. For example, I actually feel much more sexually attracted toward my brother since having had my dreams of incest than I ever did before, and am often able to express aggression openly to a person once I have been made aware of such feelings in a dream. I do not find this disturbing since emotions brought to conscious awareness are far less dangerous than those which remain repressed.

The theory of the dream as a safety valve was not a new one to Freud, and he referred several times in *The Interpretation of Dreams* to the excretion theory of W. Robert, put forward in 1886. Robert emphasized the appearance in dreams of relatively indifferent material from the previous day, rather than unconscious impulses. He described the dream as a "somatic process of excretion" which acts as a safety valve by allowing tension accumulated during the day to be discharged. "A man deprived of the capacity for dreaming," he wrote, "would in course of time become mentally deranged because a great mass of uncompleted, unworked-out thoughts and superficial impressions would accumulate in his brain," smothering his capacity for normal thought processes.

While Freud recognized that memories of thoughts and events of the previous day—day residues—could find their way into dreams, he did not attribute to them a primary function in dream activity, as we have seen. He saw them rather as vehicles whereby repressed unconscious wishes could smuggle themselves through into the dream. To Freud a man deprived of dreaming might break down because his unconscious urges had no outlet, while to Robert it is the day residues which cause the trouble. Freud also disagreed with Robert's use of the term "somatic" (physical) to describe the process of dreaming, insisting that the dream was essentially a psychological phenomenon.

In the light of modern research, Robert seems to have come closer to the truth than Freud. The regular alternating cycle of REM/NREM sleep is essentially a physiological process which occurs in the organism long before the purely subjective experience of dreaming, as we normally think of it, develops. It seems likely that at some point in the development of the human species dreaming behavior superimposed itself on the physiological background of the REM process, but whether this behavior is necessary for survival is another matter. As we have seen, human beings deprived of REM sleep for over a fortnight have shown minimal psychological disturbance, but it is certainly possible that more prolonged deprivation might eventually have resulted in breakdown.

In summary, Freud's notion of the dual function of dreaming—as the guardian of sleep and as a safety valve for the fantasied expression of repressed wishes—must be revised in the light of modern research if it is to become anything like a *comprehensive* theory of the dreaming process. Yet in spite of its limitations it was a major breakthrough in bringing back the idea that dreams can be meaningful communications—not from the supernatural but from man's own inner being. Having once opened up the idea of interpreting dreams as clues to our hidden emotional problems and conflicts, Freud paved the way for others to explore the use of dreams for expanding human awareness in a whole variety of ways, as I shall be describing later. We are probably a long way yet from having any overall theory of the dreaming process, but this in no way detracts from the fact that some dreams at least do provide us with a royal road to the unconscious, a means to the better understanding of ourselves.

CHAPTER 5

DREAMING TO SOME PURPOSE

The fact that the bulk of dream material seems trivial and uninteresting, now that we have access to so much more of it than was previously available, has led many people to abandon any notion of the dream as a creative or meaningful phenomenon. Indeed, Sir Peter Medawar, the Nobel Prize winning zoologist, rebuked Arthur Koestler for referring in his book *The Act of Creation* to dreaming as a "sliding back towards the pulsating darkness, of which we were part before our separate egos were formed." In a remark which has since become notorious, he emphasized that many dreams may be no more than the kind of meaningless "noise" that comes out of any piece of working electrical equipment—"There should be no need to emphasize," he wrote, "in this century of radio sets and electronic devices, that many dreams may be assemblages of thought-elements that convey no information whatsoever."

From my own experience, I would say that much of our hypnagogic experience at sleep onset and some of our NREM dreams certainly seem to be of this nature. For example, when we first begin to fall asleep, abstract thought rapidly gives way to sensations of falling, bodily distortions and jerks, noises and flashes of light. My own recurrent hypnagogic experience is one of slipping and subsequently waking up with a jerk. (This is a familiar phenomenon which has acquired the technical name of "myoclonic jerk"). Some people see objects hurtling toward them out of space, or grotesque faces appearing and disappearing in a menacing fashion. Repetitive or monotonous activity carried out during the day may pursue us into sleep. For example, after long and tiring car drives I find myself swerving around corners and overtaking, while cars and trucks advance upon me in an endless procession, often to the accompaniment of flashing lights and car horns. Sometimes music I have been listening to during the evening pursues me into sleep. It seems that repeated perceptual responses made during the day continue in sleep in the absense of corresponding sense-organ stimulation, and it is unlikely that this represents anything other than "noise" within the brain.

Sometimes, however, the hypnagogic imagery seems unconnected with the day's events. For example, I recently had a vision of a girl in blue wandering through a field of yellow corn which was waving gently in the breeze. This was so vivid that I attempted to reproduce it in paint the following day. On another occasion, I had a fleeting vision of a red dragon dancing in an open square. Freudian theory would, no doubt, be tempted to trace these visions back to some repressed infantile wish—particularly that of the red dragon, which is widely regarded as a sex symbol—but I believe they were merely random responses to decreased environmental stimuli as the brain passed from a waking to a sleeping state and were of no significance whatsoever.

Similar experiences occur during the day when we allow our attention to wander or fall into a daydream, and it is likely that they exist as background noise continuously in the living brain. Whether the same is true of nocturnal REM and NREM dreams is another matter. Certainly some NREM dreams seem to be of this nature, especially the ones in which the dreamer felt he was "wandering around" or "ticking over." This cannot be the whole story, however, as many dreams are detailed complex events which indicate the existence of some sort of order in the system.

As for REM dreams, far from being weird assemblages of fantastic characters and events, modern research has shown most of them to be down-to-earth representations of normal waking activity. Indeed, Dr. Frederick Snyder reported recently at the Association for the Psychophysiological Study of Sleep in America, "about 90% of REM dreams are judged to be about as credible as descriptions of waking reality, equally undramatic and lacking in bizarreness. . . . REM dream reports are generally clear, coherent, believable accounts of realistic situations in which the dreamer and other persons are involved in quite mundane activities and preoccupations. . . . Reports were considered almost entirely representational and realistic in visual form, generally involving a familiar or commonplace setting, almost always including the self, usually in interaction with other persons. . . ."

Other investigators have also commented on the lack of zip to REM dreams collected in the laboratory, and have compared them with dreams recalled spontaneously at home, which seem to offer greater promise for the uncovering of personal problems and conflicts. This observation was corroborated by a series of experiments at the University of California by Professor Calvin Hall and his colleagues, who compared samples of dreams collected under different conditions. Their results showed that home dreams contained more sexuality, aggression, misfortune, failure, success, and friendliness than laboratory dreams and were, generally speaking, more spicy and exciting.

The majority of my own experiments were carried out in my own home with subjects sleeping in a warm, comfortable bedroom under as natural conditions as possible. Of course, they were wired up to the recording apparatus and were warned that they would be awakened several times during the night in order to report their dreams—conditions which are far from natural—but an effort was made to minimize the effects produced by the cold, impersonal hospital or laboratory atmosphere. Instead of 90 percent of REM dreams being realistic representations of everyday affairs, only 65 percent of my subjects' REM dreams were of this nature; and when I divided the night into two halves, I found that over 80 percent of the dreams in the first half were dull and trivial, compared with only 50 percent in the second half of the night.

This corroborates earlier findings that dreams tend to become more dramatic and bizarre and to contain more childhood material as the night progresses. As we normally do not stay awake long enough in the middle of the night to remember a dream, it is likely that most spontaneously recalled dreams arise out of the last long REM period before waking in the morning. It is not unreasonable to suppose, too, that Freud was working with the similarly spontaneously recalled dreams of his patients, and so came to base his theory exclusively on the more dramatic and emotional of our nocturnal experiences. In fact, the common reaction of my psychoanalyst friends on reading through my subjects' dreams is how dreadfully boring most of them are—not the most encouraging remark to a poor dream researcher who has spent hundreds of sleepless nights collecting the stuff!

THE "TYPICAL" DREAM

The finding that laboratory dreams are so conspicuously lacking in sexual and aggressive activity, and indeed anything remotely hinting at unconscious infantile conflicts, has led some psychoanalysts to condemn the laboratory dream as a distorted and atypical product of the sleeper's mental activity. While this begs the obvious question of exactly what constitutes a "typical" dream, a question which will be discussed fully in a moment, can any analyst really believe that his patients' dream life remains uncontaminated by the special conditions of the therapeutic relationship? In analysis, we soon learn how to gain the attention and the approval of the analyst or, conversely, how to thwart and upset him, by learning the kind of information he is interested in and giving it to him. In one of my own periods of Freudian analysis, it did not take me long to discover that whenever I discussed sexual experiences the chair behind me creaked (with anticipation?) as my analyst came out of his reverie to listen to me. I was then rewarded with grunts of encouragement as I talked and a warm smile when I left. During the time when I was needing his approval, I obliged with many splendid dreams all teeming with sex symbols, but when I went through a negative reaction and considered changing to a Jungian analyst, I produced more than a fair share of dreams containing ancient magical symbols and mythical themes!

Dream researchers are well aware of the difficulties of obtaining a fair sample of "typical" dream reports, as almost any unusual condition is likely to bias the results. For example, even if subjects are spared the anxiety-provoking situation of sleeping in a laboratory wired up to complicated recording apparatus, the very act of even asking them to report their dreams to someone else is likely to influence both dream content and recall. These difficulties led Hall and his colleagues to consider suddenly and without warning descending via telephone or doorbell ringing on a representative sample of innocent, unknowing victims in the middle of the night, and trying to persuade them to tell their dreams for the good of science and humanity! The idea was abandoned after one of Hall's colleagues telephoned him at 3 A.M. one morning, announcing that his nationwide study on dream reports from unexpected awakenings had begun, only to receive Hall's answer: "Go to hell!" I tried this experiment on my husband with similar results.

The answer to these problems is, of course, that there is no such thing as a "typical" dream. Dreams are complex psychological products inevitably influenced by the conditions under which they are dreamed and reported. Dreams are not "distorted" by anxiety-making laboratory influences or by the special atmosphere of the psychoanalytic set-up, but are *shaped* by these and other conditions. Even at home, we are not immune to unusual influences which may affect our dream life. For example, women in the last three months of pregnancy have more dreams of babies than the rest of us, and at the time of my marriage break-up most of my dreams for a considerable period of time contained themes of disintegration and loss. And in recent detailed studies, Professor Robert Van de Castle at the University of Virginia has shown that the content of women's dreams is significantly affected by the menstrual cycle.

Long-standing personality factors also influence our dreams. For example, experiments have shown that depressed people tend to dream about depressing things; anxious people dream of personal threat; the dreams of sociopaths are full of socially prohibited activities; convicted sex offenders have more dreams of unlawful sexual activity than the rest of us; paranoid patients' dreams are saturated with themes of unjustifiable abuse and counterattack; and those who express their impulses openly in waking life show more hostility and sexuality in their dreams than those who are more inhibited.

It is not at all surprising, then, that subjects of laboratory experiments on dreaming dream about the laboratory and the anxieties it provokes in them. Approximately one-third of my subjects' dreams contained overt references to the experiment, and I believed I detected symbolic references in another third of them. The following is a typical dream expressing overt anxiety about the experiment:

We were doing this experiment. We had the dream set-up with the intercom in a hospital. I remember gray doors. I was one subject—there was another subject—and you were the experimenter, and I think there was another experimenter. It consisted mainly of you calling me through this thing, and me answering you but being in the wrong place or doing the wrong thing, or somehow annoying you for not responding on time. I woke up with things being generally wrong in the dream. I had made a mistake of some kind but I don't know what. I seemed to feel your disapproval.

This dream makes direct reference to the experimental situation and to me. The following dream of another subject depicts the same situation in a more disguised form.

> We were in a car going through some mountains. We were going to go up the mountain directly instead of going an easy way round. There were some other people in the car, and one of them, a psychiatrist, was looking over my shoulder directing the route. He seemed to be the overseer of the whole project and he was muttering approving things to me. I have the feeling that you were the psychiatrist.

While I would have guessed that this dream referred to the experiment—which the dreamer saw as a headlong attack up the face of the mountain (our direct method of obtaining dreams) under the supervision of a psychiatrist (me)—I would not have been absolutely sure had she not actually confirmed the last point. In these experiments, I did not ask for associations to the dream elements which would certainly have led us back to an underlying anxiety about the experiment. The following is an even more disguised dream, which again I guessed referred to the experiment: in this case, the subject offered no confirmation of this, and it would have remained a guess on my part had it not been for something that happened the following day, after he had gone home.

The subject reported,

> It's a country scene and there are a number of figures in the background. I seem to have some big farm receptacle that had got dirty and which had to be cleaned. And it seemed to be you in the background sending for one of these people to come and clean it. And the message came back by these people that they were so busy they couldn't spare anybody, and I said, "Don't bother, I'll do it." There was quite a large stream of

86

clear water and I immersed this object in it and cleaned it down with a brush. Then, after that, it seemed to be the end of the night and time to go home.

His last sentence gives me the clue that the dream is about the experiment, and from this I was led to look for the meaning of the farm receptacle which was obviously causing him so much concern. Now, in the early days of my experimental work I used to ask my subjects if they would mind using the pot beneath the bed instead of visiting the bathroom during the night. The majority acquiesced quite happily and the arrangement saved me much trouble in un-wiring and rewiring. This particular subject was agreeable to the arrangement on a conscious level, but I believed the dream revealed underlying anxieties about it. I interpreted the farm receptacle as the pot, and I guessed he had used it during the night and was bothered about my finding it dirty in the morning. His dream also hinted that he intended to empty and clean it before he went home. I do not know whether he actually did all this, but the following morning after he had left, I found a perfectly clean pot containing a small piece of paper on which were written the words "Ha Ha"!

Eventually, I had to abandon the pot procedure as more and more subjects produced dreams of receptacles, streams of water, and so on, most of which were accompanied by anxiety feelings. Had I been in a position to obtain my subject's associations to the above dream, we might have been led back to some infantile trauma concerned with urinating on a farm. My quarrel with the psychoanalysts is not their saying that such dreams can lead back to infantile conflicts, since obviously many of them do, but with their insistence that symbolic representation in dreams is a disguise to spare the dreamer's feelings. I believe that if my subject dreams of the pot as a farm receptacle he has a very good reason for doing so: somewhere at the back of his mind the two are inextricably linked by some process of association which has already taken place during waking life.

THE CHATTERING MIND

The layman probably has little idea of the intense mental activity that goes on continuously in the waking mind. Research on the psychology of perception has shown that even an apparently simple observation has already been thoroughly processed in terms of our past experience and present preoccupations *before we even become aware of it.* The poet William Blake was speaking the simple truth when he wrote, "The fool sees not the same tree as the wise man sees." My perception of a tree depends upon all the hundreds of experiences I have had with trees in the past—the tree in the back garden of my childhood home, the tree in the woods under which a small boy kissed me, the tree out of which I fell and broke my arm, and so on. My perception also depends on my present mood and feelings: when I am in love, a tree which I normally regard with indifference becomes suffused with light and life. Of course, our varying perceptions of the same object have enough in common to enable us to communicate our thoughts about it, but they differ in detail according to our individual experiences.

Moreover, whenever we see an object, witness an event, or think a thought a whole train of ideas is set in motion which do not seem to be connected in any logical fashion. For example, when I look at a tree and am reminded of the lilac tree in the garden of my childhood home, my mind may jump to a school friend called Lila Carlton, to memories of holidays together in Yorkshire, to the first sexual experiments, and so on. All this can go on without my conscious knowledge and may appear later in a dream as a strange cluster of apparently unrelated events. In a similar way, my subject may have reacted to the word "pot" by a subsconscious train of associations leading back to a farm experience which may or may not be directly related to some potty-training trauma.

It is worth mentioning here that another subject reacted to the word "pot" in a rather more complicated way, indicating that this had set in motion several trains of thought simultaneously. In one dream, for example, the police raided his flat after having been tipped off that he possessed a small amount of cannabis. (It was true that he possessed this.) He was in bed asleep when a policewoman marched into his bedroom, threw back the bed covers, and declared triumphantly, "I've got it." She then proceeded to reprimand him severely, and he woke up feeling anxious and guilty. He added that the policewoman seemed to be me.

I believe that the word "pot" activated at least three separate trains of thought as soon as I mentioned it. First, a present conscious anxiety that his forbidden pot would be found by the police; second, possible unconscious childhood fears that his mother, an authority figure, would punish him for wetting the bed; and third, subliminal anxieties about my disturbing his sleep and exposing his murky dreams during the course of the experiment. The dream could be said to be a condensation of three separate lines of thought, in which the policewoman, his mother, and I appear as one single person; the cannabis, pot and dreams as one object; and the police raid, his mother's discovery, and the experiment as one activity. While Freud would agree that the trains of thought were started during the day, he would insist that the condensation took place during sleep as a disguise for naughty wishes appearing in the dream. This is discussed fully in the next chapter; it is enough to say here that I see no reason why distortions and muddles should not take place in waking life as various associations link up with one another, and later appear in this form in a dream.

We can learn a great deal about associative activity by listening to children chatter to themselves as they play. For example, as my husband was rehearsing the famous speech from Hamlet, "To be or not to be, . . ." I overheard my small daughter at the other end of the room muttering to herself, "Bee, bee, busy bee, makes honey . . . bread and honey for tea . . . come on, Teddy, eat your tea . . ." Such processes, which are so often verbalized by children, go on all the time in all of us but are overshadowed by our concentration on the task in hand or logical thought processes which constantly try to maintain order in the system. When external stimulation is withdrawn during sleep and waking logic disappears, these trains of association may appear openly in a dream.

For example, I remember one of my own dreams in which a friend of mine called Kiki gave me a key which he said belonged to "that khaki-colored van over there." And a colleague of mine described the way in which such associative processes can actually lead into a dream. "As I was drifting off to sleep," he wrote, "I saw those colored balls of this afternoon's film rolling toward me. This led me to think of chocolate rolls and of woman's role in society. It was, of course, to roll her hips and I immediately found H. standing before me in the dream rolling her hips in a very seductive manner. This led me straight into a sex dream about her."

On another occasion, I noticed that my daughter had carefully arranged a paint pot, a statue of the Hindu god Krishna—which normally sits on her shelf—and a photograph of her grandma side by side on the floor. As I pondered the possible logic underlying this strange assembly, she sat down before them in lotus posture and solemnly started to chant the mantra, "Hare [pronounced Hari] Krishna":

Hare Krishna, Hare Krishna, Krishna Krishna, Hare
  Hare,
Hare Rama, Hare Rama, Rama Rama, Hare Hare ...

It was only then I realized that every time we chanted the mantra together, there flashed before her mind's eye a picture of Harry (our house painter), Krishna, and grandma, all sitting together in a row solemnly chanting each other's names! One day soon, if she has not done so already, she will question the oddity of the situation, and I should not be surprised to hear a dream in which these three characters attempt to make sense of themselves—possible solutions which have already passed fleetingly through her mind during the course of waking life without her ever becoming aware of them.

Incidentally, anyone who has tried to practice meditation is only too well aware of the mind's constant and unyielding background chatter as he attempts to clear his mind of unwanted and distracting thought.

Recently my daughter produced another good example of the kind of association muddle normally known as "Sundayschoolese" because it seems to occur particularly often with the slightly old-fashioned wording of hymns. She arrived home from nursery school, stood on a chair, and started to sing in a halting voice the Christmas carol:

> While shepherds watch their flocks by night
> All seated on the ground,
> The angel of the lord came down . . .

Suddenly she stopped and, pointing to her toy horse, said sadly, "Poor horsey—angel come and take him to God." After hearing her sing the carol several times, I suddenly realized that "*all seated* on the ground" had become for her "*horsey dead* on the ground." Quite evidently, she would go to bed that night with her mind containing a strange mixture of balancing, singing, and goodness-knows-what other associations from her school carol lesson, all bound up with a vision of some people called shepherds at night and an angel who had come down from heaven to take her poor dead horsey to God! And although as we grow up we learn to discount such misapprehensions, there is no doubt that they still go on at the back of our minds all the time, and probably play a large part in the formation of dreams.

In summary, when incoming information from the environment ceases and rational thought relaxes control during sleep, the day's background chatter comes to the fore, and if we awaken we may catch some of it. We may catch part of the day's activities and preoccupations which have not become too entangled in a net of associations, in which case we would recall a clear, coherent, realistic dream similar to those described by Snyder. On the other hand, we may pick up a whole gamut of associations, in which case our dream would probably be one of those strange, bizarre fantasies so often quoted in psychoanalytic case histories. Such associations are not mere "noise" in Medawar's sense. They operate according to a logic of their own which, as Freud realized, can tell us much about ourselves and the strange ways we have built up for coping with life, if we would only take the trouble to understand it.

It is possible that exactly the same kind of chatter is passing through the mind during REM and NREM sleep, and that the heightened activation of the former merely renders it more memorable. Hence the longer, more vivid dream reports from awakenings during REM sleep. However, no one knows the answer to this, and it may be that quite different kinds of material come to the fore during REM and NREM sleep. In the meantime it seems to me that we "dream" not only of the things which are *on* our minds—worries, preoccupations, wishes, whatever —but also of all the myriad things which have taken place below the level of conscious awareness during the course of the day and are still active *in* our minds as we fall asleep. Whether or not dreaming in this sense bears any direct relation to the underlying physiological process of memory consolidation during REM sleep, discussed in Chapter 1, is a problem for future research.

SLEEPING ON IT

Does the nightly dance of day memories and their associations have any psychological value for us if we do not become aware of them through waking? If it does, then perhaps it would be better to let it get on with its work without interruption, just like the goblins in fairy tales who spring-clean the house at night as long as they remain unobserved.

One group of workers certainly believe this. They have suggested that dreaming may be analogous to certain processes which go on in electronic computers. From time to time these machines have to be taken "off line"—that is, uncoupled from the task they are controlling—so that the programs they use can be updated in the light of new information. For example, a computer dealing with the regular calculation of pay, tax, insurance, and so on, for workers in a factory, must be up-dated from time to time to allow for the fact that a new rate of pay has been agreed on for certain jobs or a change has been made in the tax laws.

In a similar way, they say, the human brain, which is a vastly more complex and subtle mechanism than any electronic computer so far constructed, has developed its own "programs" for dealing with life's situations. These include programs for basic routines like walking and eating, programs for dealing with simple life problems like getting to work, and programs for coping with complicated emotional situations such as social and sexual interactions with others. Every day, however, life confronts us with new problems to be solved which force us to adjust our old programs accordingly. For example, when we break a leg we have to learn to walk in a new way, a change in office organization may mean relinquishing several old work routines and learning new ones, while meeting someone we find sexually attractive may lead us to reorganize much of our leisure time. The adherents of the "computer theories" of dreaming suggest that we register these new situations during the day and then, when sleep takes most of the brain out of active service, our dreaming mind runs through what has happened to us in waking life and integrates the new information into existing programs ready for the next day. At the same time, the vast amount of day memories which are irrelevant for the long-term goals of the organism are discarded, perhaps by means of some electrical discharge in the brain.

According to this view, the experiences we call dreams are no more than glimpses of this material running through our sleeping brains as they carry out their nightly operation of "information processing." It has even been suggested that the stories of our dreams are inventions of the waking mind, which attempts to impose some kind of sense and order on the isolated pieces of information being processed and bind them into a meaningful whole. And finally, it is maintained that even to awaken accidentally during sleep is to interrupt a vital process which would be better left undisturbed from the point of view of our mental efficiency. Dreaming is believed to be the actual information-processing activity, and the purpose of sleep to allow this to take place. If we are deprived of the opportunity to "dream," say the computer theorists, we must eventually break down because the brain's existing programs are not being up-dated in the light of new information. This must necessarily result in maladaptive, neurotic behavior.

While the computer analogy may be useful in many ways, I believe it is a mistake to draw too many conclusions from it. In the first place computer technology has advanced considerably since the theory was first formulated about ten years ago. Modern computers no longer have to be taken off line in order to have their programs updated: this can be done while they are still carrying on a multiplicity of other tasks. I see no reason why the brain should not do this too, and it is possible that much of the background chatter I have been describing consists precisely of incorporating new information into existing programs during waking life. Hence, while the dreaming mind may *reflect* this information-processing operation, I doubt whether any actual processing is taking place at all during sleep. It seems more likely that the sleeper is running over what has already been done during the day and that REM sleep provides the conditions for what has already been processed to be further consolidated for more efficient use. And while the mind may elaborate material recalled on waking from sleep, I believe that most of our dream fantasies were woven during the course of the day.

In the second place, REM deprivation experiments have provided no evidence that a "nondreaming" brain breaks down on account of nonclearance or faulty programs. Of course, it can be argued that the amount of deprivation so far imposed has not been sufficient to push the brain to its limits, but this renders the theory somewhat feeble.

On the other hand, our lives undoubtedly *are* impaired, irrespective of how well we sleep, by the fact that our behavior often derives from "programs" laid down in our minds in childhood which have long since become out of date or inappropriate to our life circumstances as adults. To take a fairly standard "Freudian" example, a boy with a very nervous mother may develop a program for dealing with women which assumes that they are all in constant need of placation, and there is a great deal of evidence to show that his subsequent meetings with women who are different makes very little impression on this basic program. So he continues throughout his life to react to women in this infantile and stereotyped manner. Early childhood programs like this might be likened to the basic programs with which a computer is equipped when it leaves the factory, the changing of which is a matter not of routine nightly maintenance but of a major effort of reprogramming, extending over several days, weeks, months, or even years.

The first step in digging out and changing such out-of-date childhood programs is to become aware of them and see how they are determining our behavior. As I shall be demonstrating later, my experience provides evidence, which to me seems irrefutable, that *remembered* dreams can help us do just this. They also sometimes suggest possible new behavior patterns more appropriate to our present situation. This revelatory role of dreaming may be no more than a by-product from the point of view of the brain's biological processes, but I am sure that its positive value in human life far outweighs any minor ill effects that might possibly be found one day as a result of interrupted sleep. In this, the computer theorists seem to me to be drawing a false conclusion by using their analogy in a quite unnecessarily limited way. I am not denying that there may be *something* in the folk wisdom which suggests that we may actually help to solve our problems "by sleeping on them." Merely reliving our daily preoccupations and their background chatter may well have a cathartic effect similar to that achieved by talking over some problem to a passive listener. Here again, however, it seems to me likely that when we wake up feeling that we have come to terms with a problem the solution was already present in our minds during the day among the background chatter, but external distractions prevented us from becoming aware of it. Many great discoveries and inventions have come to light not necessarily in a dream (although some of them did), but when the conscious mind relaxed and allowed the chatter to make itself heard. I believe this chatter is the source of much creative activity, as associations and ideas spread through the mind and link with new trains of thought and feeling. In this way new and unexpected connections are made, giving fresh meanings to old ideas. Metaphors, slang, puns, overlapping meanings, and figures of speech are the language used by the chattering mind to create new forms of mental life, of which the dream is only one.

Only future research can settle the question of what functions dreaming performs when we leave it undisturbed. What I am convinced of is that the dreams we recall can make available to us valuable information about ourselves. Talking over problems with a purely passive listener is on the whole of less help than discussing them with someone who applies his conscious intelligence to them. In a similar way, our conscious minds are needed if we are to make the most of our dreams: by bringing them into waking consciousness and learning to understand them we may be led to a reappraisal of our whole mode of being.

PART II

EXPLORERS OF THE DREAM

CHAPTER 6

IN THE CONSULTING ROOM

Freud's pioneering work in drawing attention to dreams as clues to inner conflicts sprang from his psychotherapeutic work in the consulting room, with the result that his subsequent method of dream interpretation became a highly specialized business. If, as he believed, a dream is essentially a *disguised* expression of what is going on below the surface of the mind, the last person to be able to understand its meaning would be the dreamer himself. Freud believed that the sleeping mind resorted to a whole battery of psychological mechanisms to dress up the unconscious wishes in forms which would prevent the dreamer's becoming aware of their true nature. To unravel the meaning of the dream therefore required, in his view, not only an expert knowledge of these mechanisms, but also a psychoanalyst independent of the dreamer who could overcome the dreamer's psychological resistance to seeing the truth.

While there is no doubt that dreams express themselves in a strange, mysterious language quite different from that of waking life, there are no real grounds for considering these transformations as disguises, as we shall see later. Although Freud's whole aim was to be scientific in his approach, there is no doubt that his disguise theory often leads to interpretations which smack more of occultism than science. Nevertheless, it is essential to examine his theory of dream interpretation in some detail because many ideas derived from it have become part of our popular folklore. Moreover, some of the mechanisms of dream "transformation" which he describes do undoubtedly occur and we can gain from him many useful insights into the picture language of dreams.

FREUD'S THEORY OF DREAM DISGUISE

Freud postulated four major ways in which the latent dream content consisting of repressed unconscious wishes becomes transformed into the "manifest" dream as we remember it on waking. He called these processes condensation, displacement, symbolization, and secondary revision, all of which are illustrated by the following incident from my own Freudian analysis.

I am lying on my analyst's couch relating a dream. I tell of floating happily through the air around the galleries of a theater, hand in hand with a man who resembles a hypnotist colleague of mine. I note with some surprise that he is wearing a bow tie, as this is not his normal custom. I have the feeling that the theater belongs to him and that he is showing me around. The seats are occupied by figures which remind me of waxworks, but as I approach them, I recognize many familiar faces from my childhood. We greet them all as we float past. Although I have no fear of flying so far above the ground, I find myself inexplicably worried that the people in the balcony seats may fall, and I wake up noticing that the whole internal structure of the theater looks extremely rickety and unsafe.

My analyst listens patiently, but is relatively uninterested in my description of the theater scene and quite unimpressed by my ability to fly. The story as I have related it is for him merely the "manifest content" of the dream, a harmless cover for the seething repressed wishes which make up the "latent content." His task, as he sees it, is to decipher the code and lay bare the underlying message of my unconscious mind. So, he asks me to start associating freely to each element in the dream. I am to relax and let my mind wander around theaters, hypnotists, bow ties, and so on, saying everything that comes into my head, however bizarre.

As he listens, the analyst may have a number of general ideas about what such activities as floating may mean, based on past experience in the consulting room, but he is also trying to tune into my particular mind in a special way. "The analyst," Freud wrote, "must turn his unconscious like a receptive organ towards the transmitting unconscious of the patient. He must adjust himself to the patient as a telephone receiver is adjusted to the receiving microphone. Just as the receiver converts back into sound waves the electric oscillations in the telephone line which were set up by sound waves, so is the doctor's unconscious able . . . to reconstruct (the patient's) unconscious." In other words, the interpretive process is an intuitive one and is often referred to as "listening with the third ear." (Unfortunately, many psychoanalysts have never developed this gift and rely for their interpretations on preconceived ideas and theories learned during the course of their analytic training.)

In associating to my dream, the gallery through which I am floating brings to mind the idea of the "rogues' gallery," and seeing the figures of my past reminds me of the analytic situation in which one relives many long-forgotten childhood experiences. The floating brings back snatches of an old German song which goes something like *"Ich tanze mit dir in den Himmel hinein, In den siebenten Himmel der Liebe,"* which translated means "I dance with you into heaven, into the seventh heaven of love." At this point, I stop in embarrassment as it is clear that my companion in the air is my analyst and that I see him as both rogue and lover. I am also extremely upset to discover that my normally down-to-earth, unsentimental mind should be secretly singing such romantic nonsense!

Continuing my associations, I am reminded that in an earlier session, I accused my analyst of hypnotizing me into accepting his ideas and values—a further corroboration of the fact that the hypnotist companion of my dream is my analyst. Since neither of them wear bow ties, I let my mind wander around this point until there flashes before me the image of an old friend of mine, Jim Savage, who is often teased for his taste in flashy bow ties. I remember that he is also teased on account of his name, "Savage," which is quite out of keeping with his gentle, courteous nature. The word "savage" to me conjures up a picture of rough, primitive sexuality, which gives my analyst another clue to the underlying meaning of the dream. It is obvious, he says, that I see him (the analyst) as a rogue who will hypnotize me into having sexual relations with him: in other words, my dream represents an unconscious wish on my part that he should rape me.

For my analyst, however, all this is only the first step in interpreting the dream, for what he is really seeking is not so much a *present* unconscious wish, but one dating back to early life. One of Freud's most important discoveries was that dreams referring to the analyst are often reenactments of much older established wishes going back to the first few years of life which have been transferred from some important childhood figure to that of the analyst himself. He called the way in which the patient projected these wishes and feelings onto the figure of the analyst "transference," and he found it a valuable technique in exposing neurotic behavior patterns built up during the early years of life.

So, at this point in my free associations, my analyst concludes that the sexual feelings I seem to have toward him really belong to someone in my past, perhaps a father, a brother, or some other family figure. In fact, my associations lead me back from the floating episode in the dream to a game I used to play with my brother when I was small, in which we jumped toward each other from chairs on either side of a large bed, clutched each other in the air, and then fell down onto the bed, rolling over and over with each other on the mattress. This probably aroused sexual feelings in both of us, and so the final interpretation of the dream, according to my analyst, is that it gives very elaborately "disguised" expression to an early wish that my brother (whom I must have thought of as a young rogue and savage) should indulge in childhood sexuality with me. Moreover, in order to escape anxious guilt feelings for such a disgraceful wish, I must have added the afterthought that he had actually hypnotized me into the forbidden activity, thus relieving me of all responsibility for my "fall."

In Freudian dream theory, this "latent" wish to be raped by my brother would be the essential motive force of the dream, but would be so horrifying to my conscious mind that I should be shocked into wakefulness if it were expressed openly. So, said Freud, the sleeping mind processes the wish in a number of different ways in order to disguise its true meaning.

In the first place, for example, the dream makes no direct reference either to my analyst or to my brother. Instead, my dream companion is the owner of a "rogues' gallery" and resembles a hypnotist colleague who is wearing a bow tie. This composite figure of rogue, hypnotist, and savage who by means of free association turns out to be my analyst/brother, is the result of what Freud called *condensation*, a special disguise mechanism whereby two or more latent dream thoughts are condensed into a single image or idea in the manifest dream. There is no doubt that such a mechanism does exist, in waking thought as well as in dreams, but in my view, far from disguising unconscious wishes, it often serves to clarify them in the most economical way possible. The whole question of disguise in dreams will be discussed fully later in the chapter: it is sufficient to mention here that the composite image of my dream companion *revealed* (not concealed) to me in a very neat fashion exactly how I felt about my analyst and my brother.

Another "disguise" mechanism, said Freud, is *displacement*, which can take many different forms in dreams. For example, an emotion really belonging to one situation may be displaced to another, in order to distract the dreamer's attention from the true object of his feelings. In my floating dream, my analyst thought I had displaced anxiety about my own sexual wishes, which I saw as a "fall" from virtue, onto the people in the balcony, who I felt were in danger of falling because the theater was unsafe.

Freud quotes a dream in which the displacement of feeling actually amounted to a total reversal. One of his patients related how he woke up laughing, yet felt miserable and depressed the following day. His associations to the dream led back to latent thoughts of impotence and death, and Freud concluded that the laughter in the dream was a reversal of the sobbing and weeping he really felt at the thought of going downhill. He also held that there might be a total suppression of feeling in a dream—for example, when we look on dispassionately as some dreadful disaster happens to a loved one. Freud thought that both reversal and suppression of emotion in a dream were disguise mechanisms utilized to confuse the dreamer and sabotage attempts at interpretation.

My analyst thought he detected the mechanism of reversal in one of my own dreams. In it, my supervisor was criticizing my work for carelessness, although there was no reason why she should have done so in waking life. My associations led to the fact that *I felt critical of her* for not paying sufficient attention to me. At a deeper level, he suggested this dream really referred to my mother, who I felt never gave me enough love.

Freud also thought that we sometimes displaced worries about the genital regions to organs further up the body. For example, a man might displace castration anxiety to fears of damage to his nose or ear, or dream about a beard when his mind was really on pubic hair. When I had a dream about a fish going into my ear, my analyst interpreted this as a wish for sexual intercourse, in spite of the fact that my associations led back to the play *Hamlet,* in which the king is killed by having poison poured down his ear. My own feeling that I was being poisoned by my analyst's interpretations, which I received through my ear, was not even considered.

We must also bear in mind, said Freud, that a common technique of dream distortion consists in representing the outcome of a train of thought at the beginning of the dream, and its starting point at the end. And finally, he added, "If a dream obstinately declines to reveal its meaning, it is always worth while to see the effect of reversing some particular elements in its manifest content, after which the whole situation often becomes immediately clear." For example, if I dream of my superior's being over-dressed, this might hide a wish to see him naked, and if I dream of my father making love to my mother, this might mean that I want him to reject her.

At this point, the whole business of displacement in dreams, as seen by Freud, becomes ridiculous, as it enables us to give a dream any meaning we wish. The idea that a dream can indicate one thing *or its opposite* would reduce any other science to an absurdity, and yet psychoanalysts are still trying to pretend that their "heads I win, tails you lose" philosophy is scientific. A basic principle in any science is that a theory which cannot be disproved is really no theory at all. While I believe that some kinds of displacement occur in dreams, just as they do in waking life, I disagree completely with Freud's view that displacement in dreams is a crafty device of the sleeping mind to lead us astray. For example, we are familiar with the man who kicks the dog after a trying day at the office, and there is no reason why such displacement of emotion should not take place in a dream. Similarly, my daughter dresses her teddy bear in nappies when she accidentally wets her own pants, probably in an attempt to ward off anxiety that I shall do the same to her.

It is possible, therefore, that my analyst could have been correct in attributing my anxiety feelings about the people in the rickety balcony in my floating dream to displacement, but in this case, I think there is a simpler, more reasonable explanation. Having established that the theater represented the consulting room in which child-

103

hood figures are resurrected, the fact that I saw it as unsafe and even dangerous means that I feel analysis to be a risky business in which many childhood idols may be toppled from their elevated status in my imagination when viewed in the grim light of reality. In this case, the anxiety is exactly where it belongs, and there is no need to invoke the concept of displacement to explain this part of the dream.

Similarly, I believe the dream in which my supervisor was criticizing my work meant exactly what it said—that I have paranoid feelings of insecurity about my abilities which lead me to feel that nothing I do is good enough. The fact that my associations led to my being critical of her was not surprising as I really did feel neglected from time to time. Whether or not this feeling was justified is a matter for analysis, but in any case it is unlikely to have anything to do with displacement.

When displacements do occur in dreams, said Freud, the waking mind is often puzzled by them and attempts to make sense of the dream by carrying out the process of what he called *secondary revision* on it. This is the natural tendency on the part of the dreamer to make sense of his dream as he recaptures it on waking. For example, in my floating dream my analyst thought I had displaced anxiety about my own "fall" from virtue to the people in the balcony, and my mind had attempted to rationalize this by seeing the theater as old and rickety. As I have said, I am sure he was wrong about this, but it offers a good example of what Freud was talking about. "It is in the nature of our waking thought," he wrote, "to establish order in material of that kind, to set up relations in it and to make it conform to our expectations of an intelligible whole." Havelock Ellis, a British dream enthusiast contemporary with Freud, described the process of secondary revision in somewhat lighter vein. "Sleeping consciousness we may even imagine as saying to itself in effect: 'Here comes our master, Waking Consciousness, who attaches such mighty importance to reason and logic and so forth. Quick! gather things up, put them in order—any order will do—before he enters to take possession.' " I am sure that a certain amount of secondary revision does take place in dreams, but I see no reason for describing this process as a disguise any more than condensation and displacement.

The fourth and most important way in which Freud believed that latent wishes were disguised in dreams is *symbolization*, a process whereby an object or idea in the latent content is represented by a substitute object or idea in the manifest dream. For example, I substituted a theater filled with childhood figures for the process of analysis, and floating for the erotic feelings I felt as a child. In addition, my analyst/brother was symbolized by the figure of a hypnotist, although in this case the substitution was overlaid by condensation. Freud wrote that "symbolization is perhaps the most remarkable chapter of the theory of dreams," and a great deal of psychoanalytic literature is devoted to it.

FREUD'S VIEW OF DREAM SYMBOLISM

Because Freud believed that one of the major motive-forces of dreaming is buried infantile sexuality, he concerned himself mostly with the mind's ability to find substitutes for the representation of sexual organs and sexual activities. By noting the associations of his patients, he came to the conclusion that almost any long, pointed object in a dream could be a substitute for a penis—sticks, umbrellas, posts, steeples, trees, bananas, and countless others. He found the same kind of phallic symbolism in dreams of objects whose function is that of penetration, such as daggers, knives, spears, firearms, and also in objects from which water flows, such as fountains, watering cans, and taps.

He found that the female genitals were often symbolized by circular objects and containers, such as pits, cavities, vessels, boxes, trunks, pockets, and so on, as well as by doors and gates, while cupboards, rooms, and stoves symbolized the womb. Dreams of vibrating or pleasurable

105

movement of almost any kind, whether riding, rocking on a seesaw, climbing a ladder or stairs, flying, and floating, he found associated with erotic activities such as masturbation and sexual intercourse.

Because of the frequency with which the patients' associations led back from these dream objects and activities to underlying sexual ideas, situations, and wishes, Freud concluded that this kind of sexual symbolism was practically universal. This meant that an analyst could guess the meaning of a dream before any associations were made to it. He recognized in *The Interpretation of Dreams* that the effect of these conclusions on many readers would be to induce incredulity. He envisaged readers asking, "Do I really live in the thick of sexual symbols? Are all the objects around me, all the clothes I put on, all the things I pick up, all of them sexual symbols and nothing else?" His reply to such possible incredulity was to ask his readers simply to look around at folklore, myths, fairy tales (in their original rather than their censored nursery versions), and slang, and find ample evidence of quite blatant sex-symbolism even in the mind's waking activities. For example, in slang we refer to the penis as a tool, weapon, prick, or cock which is used to screw, plug, or poke the female, and a pregnant woman is said to have a "bun in the oven." For this reason, said Freud, we should not be surprised to find such symbols appearing in dreams, some of which are as old as language itself while others are being coined continuously down to the present time. In the latter case, for example, the most commonly used modern symbol of sexual impulses or the penis is the car or airplane, whereas formerly it used to be the horse.

Freud also found that other symbols appeared with great frequency in dreams. For example, kings and queens often led back to the parents, princes and princesses to siblings, and policemen to authority figures and taboos of childhood. He also found whole situations occurring so repeatedly in dreams that he was led to conclude that certain dream themes were "typical" and could be interpreted as having the same meaning whenever they occurred. For example, most of us have had dreams in which we appear naked in public; to Freud, this meant the wish to recapture the earliest childhood experience of unashamed nakedness, the climate of Eden before anxiety awoke, expulsion followed, and sexual life and the tasks of cultural activity began. Dreams of a loved one's death he interpreted as the hidden childhood wish to eliminate a rival, and dreams of missing a train were "consolation" dreams: as the departing train is a symbol of death, the dreamer is reassuring himself that he is not going to die. Loss-of-teeth dreams symbolize castration anxiety, he said, while swimming and water dreams are fantasies of conception, of the womb, and of birth—the times of supreme security. Dreams of robbers, burglars, and ghosts are infantile memories of parents who come to the bedside of the sleeping child. "Analyses of these anxiety dreams have made it possible for me to identify these nocturnal visitors more precisely. In every case, the robbers stood for the sleeper's father, whereas the ghosts correspond to female figures in white nightgowns."

Nevertheless, Freud always insisted that a patient's associations to any particular dream were essential to its final interpretation. This was not only because the associations might lead to the discovery of much more personal symbols, but also because even universal symbols and themes are likely to have different specific meanings for each particular dreamer. Thus, in my floating dream, my analyst would have guessed that the floating referred to erotic feelings even before I had associated the German love song with it, but he needed my specific associations and memories to get back to my childhood jumping-game with my brother.

Another dream of mine shows vividly the process of symbolization at work. In it, I was waiting at the rear entrance of Buckingham Palace for the queen to arrive in her car from a visit to the Royal Marsden Hospital in Chelsea. In the dream, I was filled with mounting excitement until I could hardly contain myself, and when the alarm clock woke me at this point, I felt terribly cheated and let down by this mighty anticlimax. Now, in waking life, I have never had any sense of glamor or excitement attached to monarchy, even in childhood, and in much of my professional life I have been quite used to seeing the queen's car drive around this area, as she is my neighbor. So, it seemed reasonable to me from the start that the queen in my dream should be a substitute for someone else, and having read Freud, it seemed likely that it was my mother. For this I found corroboration in an intriguing way when, during the course of associating to the Royal Marden, I found myself repeating the words "the Royal Ma's den," which means, of course, the queen's house, which is, in fact, Buckingham Palace. It is possible that a train of thought which made me dream of the hospital then led onto an entirely different train of thought through association to Buckingham Palace, and thence to the queen, or vice versa.

This still left unexplained the precise reason for the excitement in the dream, although on Freudian principles I could guess that the car—a well-known sex symbol in reference to some infantile sexual experience, in this case one concerning my mother. The clue to this came from associating to the fact that the dream depicted the queen's car approaching the rear entrance of the Palace. The black bonnet of her car reminded me of the black nozzle of the enema my mother used to give me as a child, even though I had no medical need for it. Obviously, then, my excitement referred not to the arrival of the queen's car, which would actually leave me feeling quite indifferent, but to the penetration of my rear entrance by the enema. Consciously, I remember awaiting this as a child with great dread, but the dream suggests that the operation actually filled me with enormous excitement until I could scarcely "contain myself." I therefore had no difficulty in accepting the Freudian view that the dream indicated a deep-rooted confusion of feeling about my mother based on this very early experience. I am no longer surprised at some of my later dreams, in which I was sexually assaulted by my mother, who possessed a penis (the enema), and accept my analyst's view that in some way sexual climax is closely related in my mind to a feeling of anal release.

Where I found myself at odds with my analyst over this particular dream was in his insistence that the dream was a disguise for the childhood memory, for I saw it as an interesting revelation of the mind's elaborate associative processes. I had no difficulty at all in working out the Freudian interpretation for myself with no pressure from my analyst to overcome mental resistance. In fact, the whole dream was clear to me before I even arrived for my analytic session. I therefore found it hard to credit that my sleeping mind would have been shocked into wakefulness by seeing a more direct representation of the childhood experience. Also, as I have already explained, I have had dreams in which my brother is *overtly* making love to me from behind (which again probably link up with the original enema experience)—completely open and "undisguised" dreams—through which I am sure I would have continued to sleep quite happily had I not been deliberately waking myself up at the time. As my waking mind is not at all shocked by such perversions, I see absolutely no reason why my sleeping mind should attempt to conceal the dream's true meaning from me.

This difference of opinion, while only of minor importance in the interpretation of this particular dream of the queen, became much more significant on other occasions. Again and again, I found that "Freudian" interpretations were thrust upon me in spite of the fact that my own associations to the dream elements showed no signs whatever of leading to sexual wishes, either toward my analyst or toward the figures of my childhood. I have since found this to be a common experience of patients undergoing Freudian analysis, and I believe it reflects not so much on the shortcomings of particular analysts as on the unscientific character of the "disguise" theory itself, which positively encourages forced interpretations. In fact, there are many psychoanalysts today who are on their guard against this and have departed from Freudian orthodoxy.

THE VIOLENCE OF THE REDUCTIVE AP-
PROACH TO DREAM INTERPRETATION

In many ways, Freud himself was not an orthodox Freudian, and critics have noted that the accounts he gives of his own and his patients' dreams in his writings rarely go back to infantile sexual experiences. Many of them stop short at an unconscious wish from adult experience, and although in some cases he attributes this to discretion he nevertheless allowed that interpretation at several levels could be possible. "Dreams frequently seem to have more than one meaning," he wrote. "Not only may they include several wish-fulfillments one alongside the other: but a succession of meanings or wish-fulfillments may be superimposed on one another, the bottom one being the fulfillment of a wish dating from earliest childhood."

However, he remained adamant that dreams must always be interpreted back to some *objective* event in the dreamer's life, although he allowed that this objective event might well be a fantasy rather than an actual experience. (For example, my mother's sexual assault on me was a fantasy deriving from the enema experience.) He tried wherever possible to get patients to make their own connections with the objective basis of their dreams by means of the association process, but if this failed, he remained convinced that somewhere in the depths of the mind the memory lay hidden and could be brought to light if only the disguise could be penetrated. His belief that a dream would use condensation, displacement, symbolization, and secondary revision to conceal its true meaning enabled him to cling to this conviction no matter how unlikely the interpretation might seem, or how unconvinced the patient remained. In fact, he insisted that attempts to make sense of the manifest content of the dream were completely misplaced.

This has had the effect of putting Freudian dream interpretation into the same category as astrology, in which any horoscope reading can be squared with the facts because if it is not obviously true, then it is held to be true at some deeper, hidden level which ordinary uninitiated observers cannot see. When, for example, a horoscope shows that a certain person is secretive, then if he is secretive the reading is hailed as correct, whereas if his overt behavior is completely open, the reading is held to tell us something of his inner nature which neither he nor anyone else has yet noticed. In the same way, a Freudian dream interpretation cannot be faulted. If it "rings a bell" with the patient, as in my "floating" and "queen" dreams, it is claimed as obviously correct, but if it fails to do so, then the patient's resistance to the truth is held to be high and the dream's disguise is considered more successful than usual. As we have seen, the mechanism of displacement is particularly useful in this respect, since it allows the analyst to interpret a dream feeling or event either as itself or as its opposite!

It was a recognition of this that led some of Freud's most devoted disciples in the early days of psychoanalysis to begin to deviate from the master's methods of dream interpretation. Most notable amongst these was the Swiss psychiatrist C. G. Jung,* who long before the advent of modern dream research expressed the opinion that it was absurd to try to trace all dreams back to wishes. In a passage criticizing Freud's arguments, Jung wrote:

> Just as human life is not limited to this or that basic instinct but is built up of a multiplicity of instincts, needs . . . and physical and psychic conditioning factors, so dreams cannot be explained from this or that element, however attractively simple such an explana-

* In saying this, I am in no way wishing to detract from other important "heretics" of the early psychoanalytic movement, such as Alfred Adler, Wilhelm Stekel, Otto Rank, and others, who had original ideas both about therapy in general and about dreams in particular. It simply seems to me that Jung made the most important departure, especially in the area of dreams. The purpose of this book is not to describe and compare the countless different dream theories of famous people (with which I am conversant), but to pick out those ideas I consider most relevant for a simple do-it-yourself dream interpretation kit.

111

tion may seem. . . . No simple theory of instincts will ever be capable of comprehending that powerful and mysterious thing the human psyche, nor yet the dream which is its expression. . . . It is true that there are dreams which embody suppressed wishes and fears, but what is there which the dream cannot on occasion embody? Dreams may give expression to ineluctable truths, to philosophical pronouncements, illusions, wild fantasies . . . anticipations, irrational experiences, even telepathic visions, and heaven knows what besides.

The effort to trace back every dream to infantile wishes and conflicts was in Jung's view not only a highly unscientific procedure but one which could do violence to the patient's own integrity. It could also, he suggested, prevent the analyst and the patient alike from seeing that some dreams might have quite different kinds of meaning which could be no less valuable in helping the patient toward self-understanding. One such approach suggested by Jung is to see the dream elements and characters as aspects of the dreamer's own personality rather than as memories of objective events. In the course of my own analysis, I frequently had the experience of finding that my associations to a dream pointed to this *subjective* kind of interpretation rather than to the objective Freudian-type interpretation to which my analyst was committed. I shall be describing a number of such cases in subsequent chapters, but two particularly vivid examples are quoted here to illustrate my point.

In the first of these dreams, which took place soon after my marriage, I found myself waiting in a long procession of pregnant women to give birth to a baby. This was part of a Masonic ritual in which each woman went up to a birth stool and had her baby delivered by the white-gowned officers of the Lodge. (At the time, my first husband and I belonged to a Masonic Lodge.) The girl in front of me had a particularly difficult birth, with much blood and pain. I awaited my turn with apprehension, but when it came, I delivered the baby, a girl, with no difficulty whatsoever. Just before handing the baby to the Worshipful Master, I felt her head for a small bump which I knew intuitively should be there. It was, and I woke up with a feeling of great achievement and happiness.

I interpreted the dream as an "opening" (which in some religious circles means a kind of initiation into the spiritual life) out of which some form of new life had come. The baby, a girl, was a "reborn" part of myself which I was dedicating to God. (The Worshipful Master symbolizes one aspect of God in the Masonic ritual.) The bump on her head reminded me of the chakra found on the head of Buddha, another very meaningful religious symbol representing cosmic consciousness. I felt the dream had something to do with the spiritual significance of my new phase of married life, although in reality I had scorned to celebrate this with any outward show, like a church wedding. The dream was telling me, in fact, that I saw our new life together as a very meaningful kind of religious dedication, not in the usual sense of raising a happy little family but in the much broader sense of close emotional and intellectual growth. In fact, at the time my husband and I had just embarked on a course of study which was to last several years but which we hoped would enable us to work together at the end of it. The dream, I felt, was saying that this whole new enterprise meant a kind of rebirth for me, or the birth of some unfulfilled aspect of my personality, and I was greatly moved by it.

Imagine my surprise, therefore, when my analyst said that the motivation for the dream was the wish for a painless birth, and that I had displaced my fear of pain onto the girl in front of me. Moreover, he said, the bump on the child's head was motivated by my wish for a penis (displacement from below to above), and the Worshipful Master was the nanny to whom I would hand the child when it was born. (He was extremely disapproving of nannies and thought a "real woman" would want to look after her own children.) My feeling of happiness on waking, he added, was a reversal of the fear and apprehension I actually felt at the prospect of having a baby.

My reaction was, and still is, that violence had been done to the dream and to my psyche, which produced it. I felt that my analyst had not listened to me at all, but had interpreted the dream according to some preconceived ideas about women and Freudian dream theory. The religious significance of the dream to me was absolutely ignored and my feelings of joy at the sense of fulfillment reduced to a banality. True, I should have liked a painless birth (who wouldn't?) and true, I should have employed a nanny had I produced a baby, but this empty, meaningless objective interpretation taught me nothing new. As Horatio says to Hamlet, "There needs no ghost, my lord, come from the grave To tell us this."

Several years later I had another significant dream, which seemed in some way to be connected with the first and which again required a subjective interpretation. In it I was a man who had conspired with his mistress, a hard, cold-looking woman, to murder her husband. She sat guarding the unlocked coffin in some underground station, along with several soldiers in blue uniforms who murmured condolences to the weeping widow. Suddenly, she disappeared and the soldiers raised the lid and looked inside the coffin. As I fled from the scene in terror, I heard them saying, "The bitch, the bitch," and I woke up in great anxiety, crying out, "I shall kill myself in a woman's world."

Again, this was a very moving and vivid dream, and I felt that all the characters in it were aspects of my own personality—the hard, cold feminine side conspiring with the weak vacillating male side to murder what I felt to be "my real self," whose mangled remains lay inside the coffin. The soldiers, who looked like characters from the French Revolution, represented the "revolutionary" aspect of my character, which was outraged at this murder. My reason for interpreting the dream subjectively was simple: at the time, my first husband, now successfully settled in his career, was threatening to leave me unless I gave up my own work to look after him and the home. After all the long years of study, I felt this would be like destroying part of myself and yet I did not want us to separate. I wondered whether or not I could do what he wanted without too much damage to myself. The dream was telling me quite clearly that I could not, that the result would be murder, that it would be better for us to separate.

Needless to say, my analyst would have none of this subjective nonsense, which he considered to be an evasion of far more important matters. He insisted on tracing this dream back to an abortion I had had quite early in my married life, although nothing either in my associations or in my current situation of possible marriage break-up bore any reference to that almost-forgotten event. He maintained that I had really seen the abortion as a murder, in spite of the fact that I had no such conscious feelings about it at the time, nor were any guilt feelings invoked by his suggestion or my associations to the dream. I suspect that it was *he* who saw abortion as murder, not me.

Looking back on the two dreams and the treatment they received, I am angry that I allowed myself to be led away from my own train of thought by red herrings which obviously interested my analyst but had little relevance for me. The dreams clearly portrayed a situation in which the part of my personality born and nourished during the early years of my marriage was in danger of being murdered if I acceded to my husband's demands. Had I heeded this message, I would have made the break there and then, instead of giving in to him and mangling myself for a further two years.

It is this kind of "violence by interpretation" which has led some critics of psychoanalysis to describe its practitioners as "killers of dreams," and in recent years many psychoanalysts themselves have come out in support of this criticism. For example, French and Fromm, in their book *Dream Interpretation*, write:

> Each of us has his characteristic stereotypes and his characteristic blind spots. These stereotypes and blind spots are usually closely associated with the theories that we accept. To counteract these blind spots, we advise

the analyst to try to forget his theories while he is interpreting. He should concentrate his attention, rather, on resonating empathically with what is focal in the patient's thoughts.

Dr. Walter Bonime, in his book *The Clinical Use of Dreams,* quotes a story very similar to the one I have just related about myself. A patient of his told him how a very significant dream of hers had received short shrift from her previous analyst with disastrous results. In the dream, she found herself walking down a long corridor with closed doors on each side. As she walked down the old, faded carpet in the dim light, she could hear laughter and talking behind the doors, which made her feel desperately lonely and out of things. Her Freudian analyst interpreted the long corridor as her vagina and said that she felt neglected in her sex life.

Bonime quotes her reaction to this interpretation as she related it to him. "His interpretation was a shock to me. It didn't seem to ring a bell. There was nothing in it I recognized, and I didn't feel excited in the painful but rewarding way that I used to feel excited when an interpretation was recognizable and gave me something to work on in my home life. Instead I was shocked and saddened, and I felt that something was missing in the interpretation, that there was more in the dream, and that I was losing the value of the dream somehow." Relating this experience to Bonime nine years after the dream, she added, "I can still see the corridor with the many closed doors. I am certain now that the dream represented the way I felt about my entire life at that time. I felt that all doors were closed to me, that the rest of my life was going to be a long, bleak, empty journey. . . . If I had understood the dream and consciously recognized how hopeless I felt about my marriage, I would have taken steps to get out of it at that time, instead of waiting five more long, miserable years."

Bonime is one of a growing number of analysts who reject the dogmatic Freudian approach to dream interpretation, seeing the dream as an existential event which must be allowed to "speak for itself" rather than as an elaborately disguised message to be decoded. Much in Bonime's approach can be traced back to Jung (to whom he acknowledges his debt), who in the early days of psychoanalysis broke away from Freud in order to develop a much more flexible approach to therapy generally and to dream interpretation in particular. As a practiced psychiatrist, Jung was not unaware of the fact that dreams could sometimes reveal awkward facts which the dreamer might resist, but he made it a cardinal principle not to use this as an excuse for insisting on an interpretation irrespective of the patient's asquiescence. Even if the analyst sincerely believed his interpretation was correct, Jung held this would be no use unless the patient himself came, without too much persuasion, to consent to it. It seems to me that modern dream research, revealing as it does the protean character of dreams, bears out Jung's caution on this point up to the hilt.

JUNG'S APPROACH TO DREAM INTERPRETATION

While Freud's dream theory oversimplified the issue in tracing all dreams back to wish fulfillments, Jung contended, the "disguise" theory was altogether too elaborate to be plausible. He preferred, he said, to quote against Freud another Jewish authority, the Talmud, which says, "The dream is its own interpretation." "In other words, I take the dream for granted," he concluded. "The dream is a natural event and there is no reason under the sun why we should assume that it is a crafty device to lead us astray." The same point was put nicely by one of Jung's followers, Dr. H. G. Baynes, who described Freud's argument about the disguise function of dreams as like that of an English visitor to Paris who assumed the Parisians were talking gibberish in order to make a fool of him!

So Jung concentrated on the manifest content of the dream, and set out to discover what it might reveal rather than what it might be concealing. Sometimes the dream may express a hidden conflict or problem, said Jung, while at other times it may point a way toward the future by exposing some unrecognized possibility in life or in psychological development. The strange, symbolic character of dreams, he thought, is simply the natural picture language of the mind when it expresses itself outside the narrow limits of rational thought. While he accepted Freud's general approach to the understanding of this symbolic language, by obtaining the dreamer's associations to the various dream symbols and by recognizing the existence of certain "universal" symbols thrown up in the world's myths and folklore, he entirely disagreed with Freud's insistence on tracing this symbolism back to infantile sexual experience. For example, he argued, while the snake might be a phallic symbol in some dreams, in others it might represent healing, wisdom, or evil, as it does in Greek, Eastern, and Christian mythology respectively. If the waking mind can use such symbols, why should not the dreaming mind do so too? Similarly the circle, which is widely used in Eastern mythology to represent wholeness and balance (the mandala), may symbolize the integration of the personality in dreams and have nothing whatsoever to do with the female reproductive organs. I am certain that Jung would have interpreted my "birth dream," as I did, in terms of the mythological "divine birth" theme which is commonly held to symbolize a new phase of spiritual or psychological growth.

In fact, Jung believed the dream should be interpreted in whatever way the dreamer found most useful. Common sense suggests, he said, that if I dream of a person I know well, I should recognize in the person of the dream the real person in life. For example, if I dream of my father, mother, or close friend, then it is likely that the dream refers directly to these people and is dealing with a vital relationship between me and them. Understood on the objective level, the dream may reflect a worry, a disharmony, or a hidden intent against them. In such a case, the dream would express a concrete problem of interpersonal relations. On the other hand, historical, fictional, and mythological figures are probably better interpreted on the subjective level as parts of my own personality. For example, Lady MacBeth may represent the ambitious, husband-pushing aspect of my personality, while the Sleeping Beauty may symbolize the unawakened part of my nature. To Jung there was no such thing as a "correct" interpretation: a dream was successfully interpreted, he believed, when it made sense to the dreamer and could be used constructively by him.

Jung was, however, dogmatic on one point, insisting that every dream was concerned with a *present* situation in the life of the dreamer and not primarily with some past infantile wish or fantasy, as Freud believed. Here Jung anticipated the findings of modern dream research which indicate, as I showed in Chapter 5, that the overriding determinant of dream content appears to be the dreamer's current situation at the time of his dream. This situation, said Jung, *may* concern infantile wishes seeking expression in the dreamer's life at that particular time, in which case they will be reflected in the dream. On the other hand, the dream may throw light on present unconscious prejudices, attitudes, uncertainties, and conflicts. For example, in Chapter 4 I described a dream in which one of my subjects found herself pregnant with an animal and had gone to the hospital in search of an abortion. While this dream could have been expressing a repressed infantile wish for bestiality, a more likely explanation is to be found along Jungian lines. At the time of the dream, this extremely liberal-minded girl was friendly with a Negro student and was wondering whether to sleep with him or not. Her dream showed clearly that she feared becoming pregnant by this "animal," revealing an unconscious streak of racial prejudice quite repugnant to her emancipated conscious mind.

On other occasions, said Jung, the dream may act as a compensatory mechanism to balance lopsided feelings about a person or event. Jung himself, in his autobiography, *Memories, Dreams, Reflections,* describes a compensatory dream experience of his own. At the time of the dream, he was a devoted disciple of Freud, listening to, learning from, and working with the master, whom he greatly admired and esteemed. Then, to his surprise, he found himself dreaming of Freud as a "peevish official of the Imperial Austrian monarchy, as a defunct and still walking ghost of a customs inspector." Jung interpreted this dream as a corrective, a compensation, or an antidote for his conscious high opinion of Freud, indicating that something in him knew he ought to be treating the master with somewhat more caution and skepticism.

The dream, said Jung, draws up a sort of interior balance between conscious and unconscious attitudes. Whenever we are faced with an obscure dream, Jung suggested, we should ask, "What conscious attitude does the dream compensate?" In my own case, I vividly remember having a recurring dream of being beheaded at a time in my life when I was developing my intellect at the expense of my feelings. When I took a more balanced approach to life, the dreams ceased.

In fact, Jung was convinced that dreams revealed the existence in all of us of unsuspected resources and unconscious wisdom. This was a possibility at which Freud seems to have hinted in some of his writings, but the main body of Freudian analysis has tended to treat the unconscious almost wholly as a realm of infantile impulses and instincts, laying the burden of responsibility for psychological healing and "integration" entirely on the conscious, rational mind. Jung came to believe that the human organism has an inbuilt tendency toward psychological health, comparable to the body's inbuilt capacity to heal wounds or recover from disease, and he frequently found that dreams seemed to reflect the workings of this inner drive toward health and maturity, with which the conscious mind can cooperate.

It was this discovery that led Jung to pay particular attention to the world's religious myths and legends in his search for the most significant universal symbols of the human mind. Where Freud had treated myths and dreams about deity as mere reflections of the child's early experience of its parents, Jung saw them as expressions of man's awareness of the inner drive toward growth and integration. He was particularly impressed by the way many of his patients with no conscious religious conviction and little religious upbringing would produce dreams containing themes of dying and rising gods, struggles between angels and devils, divine heroes slaying monsters, and so on. He called such great universal themes "archetypes" and suggested that they revealed the existence in every human being of a layer of the mind common to the whole human race. He called this the "collective unconscious," to whose archetypal themes and images every individual gives his own peculiar stamp. When a patient was unable to find any personal associations to a dream theme or image, Jung suggested that interpretation might be found in terms of the archetypes.

The god image Jung called the "archetype of the Self," the potentiality for wholeness within every individual which might also find expression in the mandala. Jung believed he detected the influence of another archetypal image in the dream themes of the "dark double" or personal devil who haunts the hero in countless myths and legends, seeking to trip him up in some way or even destroy him. He called this the "shadow" complex, and saw it as a symbol of the dark, repressed aspects of the personality which are constantly pressing for recognition and expression in all human beings, even though its specific character is different for every person. One of my subjects, an ultrarespectable, rather uptight young woman, related a recurring dream in which a wild gypsy girl dogged her footsteps, sometimes causing her to fall over precipices or into rivers. As she could find no personal associations to this dream figure, I guessed it represented her "shadow," the unexpressed wilder, sexual side of her nature which was constantly threatening to make her "fall." Jung believed wholeness could be attained not by escaping from the shadow (which is impossible), but by integrating this rejected part of the personality into a less restricted life style.

He found this idea expressed both in myths and in his patients' dreams, when the apparently threatening evil figure was often shown to possess some vital secret or hidden treasure.

In my subject's dream, the shadow figure was a purely personal one, suggesting stories like *Dr. Jekyll and Mr. Hyde,* rather than ancient mythology. A much more striking and "archetypal" example occurred in my own dreams during my second pregnancy, when night after night, I found myself pursued by wild cats, dogs, and wolves. Sometimes, I merely attempted to run away from them, but often I stayed to fight and always succeeded in subduing the animal either by beating it with sticks or cutting it down with a knife. Now in Freudian theory, these animals are often believed to symbolize the penis, and my Freudian analyst interpreted the dreams as a wish to subdue or destroy my unborn child (which, he believed, was equated in my mind with a penis). While this may have been true at some deep unconscious level quite inaccessible to me, the interpretation failed to resonate with my feelings about the dreams, which seemed to me to be a fairly obvious example of shadow figures being thrown up to counter-balance my conscious determination not to be overwhelmed by motherhood. I was moreover struck by the fact that the first of these dreams occurred only a few days after the baby had been conceived, suggesting that my body was in some way aware of the impending uprush of "animal nature" before my conscious mind even suspected it.

Then, right at the end of my pregnancy, the recurring dream took an uncanny new turn. I dreamed that I met a wolflike dog in the road, and when it attacked me, I began beating it with a stick until it could no longer move. I knew that I had subdued it to a point where it could no longer harm me, but I continued to strike until I knew it was dying. As it died, its eyes turned golden and dangerous, and its face became that of a woman. I realized in terror that this woman had been "called up" to revenge the death of the dog, and I woke up calling out what sounded to me like "Ecube, ecube." Immediately, there came to mind the

122

names of Hecuba and Hecate, but I had no idea offhand who these figures were beyond the fact that they suggested ancient Greece. However, I was so haunted by the dream that I had to visit the library to find out their identity. My feeling of intrigue turned into one of distinct discomfort when I discovered that Hecuba, the wife of the defeated King Priam of Troy, nagged the victorious Ulysses to whom she had been given until he turned her into a bitch with a curse and drove her into the sea, while Hecate was a Titan, the great Mother, who presided over vegetative nature and births, and had three animal heads, one of them that of a dog.

I have never pursued these mythological allusions in detail, but it seemed to me that these dreams had somehow tuned in to a layer of my mind which spoke in mythological terms to warn me that the instinctual side of myself, above which I was trying to rise, was far more powerful than I realized. In fact, it seemed that I was pitting my strength against the whole force of maternal nature, which would have its revenge if I went too far. I was being warned that I had to learn to live with and accept forces in myself far older and more powerful than my personal ambitions for a career and intellectual knowledge, however important these latter might be in my individual life plan. I suppose I may have read about the dog associations of Hecuba and Hecate at school, although I certainly had no conscious recollection of them at the time of my dream. Even so, it seems to me significant that my dreaming mind eventually used a neat condensation of these two extremely powerful ancient images to make clear to me, as the earlier dreams did not, that the shadow forces I had to learn to integrate into my life were not merely certain personal character traits I had been ignoring hitherto, but something much stronger. The body language of my Freudian analyst was quite inadequate to do justice to this dream's force and feeling.

Another archetypal theme to which Jung believed Freudian analysis failed to do justice was that expressed in the worldwide myths of the demon lover/fairy prince and the

123

siren/goddess-of-love. He frequently found the male images appearing in the dreams of his women patients, and the female images in the dreams of his male patients, in both cases with emotional overtones suggesting something much more profound than mere sexual wish fulfillment. He called them respectively the animus and the anima complexes, and suggested that they represented another kind of compensating principle essential to personal wholeness— the need to come to terms with the fact that we all possess inside ourselves many characteristics of the opposite sex which our culture teaches us to ignore. Thus a woman must cultivate, in her own unique way, the "masculine" attributes of initiative and intellect which will help her to grow into wholeness, while a man might have to integrate the essentially "feminine" qualities of tenderness and intuition into his personality. On the other hand, if a woman is possessed by her animus, she may become hard and opinionated, while an anima-dominated man may become a moody fusspot—the kind of man we refer to as an "old woman." We must watch our dreams, said Jung, to discover what message the inner man or woman is sending us, so that we may restore balance within the psyche.

Jung's theory of archetypes and the collective unconscious is a complex one and cannot be discussed in detail here. Instead, I have provided a reading list at the end of this book for those who would like to pursue the subject further. My purpose in this chapter is not to discuss all aspects of Freud's and Jung's theories of dream interpretation (this would require several volumes), but only those which are considered relevant to the comprehensive method of dream interpretation I shall put forward in later chapters. My reason for touching on Jung's theory of archetypes is that he saw, as I do, the necessity for a special approach to certain dreams of an awesome or "numinous" character. I do not know whether these dreams arise from a deeper layer of the psyche, as Jung believed, but the fact that *they feel as though they do* cannot and should not be ignored. My own treatment of such dreams is discussed fully in Chapter 10 of this book—"Looking Inward."

Whereas Freud firmly believed that he had discovered

the secret of dreams, Jung remained humble before what he felt to be a phenomenon larger than the individual human mind. "I have no theory about dreams," he wrote, "I do not know how dreams arise. I am altogether in doubt as to whether my way of handling dreams even deserves the name 'method.' I share all my readers' prejudices against dream interpretation as being the quintessence of uncertainty and arbitrariness. But, on the other hand, I know that if we meditate on a dream sufficiently long and thoroughly—if we take it about with us and turn it over and over—something almost always comes of it. This something is not of a kind that means we can boast of its scientific nature or rationalise it, but it is a practical and important hint which shows the patient in what direction the unconscious is leading him."

Because Jung believed that the unconscious had a "prospective" or forward-looking function, he always tried to work with dreams in series rather than in isolation. In the first place, one dream often throws light on another, more ambiguous one; and secondly, a patient's progress or otherwise can be gauged from changes in his dreams over a period of time. A good example of a short series of dreams is the one I experienced during my pregnancy, when I started by fleeing from my animals, then fought and subdued them, resulting in a confrontation with the forces of nature when I killed them. This is not a series of dreams with which Jung would have been pleased, as it foreboded possible psychic tragedy unless I changed my ways. Even more interesting are dream series extending over several years.

Not the least significant outcome of Jung's work was to open up the possibility that some use may be made of dream interpretation by ordinary people outside the professional atmosphere of the consulting room. In particular, he advised his patients and readers to meditate on their dreams until meaning came. One special method of meditation he advised was that of "interior dialogue," whereby the dreamer converses with one of his dream characters. This technique, in my experience, can sometimes give remarkable results. At first, the conversation may appear to be stilted and decidedly artificial, but there usually comes a moment when the imagined dream figure seems to take on a life of its own and say surprising things—a real speaking out of some repressed or alienated aspect of the personality. This is essentially the approach to dreams of Frederick Perls, discussed in the next chapter, who along with Calvin Hall, another modern dream pioneer, followed Jung's lead in bringing dream interpretation out of the consulting room into the marketplace.

CHAPTER 7

INTO THE MARKETPLACE

Since the middle years of the twentieth century, there has been growing interest in the possibility that ordinary people might be able with advantage to interpret their dreams at home without having to resort to the services of a professional psychotherapist. This trend was started by Jung when he showed that dreams could have meaning without being interpreted as disguises for unpalatable repressed wishes, thereby dispensing with the necessity for an unbiased interpreter to break through the dreamer's resistance to the truth. On the other hand, Jung's system of dream interpretation is a complex and somewhat mystical one, implying a knowledge of ancient mythology and a degree of intuition beyond the reach of ordinary people.

Since World War II, however, two psychologists in America—Calvin Hall, an experimental dream researcher, and Frederick Perls, a somewhat eccentric psychotherapist—have taken the whole subject right out of the consulting room into the marketplace and made dream interpretation a possibility for all of us in everyday life. Although they approached the subject from completely different points of view and developed very different theories about the use of dreams, I see their methods as complementary. In later chapters, I shall show how some dreams respond to both methods with beneficial results, while others appear to be more suited to one type of interpretation rather than the other.

HALL'S "CONTENT ANALYSIS" AND INTERPRETATION OF DREAMS

Calvin Hall, who was Director of the Institute of Dream Research at Santa Cruz, approached the problem of dream interpretation primarily from a scientific point of view. During the 1940's, Hall became dissatisfied with the dream theories of the psychoanalysts on the ground that they were based mainly on an atypical sample of dreams presented by patients undergoing treatment. So he set out to collect a really large sample of dreams from "normal" people, recalled spontaneously under ordinary circumstances at home. These subjects were asked to record any dreams they remembered on a printed form which included specific questions about dream settings, characters, plots, and emotions. Thereafter, these features of the dreams were cross-correlated with objectively ascertained information about the dreamers' age, sex, occupation, and so on to produce for the first time a full-scale report of what different people dream about.

In this first major study, which heralded an important new trend in dream psychology now known as dream-content analysis (not to be confused with dream interpretation), Hall collected and analyzed no less than 10,000 dreams of normal people. The results of his analysis, together with the conclusions he drew from them regarding the nature of dreams and their meaning, are given in his book *The Meaning of Dreams,* published in 1953, the very same year as the great breakthrough in dream research when the "objective indicator" of dreaming, the REM period, was discovered. I see this as a happy coincidence which has had the effect of revolutionizing our ideas both of the dreaming process itself and of its psychological equivalent, the dream. As I can give only a very brief account of Hall's findings and conclusions, I recommend the reading of this important and entertaining book, which was probably the first of its kind to bring dream interpretation within realistic scope of ordinary people.

Briefly, Hall found that dream settings were on the whole very prosaic, usually a house, a car, a street, or a shop. People rarely dreamed about places of work, such as offices or factories, which forced Hall to conclude that in our dreams we tend to show an aversion toward work, study, and commercial transactions, and an affinity for recreational activities. At the same time, aggressive acts and negative emotions such as apprehension, anger, and sadness outnumbered friendly acts and positive, happy emotions. Most of the dream characters were people with whom the dreamer was intimately involved in waking life, public personalities appearing much less frequently. Hall concluded from this that dreams rarely concern themselves with public affairs, a conclusion which seemed to be corroborated by the fact that although he was collecting dreams daily from students during the last few days of the war with Japan, he did not find a single reference to the dropping of the atomic bomb.

"A dream is a personal document, a letter to oneself," wrote Hall. "It is not a newspaper story or a magazine article." The expression is similar to a statement made by Alfred Adler that the dream is "a message to oneself," containing clues about personal problems and unresolved conflicts. Hall was also forced by his evidence to conclude, along with Jung, that dreaming is simply the sleeping mind's natural picture language whereby thoughts are translated into images, without any intent to mislead or deceive the dreamer. He agreed with Jung that the dream actually reveals in the clearest, most economical way possible the *present* state of the dreamer's inner life and is not primarily concerned with some long-repressed infantile trauma, though on occasions this may be reflected in a dream. In fact, said Hall, the dream gives a very clear and precise account of exactly what the dreamer is thinking as he sleeps. On the whole, he is concerned with himself, his relationships with those close to him, and his conflicts and anxieties. For much of the time, the dreamer could be said to be acting out his worries during sleep—worries about the sort of person he is, how others see him, how he sees others, and what he feels the world is going to do to him.

For example, the way in which the dreamer sees himself is expressed in dreams by the parts he gives himself. Is he the victim or the aggressor, strong or weak, the cowardly or the brave? The way in which he sees others is shown in a similar fashion; for example, a person who conceives of his father as stern or autocratic may in his dreams turn him into an officer or a policeman. When strangers or public figures appear in dreams, says Hall, they almost always turn out to be personifications of our conceptions of people we actually know. These conceptions vary, so that on one night I may dream of my mother as a witch and on another night of her as the queen. Hall had little difficulty in tracing the true identity of such figures from the dreamer's associations.

Similarly, the dream setting seems to portray the dreamer's feelings about the world by converting his thoughts into picture language. If he constantly dreams of cramped spaces, he feels the world is closing in on him; if he dreams of raging seas, air raids, thunderstorms, and so on, he sees the world as threatening and destructive. (Many people dream of nuclear bombs now that the idea of nuclear threat has become part of our general mental furniture, but associations almost always demonstrate that the dream bomb symbolizes a much more personal sense of anxiety in the dreamer's life than a worry about war as such.)

The sleeping person, says Hall, can see his most intimate personal thoughts embodied in the form of pictures, and we study dreams in order to discover what we are thinking during sleep. Dream thoughts are often more startling and revealing than waking thoughts, which tend to be censored by the conscious mind so that they are more in keeping with the image we have of ourselves than with our true selves.

Like Jung, Hall is adamant that the dream has no intent to disguise or distort dream thoughts, and he puts forward cogent arguments for his point of view. In the first place, he found as I did that many dreams reported by subjects could be identified readily by the dreamer as symbolic representations of sexual events without the help of a professional analyst. What is the point of disguising something in a dream if the person sees straight through it when he wakes up? One of the reasons we are able to translate our dreams is that the symbols they use are exactly the same as those we use in everyday slang—gun, tool, cock, or prick for penis, and so on. Hall argues that Freud's appeal to the ubiquitous sex symbolism of slang actually tells *against* his disguise theory, since it is not very sensible to speak of the dream's using the image of a gun or screwdriver to disguise the thought of a penis if the dreamer regularly thinks of his penis as a weapon or "screwing" tool in waking life.

Hall also found, as I did, that a dreamer may have a symbolic dream of sexual activity on one night, and a perfectly overt one the following night. Is it sensible, Hall asks, to think of the sleeping mind's preparing an elaborate disguise on one night only to discard it on the next? (Hall does not answer the question of why some dreams should be symbolic and some overt, but my feeling is that it has something to do with the depth of sleep or brain conditions at the time of dreaming—conditions perhaps which are not yet detectable on the EEG.)

Finally, Hall argues that the sheer multiplicity of sex symbols in psychoanalytic theory makes the disguise theory rather absurd. In a search of the psychoanalytic literature, he found 102 different dream symbols quoted as disguises for the penis, 95 for the vagina, and 55 for sexual intercourse. If all these are merely masks for forbidden sexual thoughts, says Hall, dream interpretation is reduced to a boring discovery that we are all sex-obsessed, which even if true would scarcely be very helpful. A more sensible procedure is to accept the link between pointed objects and penises as self-evident and to ask why a particular person tends to choose one kind of symbol for sexuality—say an aggressive symbol such as a gun or a spear—while another person (or the same person on another occasion) chooses a quite different kind of symbol, say a fountain. Hall concluded from his own investigations that the sex symbols appearing in different people's dreams correlated directly with the dreamer's feelings about sex at that time, some seeing it as aggressive, others as life-giving, and so on.

Hall agrees with Jung that the symbolic language of dreams is a remarkably condensed form of expression which, once we have learned to understand it, can show us many aspects of our thinking that escape notice during the day, when we are busy organizing life and expressing ourselves in the abstract concepts of language. Hall quotes the Russian writer Turgenev, who observed, "A picture may instantly present what a book could set forth only in a hundred pages."

Hall is convinced that anyone who can follow a few simple rules can interpret his own dreams. Dreams, he says, are pictures of what the mind is thinking during sleep, and "anyone who can look at a picture and say what it means ought to be able to look at his dream pictures and say what they mean. The meaning of a dream will not be found in some theory about dreams: it is right there in the dream itself." While Hall does not advocate do-it-yourself dream interpretation for mentally disturbed people, who are advised to seek treatment, he does believe that any clear-headed person can become proficient in the art, a conclusion which my own work thoroughly bears out, as later chapters of this book will show.

There are four basic rules of dream interpretation according to Hall, which must always be borne in mind:

1. The dream is a creation of the dreamer's own mind and tells him how he sees himself, others, the world, his impulses, and so on. It should never be read as a guide to objective reality—that is, it does not give us the truth about things, but merely a picture of how they *appear* to us.

2. The dreamer is responsible for everything that appears in his dream. If he dreams of something, however terrible or stupid, he must first have thought it.

3. A dreamer usually has more than one conception of himself, others, the world, and his impulses, and these multiple conceptions will appear in his dreams. They tell him how he sees something at a particular point of time in his life.

4. Following Jung's lead, Hall advises that dreams be read in series rather than in isolation. A dream, he says, ought never to be interpreted without the consulting of the other dreams of a series, in order to see how the thoughts of a person are tied together. Very often, the meaning of a dream is completely obvious, and such barefaced dreams can often throw light on the more complex, symbolic productions of the dreamer's mind. The dreamer's associations should always be used to corroborate conclusions.

My own work with dreams has convinced me of the value of Hall's very down-to-earth, commonsense approach to dream interpretation, as is shown from the following examples taken from my own personal dream record and those of my subjects. The dreams are concerned with:

a. *How I see myself*

A woman subject, the wife of a business executive who spent a great deal of her time successfully entertaining her husband's colleagues, experienced recurring dreams of accidents spoiling these social occasions. In one dream, the maid poured the soup all over the table; in another, she found herself speaking in a broad country dialect, although her normal accent was impeccable; and in another, she discovered that the dinner she was about to serve consisted of sausages and baked beans.

When she came to think about these dreams, along the lines suggested by Hall, this executive wife realized just how insecure she really felt beneath her polished surface confidence. She came from a working-class background, and although consciously she had no qualms about her ability to fit into her husband's environment, part of her constantly feared humiliation on account of her humble origins. Further associations showed that she resented the strain imposed upon her unthinkingly by her husband.

A woman scientist related a vivid dream of taking an English literature examination in territory where there were threats of a Negro uprising. Entering the hall, she found to her dismay that she had done no work for the examination and could not answer a single question. Looking out of the window, she saw the natives arming themselves with spears and hatchets, so she decided to leave immediately and woke up running away from the scene of war.

Since there was no impending examination in her real life, I asked her to associate to this part of the dream. She said that the dream of failing an English literature examination was a fairly common one. This puzzled her because outwardly she was very scornful of the literary world which she had totally neglected over the years in her pursuit of a scientific career. The dreams, however, told a different story by throwing up anxiety and inadequacy feelings whenever she failed to "pass the test" in some particular life situation. In this case, she was reminded of an evening class she had recently started to attend, in which the lecturer, although himself a scientist, frequently quoted Shakespeare and the poets. The next part of the dream showed clearly why she was so anxious not to fail his test and appear inadequate in his eyes. The Negro uprising made her think of an "upsurge" of sexual impulses, and at my suggestion, she reluctantly admitted that her feelings toward the lecturer were rapidly becoming more than friendly. The dream showed her attempting to deal with the situation, which she saw as dangerous and threatening, by running away—that is, by denying her sexual feelings. She agreed, adding that other dreams in which she was chased by men or animals probably referred to a deepseated inner fear of sexuality.

These are just two examples illustrating Hall's assertion that anyone who takes a hundred of his dreams and examines the parts he plays in them will at the end be able to write an essay on "What I Think of Myself."

b. *How I see others*

One of my colleagues dreamed of a man running down a street dressed in chain mail. He bumped into her, knocked her down, and bruised her slightly. He continued running as though nothing had happened. She was furious with him for his roughness and disregard for her and decided to feign much greater injury than she had actually received, in order to get compensation for which he would have to pay.

She told me that in real life her husband had just informed her that he was having a love affair with another woman, whom he wanted to marry. My colleague felt terribly hurt and upset, particularly with his apparent unconcern for her welfare. She quickly identified the dream figure as her husband, and expressed surprise that she had ever thought of him as a "chained male." She was also horrified to learn from the dream that she was far more angry than hurt at his behavior and fully intended to make him pay for it. She reluctantly admitted that the dream was correct in that the very last thing she had ever expected to happen was that the "chained male" should escape from her domination and make a break for independence. She also resolved to watch her own behavior for destructive, revengeful tendencies, which she knew would only serve to aggravate the situation.

I had an amusing dream in which a male friend and I were driving toward the customs barrier on the border between two countries. As we approached, my friend insisted that I stop the car outside a sweet shop, while he went into buy some sweets. He came out carrying a large chocolate cannon, and when I asked what he intended to do with it, he beckoned me to follow him into a field through which ran a fence representing the boundary between the two countries. He carefully placed the cannon in front of the fence, lit the fuse, and stood before the mouth of the cannon, saying that the only way to cross the border was to fire himself over the fence! I assured him that our passports were quite in order and that we had nothing to declare. He remained unconvinced, and when the cannon fired in a rather desultory way, he was propelled toward the fence, just managed to land on top of it in a very undignified manner, and fell down onto the other side.

My associations led to a childhood memory (or fantasy) of a clown being fired out of the mouth of a cannon, indicating that at this particular moment in time, I saw my friend as a clown who insisted on taking the most difficult course of action in spite of the fact that there were much easier ways of doing things. My dream picture of him firing himself over the fence could not have expressed my feelings in a more apposite and economical manner.

This second example illustrates a point which I shall be examining in some detail in the next chapter, namely that while dreams are concerned with what the dreamer thinks and feels about various people and events, they can sometimes be found on examination to reveal some objective truth which either the dreamer or the person he dreams about have been trying to avoid in waking life. In the case of this dream, my friend was so amused by it that he reluctantly admitted to irrational persecution feelings, which often made him indulge in what appeared to others as ridiculously elaborate and roundabout avoidance techniques.

c. *How I see the world*

One of my male subjects dreamed of being examined prior to an operation for high blood pressure. The pressure-measuring apparatus in the dream was a large wooden cross to which he was strapped by the wrists, with his arms outstretched along the horizontal bar. The nurse standing by one arm was his wife, while the doctor on the other side was his boss. He woke up hearing a voice say, "We shall have to operate immediately or the pressure will burst his heart."

In real life, he was not only in good health but had just had a medical checkup, which probably suggested the form of the dream to his mind. He had little difficulty in seeing from the dream that his mental state was not as healthy as his physical body had been declared to be. Although he thought of himself as living a normal sort of life, the dream showed clearly that he felt himself being "crucified" by the tensions between work and home. The words he heard on waking suggested that he should make some radical changes in his life style before it was too late.

Another subject dreamed he was walking happily through a peaceful valley, hand in hand with his girl, when suddenly a crack appeared in the ground in front of them. This became wider and wider, and he tried to jump across dragging her with him. She was frightened and struggled, with the result that he let go of her hand and she fell down what by this time was a gaping precipice. As he stood on the far side and watched her disappear under a shower of stones, the whole landscape began to crumble and he feared that he too would be dashed to death by the boulders which rolled toward him down the mountainside.

Associating to the dream, he said that for the past two years, he had shared a happy, carefree relationship with his girl, who had just informed him that she was pregnant. He had offered her an abortion, which she had refused, saying she wanted to marry him and have the child. My subject felt strongly that he was not ready for marriage, but because he was fond of the girl, he agreed to her request. The dream showed clearly how desperate he felt about the whole situation: he saw the world crumbling beneath his feet and all around him, with the result that neither he nor the girl survived.

Pursuing the interpretation further, if we accept Hall's dictum that the dreamer is the sole author of his dream and is responsible for all that happens in it, then obviously my subject wanted to destroy the girl for not "going along with him" over the abortion, for he caused her to fall down the precipice. Probably as a self-punishment for such a wish, he then brought about his own demise in the dream. I do not know whether or not he married the girl, but the dream clearly indicated that he would be ill advised to do so.

d. How I see my impulses

While there is no doubt that Freud was correct in seeing many dreams as expressions of sexual and aggressive urges, Hall argues, most of us do not need to turn to dreams in order to discover that we have such urges. What we can learn, however, is the way in which we conceive of our impulses at any particular time and how we hope to gratify them.

One of my subjects, a very mild-mannered man, had recurrent dreams in which he was compelled to witness tortures and acts of brutality, against which he would protest to no avail. He found this very disturbing and asked me to try and help him understand the dreams. I suggested he reflect on Hall's contention that we ourselves are the authors of all that happens in our dream world, and he realized with a shock of surprise that one part of him at least actually wanted to see others hurt and humiliated. His dreams showed that his method of giving relief to this "dark side" of his nature was to manipulate situations in which other people carried out the acts of aggression which he himself would "never dream of committing."

A young woman subject dreamed she was skiing down a mountainside. To her horror, she found herself hurtling toward the edge of a precipice. Just when she felt herself about to plunge to death, her skis swerved and brought her back to safety. Her associations revealed that skiing made her think of pleasurable excitement and thrills, which reminded her of intercourse with her new lover. She told me that she was starting to fall in love with him, but he did not appear to return her feelings. There was something cold about the relationship, she said, which the dream depicted by staging the action in the snow. The dream also indicated that she was afraid to "let herself go" completely as she feared she would get hurt. So she prevented her feelings from "running away with her" by holding back in bed with the result that her sexual satisfaction was far from complete.

e. *How I see my conflicts*

Hall came to the conclusion from the analysis of thousands of dreams that every human being is constantly striving for the resolution of five basic conflicts. He characterizes these as the conflicts between freedom and security, right and wrong, masculinity and femininity, life and death, and finally love and hate in the parent/child relationship. Dreams, he says, often provide us with valuable information about the conflicts with which we are coping at any particular time, and about our attitudes toward these conflicts. I propose to give here just two examples from my own experience.

I used to have a recurring dream in which I had to choose between a modern house made almost entirely of glass situated in open country high on a hilltop, and a small, cozy cottage by the sea against which the waves beat fiercely in stormy weather. My associations revealed a conflict between the choice of a "public" career (glass house) in which I would rise in the academic world (hilltop), and a cozy home life of warm domesticity close to the emotional, primitive roots of being (the sea). The stimulus was obviously the fact that at the time my husband was threatening to leave me unless I gave up my career to devote myself wholeheartedly to the family. The dream indicated clearly how I felt about this predicament: I could retain my freedom and independence (career) only at the price of loneliness and isolation, while if I opted for safety and comfort (home) I ran the risk of being in some way emotionally overwhelmed. The dream seemed to be a clear case of a conflict between freedom and security. My analyst, however, insisted that it was more likely to be a conflict between masculinity and femininity, a choice of career representing my wish for a penis, and a choice of home full of close emotional relationships indicating my desire to be a "real woman"! (I shall return to this dream later in the chapter.)

At the time of my final marriage breakup, I had recurring dreams of losing teeth, appearing at a rich friend's house wrapped only in an old blanket, and wandering gray streets full of old, shambling figures. I used to awaken in the mornings with a dull, heavy feeling of disintegration so that I could scarcely get up. Associating to all these dreams, it was clear that I felt old, unattractive, and finished, in spite of the fact that I was young and in excellent health. As time went on, new elements began to appear in my dreams as though trying to shake me out of my inertia. For example, one night as I shuffled barefoot through the gloom, a car stopped and the driver asked if I would like to go to the theater. When I pointed out that I had no shoes or proper clothes, he said I would find these in the car. I hesitated before accepting, and woke up feeling like Cinderella at the ball. Gradually, my conception of myself changed as I realized that life was far from finished, and subsequent dreams depicted my growing awareness of new possibilities. I would interpret these dreams in terms of the life and death conflict, even though in this case it refers to a symbolic death. Very often this kind of conflict is reflected in the dreams of old people, who in reality are having to face the problem of approaching death. In my case, the obvious solution lay in the direction of life, whereas in the case of old people, a gradual acceptance of the inevitable might be the better way.

It must be remembered that *The Meaning of Dreams* was written before the discovery of REM and NREM sleep in 1953, so that Hall had no knowledge of the different kinds of dream thrown up by the sleeping mind at these times. His work was based solely on dreams recalled spontaneously at home, which, as we have seen, are likely to consist of the more entertaining and exciting REM dreams. Had Hall been aware of the ramblings of NREM sleep and the blandness of most REM dreams, it is possible that he would not have insisted that dreams are the product of good hard thinking. As I discussed in Chapter 5, the new evidence suggests that the sleeping brain is merely turning over, in a rather disconnected and haphazard manner, material that has already been processed during the course of the day.

On the other hand, Hall's *interpretive* approach is not really affected by the new evidence, as it is only the more interesting REM dreams which contain useful material for interpretation. However I doubt whether the dreaming mind reviews our attitudes toward ourselves, others, and so on in any systematic way. So in my own attempts to apply Hall's method to dreams, I do not find it very useful to work through all his categories systematically. Nor do I find it necessary to press the point that the dream should never be read as a guide to objective reality. In fact, I prefer to tackle a dream *in the first instance* as a picture of some objective event which has escaped the dreamer's notice during waking life. I have found during the course of my work that dreams can sometimes be extremely useful in bringing to our attention facts we have brushed aside during the day either because we do not want to face them or because we were too busy at the time really to notice them. I shall be dealing with such dreams in the next chapter, entitled "Looking Outward." Only when I am convinced that a dream does not contain any objective truth by checking it do I turn to Hall's method for guidance, as I feel that his straightforward approach is ideal for exploring the world of subjective reality.

Hall, however, uses only one method of understanding dreams—that of idea association—and while I agree that this is essential in most cases, there are other methods which produce additional valuable information. One of these is Jung's "interior dialogue" approach to the understanding of dreams, which Hall does not use at all. This is the essence of the Gestalt approach developed by

Frederick Perls, which I find particularly useful when a dream refuses to yield its meaning by free association, or when a deeper interpretation is needed.

PERLS' GESTALT APPROACH TO DREAMS

Frederick Perls (known as Fritz) died in March 1970. Austrian by birth, he trained as a Freudian psychoanalyst in Vienna and came to live in America during the 1940's. He soon became convinced that professional analytic psychotherapy had developed in a wrong direction by concerning itself mainly with neurotic patients who were prepared to undertake many years of intensive analysis merely to get themselves adjusted to the norms of a far from healthy society. He felt that individual therapy constituted an unreal situation and that work on oneself, like all other activities in life, should be conducted in groups. So, he set about devising more intensive, short-term methods of therapy in groups for "normal" people who wanted to lead fuller, healthier lives. "It is always a deeply moving experience for the group and for me," he said, "to see the previously robotised corpses begin to return to life."

Perls' methods, now known as Gestalt therapy (from the German word meaning "whole" in the sense of a completed pattern), have become part of a major popular movement in America, the Human Potential Movement, which includes encounter groups, sensory awareness workshops, and so on, all geared toward promoting personal growth. For the last few years of his life, Perls lived and conducted Gestalt therapy workshops at the famous Esalen Institute in California. (For further information about the Human Potential Movement and the Esalen Institute, see the reading list at the end of this book.) Toward the end of his life, he came to the conclusion that even group therapy was obsolete, and in 1970, just before he died, he opened a commune in British Columbia where residents would be able to practice openness and honesty in their ongoing relationships, according to the Gestalt prayer:

142

I do my thing, and you do your thing.
I am not in this world to live up to your expectations
And you are not in this world to live up to mine.
You are you and I am I,
And if by chance we find each other, it's beautiful.
If not, it can't be helped.

It has been said that every philosophy worth considering must have a practical application, and Gestalt therapy has become known as the active component of existentialism which concerns itself with "being in the here-and-now." Perls had no time for tracing back associations to some dubious infantile trauma, but concentrated, like Jung, on discovering buried treasure within the personality. He believed that the patient's free associations to an idea or dream merely led the therapist a merry chase around and around the problem without ever reaching it. He called the process "free dissociation," a flight of ideas used by the patient to avoid facing his neurosis. So instead he focused his attention on actual behavior in a group situation—facial expression, tone of voice, posture, gesture, reactions to other members, and so on—in order to discover the "holes" in a person's present personality. These holes, said Perls, have been caused by the rejection of certain parts of the personality in order to avoid pain. So the task of the therapist is to concentrate on what the person is avoiding in his present existence, help him act out painful situations, and reintegrate the alienated parts of the personality into his life.

Perls rejected any notion of an unconscious mind, preferring to think of the personality as a rubber ball floating and turning in the water, so that only one portion is visible at a time. The Gestalt therapist works with the portion that is visible in the context of the moment. So instead of trying to trace a symptom back to some childhood trauma, he always asks the person what it is "doing for him" in the here-and-now. For example, in one Gestalt therapy group I attended, it became apparent that a member was using his stammer to express hostility to others without fear of retaliation, for who would be unkind enough to attack a man with such a disability? Another member was using his rash as a means of avoiding sexual relationships, and yet another had learned that headaches relieved her of the chore of entertaining and accompanying her husband on social occasions.

Perls saw the dream as an added bonus in the form of an existential message which tells us exactly where we are in relation to ourselves and to the world at the present time. Whereas Freud called the dream the "royal road to the unconscious," Perls called it the "royal road to integration" because he saw in it the possibility of reclaiming the lost parts of the personality and becoming whole.

His method of dealing with dreams is to regard every image in the dream, whether human, animal, vegetable, or mineral, as an alienated portion of the self which we have projected onto that image. The dreamer is asked to act the part of each image in turn and reexperience the events of the dream from the standpoint of each. Encounters are then conducted between these images, and when they fight, the dreamer knows he has hit on something important. Whenever the mind goes blank or he feels sleepy, he knows he is trying to avoid something. For this reason, it is good to work out a dream in a group or with another person who can point these things out. The aim is to bring the fragmented parts of the personality into harmony with each other so that they help, not hinder, our growth. The best way to use a dream said Perls, is not to cut it to pieces and interpret, but to bring it to life and relive it.

As a first step, Perls asked the dreamer to retell his dream in the present tense in order to bring it into the here-and-now and reexperience the actual feelings of the dream. When this took place in a group, Perls noted the facial expression, gestures, and so on of the person as he recounted his dream, as these often provide clues to particularly conflictual areas of the dream. For example, a Gestalt therapist told me of one of his group members who recounted a long, elaborate dream which began with his entering his office building and taking the elevator. Quite near the beginning, the therapist noticed that when the elevator was first mentioned, the storyteller's eyes flashed rapidly to the left and back again, so he asked whether there was anything he had failed to mention just before taking the elevator in the dream. The man tried to brush it aside by saying that he had merely glanced at the door of a little room beside the elevator, which was of no importance since it was simply full of rotting garbage. The therapist, of course, promptly asked him to act the part of the garbage in the room, and there followed some most interesting revelations of parts of the dreamer's life that he was trying to ignore because he considered them "rotten."

While Freud himself observed that those parts of a dream which are forgotten or ignored on first telling are often the most important, his method of placing the patient on a couch with the analyst behind him actually reduces the number of clues available for work. Jung's method of treatment, in which therapist and patient sit facing each other, enables the therapist to observe any facial and bodily expressions which provide clues to ongoing conflicts, and the Gestalt method gives the whole group an opportunity to do this.

Many Gestalt therapists find it useful to place an empty chair facing the "hot seat," which is occupied by the group member acting out his dream, so that when two dream images meet in dialogue, he can move from one chair to the other as he acts out their different parts. The point of this is to break any bodily posture or tension built up by playing one part, and to start afresh in the other chair with the new part.

As an example of how the Gestalt approach can work, I propose to work with my own recurring dream of the two houses which I described on page 139. It has been my experience that the totally *subjective* Gestalt approach, taking all dream elements as aspects of the dreamer's personality, is particularly valuable with recurring dreams, since they are likely to reflect long-standing conflicts triggered off from time to time by some relevant external situation. I also find that the Gestalt method is useful when the more direct approach of free association has failed to yield anything significant, or has left the dreamer with the feeling that something important has not been clarified.

In the case of my "two houses" dream, I could see clearly enough, looking at it as a picture, that I was in some way torn between freedom and security. If I chose a public career in the academic world (the glass house at the top of the hill), I was afraid I might feel lonely, isolated, and exposed, yet I equally feared that if I chose the warm domestic house at the bottom of the hill, I should in some way be overwhelmed by feeling (the sea). This was a useful insight, as far as it went, in suggesting that I would be well advised to avoid being forced into either extreme, which at that point in my life meant not allowing my husband to force me into a total abandonment of my career. However, I felt strongly that this was not the whole story and I was particularly puzzled about the emotions which were supposed to be overwhelming in the domestic situation. My Freudian analyst took it for granted that these were the feminine emotions of tender, loving feeling, which I was resisting out of a neurotic wish to compete with men, but I could not bring myself to believe that I was really repressing a deep yearning to become totally immersed in domesticity. So, I applied the Gestalt techniques, starting by retelling the dream in the present tense:

I have to choose between two houses, one made almost wholly of glass, situated on a hilltop, and one on the beach by the sea built of stone with tiny windows. I am inclined to choose the former, as it is light and airy and has a marvelous view over the valley and sea. It would be lovely as a summer retreat as there are no other houses around, but in winter it might be cold, exposed, and rather frightening, and not very stable on a windy day. The other house is far too near the sea for comfort, and I can't help feeling that although it looks sturdy enough, an angry sea could easily knock it down.

Merely retelling the dream in this way at once makes something clear that I had not understood before, namely that it is an "angry" sea which threatens to destroy the house on the beach; in other words, the repressed emotions

146

I fear in the domestic situation are almost certainly those of anger as well as love. So in order to probe more deeply, I allow the house by the sea, and then the sea itself, to speak out. The house says:

I am the house on the beach. I am very old and very strong. I have thick, sturdy walls, but although I have withstood the onslaught of the sea so far, wet rot has set in at my foundations and I am in grave danger of collapse. I do my best to protect those inside me. Yes, there's a family inside me—a sort of extended family, lots of them. When the sea beats up against my walls, they close the curtains, make a cup of tea, and sing songs around the fire. In this way, they drown the noise of the waves and forget the danger.

The sea says:

I am the sea. When I'm calm, I roll gently up and down the beach, and I don't threaten this little house at all. But when a storm rises and my waves are whipped into a frenzy by the wind, I wish the house weren't there because I can't let myself go without hurting it. The house shouldn't be on the beach at all: the beach is mine and I need the space to roll over. I don't want to destroy the house or the people in it, but they are encroaching on my territory, not I on theirs. I try to hold myself back for their sake, but this isn't good for me. I need to dance and fling myself about and express myself in vigorous movement. I need to be noisy sometimes. A sea can't always be calm—it's not in its nature. And when I'm stirred up, above all, I need space.

Already an important new insight has emerged. It is not some neurotic, defended, career-oriented self which fears being overwhelmed by emotion; my fear is that *my* emotions, whose expression is essential to my well-being, will prove too strong for anyone (myself included) who tries to contain them in a cozy, restricted domestic situation. There is an immediate "existential message," as Perls called it, namely, that I see domestic life as a realm where emotions are not really allowed *true* expression at all. The people in the house by the sea like to get a nice, glowing feeling out of listening to the waves but they do not really want to come into contact with them. They have built walls to keep them out and are frightened if they get at all fierce; in fact, the whole domestic way of life, to my mind, represents a pretense which can be maintained only by trying to force the sea to deny its nature by staying calm. This showed me that I feel much of what passes for the "warm, domestic emotion" so valued by my husband (and earlier my parents) is distinctly bogus, in that any discordant notes which threaten the game of "happy families" are promptly squashed by a display of false jollity (singing around the fire). Discordant notes in this context are struck not only by outbursts of angry feeling, which the cozy family circle automatically interprets as destructive and evil, but equally by any really vigorous expression of joy, sexual feeling, or even grief.

This came out even more clearly when I acted out a dialogue between the sea and the family who lived in the house on the beach. As I took the part of the family, my voice changed, and I began to speak in the high moral tone so reminiscent of my parents and my husband, reproaching the sea for getting "stirred up." What they wanted was a sea which simply lapped gently on the beach, rising and falling with the tide and barely touching their house. Obviously there is a part of me, taken originally from my parents, which feels this fear of strong emotion, but equally, the sea itself is a part of me which in the dialogue protested that it simply needed to dance, roll, and splash with the wind:

I'm not destructive; I just need space. You interpret my movement as destructive because I bash against your house, but if you built your house above the beach, you would see exactly the same movement as a dance. I've suffered agonies trying to hold myself back from destroying your house; but this kills me, and I can't go on doing it forever.

148

Perls wrote, "Emotions are not a nuisance to be discharged. The emotions are the most important motors of our behavior: emotion in the widest sense—whatever you feel—the waiting, the joy, the hunger. . . . Emotional excitement mobilizes the muscles. . . . You can't imagine anger without muscular movement. You can't imagine joy, which is more or less identical with dancing, without muscular movement. In grief there is sobbing and crying, and in sex there are also certain movements, as you all know. And these muscles are used to move about, to take from the world, to touch the world, to be in contact, to be in touch." If these emotions are denied their proper physical expression, they lead, says Perls, to a state of anxiety in which the person becomes desensitized; his sensuous awareness of sight, sound, taste, smell, and touch is dulled, and he becomes frigid. The purpose of Gestalt therapy is to restore such a robotized corpse to life.

A Gestalt therapist would have had no difficulty in identifying the voices of my parents and husband which spoke in such moralistic and condemnatory tones whenever my emotions expressed themselves strongly, as the "topdog" of my personality. Topdog is always righteous and authoritarian; he knows best. His favorite words are "You should," "You ought," "You must never," and so on. He works with threats of catastrophe—in my "two house" conflict it might be, "If you express your feelings and emotions, no one will love you or come near you," or "You will destroy yourself and those you love." These voices, which have become part of me, constantly nag, "calm down, control yourself, don't stir things up, keep the peace" and criticize me as "destructive, a troublemaker, a monster who should be ashamed of herself."

The recipient of such internal criticism is the part of the personality known as "underdog" in Gestalt terms. He protests against the nagging but never seems to be convinced he is not all the things topdog calls him. He is usually apologetic, defensive, wheedling, and manipulative, but he has no power. He says, "Yes, yes, I know you're right. So I'll try to do better. But I can't help it if I fail." In my case,

I would try to dam up my emotions, which invariably burst forth later with much more vehemence than they would have done had they been allowed normal expression at the time, convincing everyone, including myself, that I was indeed a monster.

Perls calls topdog and underdog the two clowns of the personality, constantly acting out their self-torture game beneath the level of conscious awareness. We have a topdog and underdog for each specific conflict, so whenever a conflict is sparked off by some present problem or event in life, the two clowns emerge and start their self-torture game. Both strive for control, and it is a battle to the death, dissipating all the energy which should be used for constructive and positive living.

In acting out my dream, my underdog sea was beginning to speak up for himself, and had I been working in a group, the leader might have asked me to stand in front of each person in turn and say as convincingly as possible, "I am not destructive, I have a right to express myself," until the group really felt I meant it. Or he might have asked the group to form a closed circle around me and slowly advance upon me, in which case I would have had to shout, "Don't fence me in, don't crush me," and try to fight my way out. The aim is to reduce the power of topdog and allow underdog to express his needs openly, which in my case meant not allowing myself to be bullied into accepting a restricted life-style on the grounds that this was what any "normal" person would want. In terms of my dream, this would mean the house on the beach moving itself inland and allowing the sea to express itself naturally upon the open beach.

Perls said that it was unnecessary to work with every element or event in a dream, so long as the dreamer was able to receive at least one existential message from the dream. So in my case the matter might well have been left at this point had I not been intrigued to notice that the dialogue between the sea and the people in the house brought to light a hitherto unnoticed character in the dream, namely the wind, without which the sea would have remained the placid thing they wanted it to be. I therefore decided to allow the wind to speak, and the result was distinctly surprising. It said,

I am the wind. I'm not sure where I come from but I feel I'm the breath of God—you know, the spirit of God that moved upon the face of the waters and caused them to dance with life. I am the breath of life that God breathed into Adam, turning him from a piece of clay into a living soul. I breathe life into man and scatter seeds over the earth. Sure, I'm sometimes like the whirlwind from which God spoke to Job, but it's silly of people to call me destructive or to get irritated with me when I blow off their hats or rattle their windows. If they insist on building houses right by the sea, it's their own fault. And that chap who builds his glass house on the top of the hill is just as foolish, because he's forgotten how strong and elemental I am. I want people to listen to me because I bring messages from God, but they should do this from a sensible vantage point as I am extremely powerful and unpredictable. A house halfway up the hill would be a good place for man to live, as he could then listen to me in safety without being overwhelmed, and he could even build a windmill to harness some of my energy. But I can never be tamed or controlled by man because I am bigger than he is.

Here I recognize another existential message, namely that the energy of my emotions (the wind on the sea) is the same life-giving force which permeates the whole of nature and inspires man to creative imagination. Consequently, it would be just as foolish of me to immerse myself totally in academic intellectualism (the glass house on the hilltop) as it would be to devote my life to unthinking domesticity (the house on the beach). In either case, the wind, far from being a source of creative energy, would merely become a nuisance, disturbing my rigid, controlled life style. The creative life I desire must be constantly open to uncertainty: "The wind bloweth where it listeth . . . so is everyone that is born of the spirit." I need close relationships and intellectual stimulation, but I must have them in a form which is constantly open to new possibilities and growth.

I hope I have made it clear from this example how a dream can be used at home, without the help of a group. The advantage of having other people around, particularly a group leader whose experience alerts him to almost undetectable nuances of feeling as the dreamer acts out his dream, is obvious but not absolutely necessary. In his book *Gestalt Therapy Verbatim*, Perls gives many hints how the dreamer can become sensitive to his own blocks. For example, if you find difficulty in playing the role of a particular character in your dream, you can be sure that you are dealing with an alienated part of your personality which you are reluctant to reclaim. You are saying, in effect, "That's not me." The more fragmented you are, the more nightmares you are likely to have. As you become more integrated, these should gradually disappear.

On the whole, Perls preferred to work with short dreams as they are less confusing than long ones, and he insisted that even a half-remembered dream fragment could be enough to start off the creative process of opening up the personality. The following dream fragment was presented at one of the British Gestalt workshops I attended by a rather self-important, uptight businessman who said it was unlikely that we should be able to get anything out of it. "All I can remember," he said, "is urinating on the carpet." Having some knowledge of Freudian theory, he offered to interpret this as a wish to return to a state of uninhibited, infantile freedom in which urges receive immediate gratification, adding that this was hardly the most illuminating of insights.

The group leader asked him to conduct a dialogue between himself and the carpet, moving from one chair to the other as he played the respective roles. This rapidly revealed a "topdog" and "underdog" element in his personality, the dialogue going something like this:

152

CARPET: Why are you pissing on me like that?

MAN: Good heavens, I didn't even notice you. Now I come to take a good look at you, you're pretty old and worn out anyway—dirty as well—not good for much else than pissing on, I'd say.

CARPET: Well, it's not fair. I protest . . .

At this point, the group leader intervened to ask the "carpet" to protest with some conviction, as though he really meant it. So, the businessman went around the group, repeating, "Stop pissing on me," hesitantly at first, gradually gaining confidence until at the end he was positively dancing with fury as he shook his fists and shouted the words at the top of his voice. The leader then asked him to return to his seat and continue being the carpet.

I may be old and a bit worn, but I won't have people pissing on me. I'm made of good stuff and I'm hardy. I'm useful and I'm really quite warm. In fact, I'm a pretty good carpet really.

The existential message was clear. He suffered in his business life from a continual sense of being slighted and put-upon, which he positively invited because he had an inner feeling that he was worth nothing better. This dream fragment served to bring to light a large "hole" in his personality, and encouraged him to reclaim the "buried treasure" of his missing self-confidence.

If a person rarely recalls whole dreams, Perls suggested that we ask, "Dreams, why do you always come to me in bits and pieces?" One group member received this answer from himself, "Because we want to tantalize you, make you wonder about the rest of us. We want to get your interest. If we gave you the whole of ourselves, you might find us dull and boring." "Is that why *you're* not participating fully in the group?" asked the leader. Similarly, with nightmares we should ask, "Dreams, why are you trying to frighten me?" Another member of the group gave herself this answer, "Because you shouldn't have a nice life all the time. If you have a happy, successful day, it's only right that you should suffer at night. If you have a miserable day, then we shall come and cheer you up at night." Something like this may well be the reason for what Jung called compensatory dreams—the inner feeling that we are not entitled to experience too much happiness, nor should we be allowed to suffer more than our fair share of misfortune.

Perls also used this technique with people who rarely or never recall a dream. His theory was that dream forgetting is a ruse to avoid coping with unpleasantness and is usually used by people who think they have come to terms with life. He tells them to talk to their missing dreams: "Dreams, where are you?" The answer is always interesting. As I write this, I am reminded that I have not recalled a real dream for several weeks, which is most unusual for me. I ask my dreams what has happened to them, and they reply, "We don't want to confuse you with more material at this stage, so we are keeping away for a little while. We'll come back when the book is finished. You have plenty of material to work with and we don't want to confuse you with more. If we come to you now, you will only spend your time interpreting us, and even confusing yourself with possible new ideas. You've got everything pretty well worked out, so we are going to help you keep things this way." It is easy to see how a chronic nonrecaller of dreams might receive a similar answer in relation to his life as a whole.

Gestalt techniques do not tell us much about the dream itself—its source, nature, and purpose—but there is no doubt that they can often tell us a great deal about ourselves. In my experience, they do not work for everyone, particularly those who have difficulty in contacting their inner world of fantasy, and in these cases I would recommend Hall's method of working with dreams. I have no doubt, however, that there are many occasions when the Gestalt approach fully justifies Perls' claim that with it he can get to the heart of the personality in half an hour, whereas a psychoanalyst often take months to get warmed up. As I have said, the best results are obtained from work in groups with an experienced leader, but there is absolutely no reason why they should not also be used at home to the benefit of all concerned.

TOWARD A COMPREHENSIVE METHOD OF DREAM INTERPRETATION

While Hall and Perls take quite different approaches to dream interpretation (Perls is reluctant even to use the word "interpretation"), their dream theories have much in common.

1. Both recognize that dreams use symbolic picture language, but are concerned with what this *reveals* about the dreamer and his problems, instead of treating it, as Freud did, as a disguise mechanism whose purpose is to prevent the dreamer from understanding his dream.

2. Both insist, as Jung did, that any particular dream has reference to the dreamer's *present* life situation, as well as to his basic character structure formed by early childhood experiences. Both look for the dream's "existential message" in the here-and-now, and bring in references to the character-forming experiences of the past only incidentally.

3. Both agree with Jung that the dream should be interpreted in whatever way the dreamer finds most useful. If it throws up what looks like an unconscious infantile wish, this should be examined for how it is affecting our lives now. On the other hand, dreams contain far more than mere wishes and we should always look for their most relevant message, whatever it may be.

4. Because both methods are simple and straightforward, they can be used by ordinary people at home to gain insight into personal problems and conflicts. They are not specialized disciplines to be used only by experts in the consulting room, nor are they concerned with the treatment of mental illness.

All these points seem to me to have been vindicated by the findings of modern dream research, but I do not wish to deny that dreams may also be of use in the professional treatment of mental illness. In fact, I would advise anyone who becomes seriously disturbed by the things he finds in dreams, or anyone who has any reason to suspect that they are connected with mental instability, to seek professional advice. In particular, I would advise those who cannot cope with the experiment I am suggesting in the following chapters either to abandon it or to seek help, particularly if there is any serious feeling of being overwhelmed in any way. In such a case, the dreams, would be saying, in Perls' terms. "We are too much for you to cope with. Go and get help."

In particular, I do not wish to imply that orthodox Freudian psychoanalysis has nothing to offer. I am prepared to believe that there are occasions on which a seriously disturbed person undergoing professional analysis may benefit from a Freudian treatment of his dreams if it succeeds in bringing to light the infantile conflicts responsible for his neurosis. On the whole, however, I think that "normal" people feel restricted by the whole Freudian approach, especially when its practice is influenced by what is now generally considered to be an outmoded and mistaken theory. As I have shown, a rigid approach to dreams can do great violence to both the dreamer and his dream. I believe our debt to Freud lies in the fact that his pioneering work gave importance and significance to the dream at a time when science was doing its best to reduce it to a triviality unworthy of investigation.

Freud's further contribution was to furnish us with a wealth of ideas for consideration, many of which have found their way into our everyday language and life. Nowadays we can all converse glibly about the "Oedipus complex," "penis envy," and "castration anxiety" even if we disagree with the strict Freudian viewpoint, so it is not surprising that we should find elongated objects symbolizing the penis in dreams and so on. However, it is not enough, as Hall argues, merely to leave the matter there; we should ask ourselves why we have chosen that particular symbol at that particular time. Freudian analysis is often called "deep" analysis, but in my view, it often does not go deep enough.

The Freudian approach to dreams may have its uses within the consulting room but as a general practice it is not suitable for work with dreams at home. I am concerned to show how dreams can help ordinary "normal" people in everyday life to get to know and understand themselves better. On the whole, I shall restrict myself to the approaches of Hall and Perls (which both owe much to Jung), and show how I think they can be used to the best advantage at home. My main debt to Jung is that he led me to see that there are a small number of rather special dreams requiring interpretation along quite different lines, and I discuss these in Chapter 10. The very first rule of dream interpretation is to ask not "Which method of interpretation is correct?" but "When should I use one particular method in preference to another?"

During the course of my dream research over many years, I have found it helpful to recognize three distinct kinds of insight which can be obtained from dreams:

a. Insight about facts in the outside world which have been perceived below the belt, as it were, during the course of the day but not assimilated into conscious awareness. So the very first question I ask about a dream is "Does it contain any objective truth?"—that is, does it reflect any factual information about present events, or does it merely reflect a subjective impression of how the dreamer sees his world? I call this first step *Looking Outward.*

b. If I can find no evidence of objective truth in a dream, I apply Hall's "looking at a picture" method in order to discover the dreamer's conceptions of life. In this case, I use the dream as a distorting mirror which has twisted external reality according to the dreamer's inner attitudes and conflicts, giving a picture of his own unique inner reality. I call this second step *Through the Looking Glass.*

c. Finally, dreams can give insight into the dreamer's deepest inner self. Sometimes this is true of dreams which have already yielded insight at the other levels, as I have shown in my treatment of my "two houses" dream. At the same time, there are some dreams which seem to demand this deeper interpretation straightaway, in that they consist of bizarre, magical or mythical images and themes which "feel" as though they have arisen directly from some deep layer of the personality. Such dreams, like all others, are stimulated in the first instance by events in the dreamer's waking life, but they ultimately appear to be concerned more with an inner, psychological state than with external reality. I call interpretation at this level *Looking Inward* and find Perls' and Jung's methods particularly appropriate to it. Where "looking glass" interpretations tell us *how* we see ourselves, others, and the world, "looking inward" can often tell us *why* we built up such attitudes in the first place.

I believe that something like a comprehensive approach to dream interpretation may be achieved by examining any dream from each of these three standpoints in turn and using the method of interpretation most suitable in the circumstances. Guidance will be given in the next three chapters, the cardinal rule in all cases being never to impose a meaning on a dream but to allow it at all times to "speak for itself."

PART III

THE THREE FACES OF DREAMING

CHAPTER 8

LOOKING OUTWARD

In earlier ages, it was taken for granted that dreams could bring messages or warnings to the dreamer of events that were actually happening or about to happen in the external world. With the rise of the scientific outlook, this idea came to be discounted as nothing more than primitive superstition. From time to time newspapers and magazines still try to arouse interest in stories of dreams which seem to demonstrate some kind of clairvoyance or precognition of real events quite outside the dreamer's conscious awareness, but the scientifically minded public tends to treat all such stories with suspicion, as attempts to use coincidence to recapture belief in mental powers.

On a humbler level, psychologists have come to recognize that we all have a tendency to project our fears, hopes, and wishes onto the outside world and have therefore actively discouraged people from looking for objective truth in any dreams they have about relatives, friends, and life situations. Calvin Hall is typical here when he warns, "The dream is not a picture of objective reality and should never be treated as such. It is, however, an accurate picture of reality as it appears to the dreamer. This kind of reality is called subjective reality. Often one's subjective reality does correspond with objective reality, but from dreams alone it is not possible to determine the extent of this correspondence."

While I do not disagree in principle with Hall's statement, it seems to me that there is a real danger here of scientific and psychological caution's allowing a baby to be thrown out with the bathwater. Modern dream research has shown that dream content derives mainly from recent waking experiences, and my own work has provided many examples of dreams throwing up information which the waking mind has brushed aside on account of a preoccupation with more immediate problems or because the information was too disturbing to accept. In such cases, the dream may provide us with very valuable information about the external world, and it is for this reason that I believe we should examine all dreams for elements of objective reality. These may act as reminders, warnings, or even predictions, and I feel it is as foolish to ignore this possibility as it is to make the opposite mistake of seeing all dream events as accurate revelations of real people or situations.

The sensible procedure, as I see it, is to look at any dream first of all to see if it *could* be throwing up real information about external events which have not been assimilated by the conscious mind in waking life, and to examine every such possibility critically in a commonsense way to see if there is anything in it. This in no way precludes the possibility that the same dream contains other levels of insight as well, and often the objective references will need to be teased out from the dream story as a whole. Normally they are represented directly, but sometimes they appear in a symbolic form which has to be translated before the information becomes clear. It is my experience that where such "subliminal perceptions" appear in dreams they can often be more immediately useful to the dreamer than their more complex subjective counterparts.

I shall begin with some very simple examples and gradually lead into more complex ones.

A few nights ago, I had a dream which acted as a very simple, direct, reminder of something I had forgotten. I dreamed that the door to the garden was open and banging in the wind. I woke up actually hearing it bang, but when I went downstairs I found it fixed open on a hook which would certainly have precluded any banging. Moreover the night was calm and no other doors were banging. Somewhere along the line, my brain knew I had forgotten to lock the door, and this subliminal worry was in the process of being turned over when I woke up. It seems almost as if some alerting mechanism in the brain had manufactured the banging in order that I should wake up and close the door.

A slightly more complicated reminder dream occurred a few years ago when I dreamed of arriving for a psychoanalytic group session only to find all the members in the middle of a party. I was cross because all the best food had been eaten and they seemed to have had most of the fun. I looked across the table and saw the group leader staring at me in a most disapproving fashion. I asked the girl next to me why they had started so early without me, and she replied, "Didn't you remember? He asked us all to come earlier this week." I woke up remembering that my weekly group session was to take place that very day and the leader had in fact asked us all to come one hour earlier than usual, although I had quite forgotten it. The dream was propitious, if not exactly correct, in that I was due for an individual analytic session before the group met, so that had the dream not reminded me of the earlier time I should actually have arrived in time for the group but missed my individual session. This would have wasted a much larger fee than that payable for the group and would also have entailed a very boring and irritating interpretation in terms of my resistance to analysis! So I was very glad that the dream had given me a reminder, and found this much more useful than the obvious psychological interpretation that I evidently saw the group sessions as parties, a sentiment of which the group leader (my analyst) would have greatly disapproved.

A similar "appointment" dream whose message was not quite so obvious occurred recently. In it, I was with a group of people playing strip poker, and when the moment arrived for me to remove my tights, I noticed with horror that my legs were covered with thick, black hairs. On waking, I immediately examined my legs and found that although the dream had grossly exaggerated (my hairs are blond anyway), I was in need of a waxing treatment, which I usually have done at approximately six-week intervals. As an appointment normally has to be made at least two weeks in advance, I telephoned the salon immediately only to be told that I had in fact made an appointment on my last visit for that very afternoon.

In a case like this, I find it hard to believe that the psychoanalytic ("penis envy") or even Hallian interpretation ("I see myself as masculine") need be given much value. It seems more sensible to assume that my brain had somehow registered the fact of the appointment and had thrown up a reminder in the dream which my waking mind had been too crowded to notice. Why does this sort of thing not happen more often? The answer is that it may well happen far more often than we realize, since we remember only a fraction of our dreams, so an appointment book or diary is the more efficient method of recording our dates. In fact, it is possible that we dream of appointments only when the brain has at some point in the day registered, without the conscious mind's being aware of it, some kind of discrepancy between our plans for the next day and our stored information, which then becomes a puzzle to be worked over at night. It would be quite unfair to the already overworked brain to present it with even more puzzles than it normally has to cope with!

In these last two "reminder" dreams, it seems as if my brain had been turning over the puzzling discrepancy by following out a "story" of the kind of thing that might happen if the appointment remained forgotten. A rather more dramatic instance of this occurred to one of our group members who dreamed she was in a labor ward of a maternity hospital giving birth to a baby. This dream took place in the early part of the night, and as she pondered its possible meanings—a "Freudian" wish to have another baby or a "Jungian" rebirth into a new phase of life—she suddenly remembered she had forgotten to take her contraceptive pill before going to bed that night. She immediately leaped out of bed and took it. It seems clear to me that the dream was actually the result of her brain's exploring the consequences of this slip from normal routine.

Another similar experience was produced by a group member who dreamed she was crossing the barrier between two countries, only to discover that she had no passport. Remembering our first rule of dream interpretation, she looked for her passport on waking as she was due to leave on vacation the following week. To her relief, it was exactly where she expected it to be, but just as she was about to start interpreting the dream in terms of crossing barriers into the unconscious, she noted that the passport expired halfway through her holiday. This could have been extremely inconvenient, as she intended to drive through Europe—and I believe the dream was a plain reminder to get her passport renewed.

I find this a fairly common feature of dreams, but in most cases it happens not with specific events which have been forgotten, but with ongoing conscious worries which are being ignored. In such cases the dream seems to reinforce the worries by depicting what might happen if we continue to ignore them, and I call these "warning" rather than "reminder" dreams. By this, I do not mean to imply any hard-and-fast distinction in the dream mechanism, which is probably the same in both cases.

Dr. William Dement, the modern dream pioneer mentioned in Part 1, tells of waking one morning in great anxiety after a dream in which he had been diagnosed as having lung cancer. The dream and its attendant emotions made such an impression on him that he stopped smoking for two years. He writes that he has recently resumed the habit, in spite of all the anti-smoking propaganda and his own conscious anxiety about it, and is awaiting a second similar dream to stop him smoking altogether!

A Freudian analyst would have difficulty in interpreting such dreams as "wishes," and this was one of the points on which Adler insisted on taking a more commonsense view. Dr. Rudolf Dreikurs illustrated the Adlerian approach by telling the story of a patient who dreamed of being in jail the night after filling in his tax return falsely. He made no connection between the two occurrences until several days later when he presented the dream for analysis. He then remembered that on waking he had decided not to send in the false declaration. The dream seems in this case to have given the warning at a purely emotional level by making the dreamer feel uneasy about trying to cheat the law, without actually bringing the problem itself directly into consciousness at all! The general principle which concerned Adler, however, was that time and again the dream seemed to be "rehearsing" the dreamer's worries and, in so doing, sometimes gave warnings of perils that were in danger of being overlooked.

When my daughter was born, I had several anxiety dreams about losing her, as many new mothers do. Such dreams are usually interpreted psychoanalytically as a wish to get rid of the child, which may contain a germ of truth as new babies do restrict our freedom, keep us up at night, and often drive us frantic with irritation. In most cases, however, we are perfectly aware of such fleeting wishes, so this interpretation tells us nothing new. On the other hand, what such dreams can tell us is exactly *how* we fear our children may come to harm, and it is often fruitful to examine the dreams for hints of possible real danger. For example, I dreamed one night that the cat knocked over the nightlight in the nursery and set the house on fire, with the result that the following morning, I gave the cat to a friend and stopped using the nightlight. The dream seemed to be an amalgam of two very possible real dangers—the cat, which might have jumped onto the baby in her cot, and the light, which could be knocked over in a number of different ways.

On another occasion, when my daughter started to walk, I dreamed she fell through the railings of a flight of stone steps to the garden, and I subsequently took precautions to see that she could not reach them. I also dreamed that I fell down the stairs with her in my arms after catching my foot in a piece of torn carpet. In waking life, I had actually caught my foot in this more than once and sworn to remedy the situation immediately. In both cases, the worries had been more or less conscious most of the time, but I had been ignoring the possible implications of further neglect. Dreams like this which picture a disastrous outcome and make us experience all the relevant emotions do more to remedy the situation than all the conscious good intentions in the world. However, as I have stressed, we sleep through so many of our dreams that it is more efficient in the long run to make a tangible note of our anxieties as they arise in waking life, instead of putting them to the back of our minds, where they become the raw material for nightmares.

An amusing dream was related by a friend of mine when I asked one day if I could borrow her comb or hairbrush, as I had forgotten my own. She handed me a comb, saying, "That settles it. I shall wash my hairbrush this minute," and did. When I queried the significance of this strange and sudden action, she said, "For weeks now, every time I've used my hairbrush I have sworn to wash it as it was getting quite filthy—but I was always too busy at the time and forgot. Then a couple of nights ago, I had a dream in which the queen came to tea. Just as we were about to sit down, I noticed with horror that my dirty old hairbrush was lying faceupwards full of hairs right in the middle of the tea table. I tried to whisk it away quickly before she noticed, and woke up feeling extremely anxious." Now while I was not the queen and the dream had exaggerated the possible consequences of not washing the brush, it was clearly a warning of the kind of embarrassing situation which could arise. A Freudian interpretation of the queen as a mother symbol would add little or nothing to the dream's practical value as we all know that our mothers disapproved of our dirty habits. In this case, the dreaming mind simply chose the most illustrious figure it could think of in order to make its point.

"Reminder" and "warning" dreams refer to some situation or event of which we have at one time or another been consciously aware but which we have pushed to the back of our minds. There are some dreams, however, which actually refer to present situations of which we have never been consciously aware. For this reason, I call them "clairvoyant" dreams (clairvoyance is the faculty of seeing mentally what is happening or exists out of sight), although, as I shall show, these usually turn out to have a natural rather than a supernatural explanation.

"CLAIRVOYANT" DREAMS

I have come across many cases of dreams which "speak the truth" about something which at first sight seems to have been communicated to the brain by paranormal means, and they often give the dreamer feelings of distinct discomfort and unease. My first experience of this, as far as I remember, occurred at school when the headmistress announced one day that Miss R. had left to nurse her mother, who had suddenly been taken ill. That night I dreamed that Miss R. and the school gardener were getting married. I told the other girls next morning and we all giggled at the thought of our rather uptight Miss R. marrying our rather handsome young gardener. However, when he was not to be seen for several weeks afterward, we made inquiries and discovered that my dream had indeed "spoken the truth." We were all frightfully impressed, and I received requests to dream examination questions, my friends' futures, and so on. The results were usually disappointing, but had I persevered I might well have become a prophetess instead of a psychologist!

However, when I came to reconsider the experience later, I recalled that I had in fact once or twice noticed Miss R. walking with the gardener in the grounds, and several days before her departure some of the girls had remarked that the gardener seemed to be missing. I also recalled hearing Miss R. humming beneath her breath, "If you're in love the whole world sings a melody . . ." as she passed me in the corridor the day before she left. Although I did not consciously think about these things when the headmistress made her announcement, something in my brain must have registered a small puzzle that Miss R. had been so cheerful at facing the prospect of nursing a sick parent, and somewhere at the back of my mind I had run over a possible solution in terms of a romance with the gardener. My sleeping mind then picked this up in its nightly turnover of the day's material and presented it in terms of a picture story.

A rather more distressing "clairvoyant" dream was reported by a member of my own dream-study group, Joan, who arrived one evening in tears and reported a dream in which she had found a letter in the breast pocket of her husband's sports jacket. Although she woke up before discovering the contents of the letter, she had a strong feeling of anxiety, and knowing my view that any dream should first be examined for signs of objective truth, she had gone with some trepidation—and more than a little guilt—to look in her husband's wardrobe after he had left for work. To her amazement and horror, she found a letter in the breast pocket of his sports jacket from a girl she had never heard of, indicating quite clearly that an affair had been continuing for some time.

When the group pressed Joan to try and recall possible subliminal perceptions to account for the dream, she admitted that her husband had spent frequent nights away from home over the past few months, had quite often arrived home later than usual from work, and had once or twice put down the telephone receiver abruptly as she entered the room. His story was that his job entailed extra work, and her conscious mind had accepted this. We concluded that she must have noticed little discrepancies which she thrust to the back of her mind because she did not want to face the possibility of her husband's being unfaithful. It is possible that she actually caught a glimpse of a letter in his pocket as he took off his jacket, a perception which clicked with the worries already at the back of her mind, whereupon her dreaming mind presented a picture story of her anxiety. On the other hand, the actual occurrence of the letter in the dream may have been a real coincidence, her sleeping mind simply expressing her anxieties in terms of a fairly standard drama about the ways in which wives discover their husband's infidelities.

This incident naturally led to a great deal of discussion in the group about the possibility of someone's having a dream which expressed anxieties having no foundation in fact whatever. Might not the principle of looking for objective truth in dreams lead to much unnecessary misery and suspicion? Do we not have to guard against a paranoid tendency to believe other people are deceiving us when our fears may be quite irrational? The simple answer seemed to be that if Joan had found no letter or anything like it, her next step should have been to tell her husband about the dream instead of watching his movements suspiciously. If one person in a relationship is being dishonest, there is no reason why the other person should retaliate in kind. If such a discussion had revealed that her husband was in fact feeling frustrated in the marriage, then nothing but good could come from talking about it. On the other hand, if the discussion revealed the presence of totally paranoid, irrational feelings on Joan's part, there would be a clear case for exploring her dreams further for hints about the possible origins of such fears. This is discussed fully in the next chapter.

The following week, another group member, David, reported a dream in which his fiancée had received a sum of money from her ex-husband, although she had promised to stop this practice since going to live with David. This issue had been a bone of contention between them in the early days, as he wanted her to cut herself off from her husband completely, while she wanted to take the money until they could marry. David was very upset by this dream because he felt that there could be no truth in it and that it indicated the presence of irrational feelings of distrust on his part. He told his fiancée about it the following morning, and together they explored possible weaknesses in his personality. That night he came home to find the table laid for two by candlelight and a bottle of champagne on ice. The dinner was delicious, and as he sat back glowing with good food and wine, his fiancée leaned across the table and said she had something to tell him. His dream was correct, she said: she had in fact accepted money from her husband and hoped David would forgive her because she had already spent it. She confessed to feeling very disturbed by his apparent power to "read her mind" in his dreams, and said she would never think it worthwhile to try and deceive him again.

The group was prepared to regard this as a happy development in the relationship, but were disinclined to attribute any supernatural powers to David. We saw it as another case of the brain's "playing detective" by putting two and two together from the many small hints it had received below the level of conscious awareness from his fiancée's behavior. Being wise after the event, David agreed that she had probably given herself away to him subliminally, perhaps by not asking him for money for a long time or by buying something he felt she could not afford, and his conscious mind had shied away from drawing the obvious conclusion.

All the examples I have given so far show direct and straightforward "clairvoyance," but I have also come across many cases of dreams depicting the essence of the truth while being somewhat off the mark about the details. For example, I once dreamed that I opened the morning paper at breakfast and saw a large photograph of a rather humorless psychoanalyst friend of mine. He stood smiling broadly between the figures of Frank Sinatra and Tony Curtis, and the caption below read in large letters "The Singing Psychoanalyst." The newspaper said he had been chosen from hundreds of applicants to play the romantic male lead in a new musical film with the two famous stars. In the dream, I felt a mixture of emotions—amusement at the thought of his playing this role, admiration for his initiative, and annoyance at the thought that he was getting himself into the public eye and encroaching on what I considered to be my own territory—for I saw him as the dry, highly academic psychoanalyst and myself as the popularizer of psychological issues on television, on radio, and in magazines. I felt in the dream that it was most unfair of him to do this, especially in view of his normally superior attitude to my activities.

Of course, I checked my dream and discovered that far from landing the male lead in a new musical, he had neither broadcast, televised, nor even published an article in the popular press. I wondered what on earth my dream was up to in concocting such a story, and toyed with various psychological explanations in terms of "how I see my analyst friend," none of which rang true. A few days later, however, I heard from a friend that she had written to a box number in a magazine advertising encounter and sensitivity-training groups, and had received a reply from this analyst informing her that he had recently taken up this new form of therapy and was now running his own groups. He was indeed encroaching on my territory, but not quite in the sense depicted by my dream, for I had in fact started my own encounter groups using the principles of Gestalt therapy and dream interpretation several months earlier. I considered myself one of the pioneers of the Human Potential Movement in England and had lost no time in pointing out to my analyst friend that his kind of orthodox therapy was on its way out and would soon be replaced by the new group techniques. In his usual manner, he had poured scorn on the whole idea and had apparently remained totally unconvinced in all our subsequent conversations.

Looking back, I was able to see that he had quizzed me about groups, books, and all relevant information on the subject to a degree which was quite out of keeping with his apparent disinterest. I had obviously registered this discrepancy at the back of my mind and my dream had thrown up a story around the subliminal suspicion that he was encroaching on my territory. The dream also incidentally told me something about this man's general character of which I was not consciously aware. Beneath his apparently rigid and uptight exterior, there lurked a desire to break out and "get with it" on the psychological scene, as well as a possible envy of my own position in the field of popular psychology. It is also possible that my dream picked up from him a ruthless streak of ambition which would cause him to jump on any bandwagon likely to further his prospects.

This dream probably taught me more about the analyst than about his actual activities, and I find that many dreams throw up elements of objective truth about a person which have bypassed the conscious mind in waking life. These dreams are on the whole less uncanny than their apparently "clairvoyant" counterparts about specific events, but are no less useful. Over the years, I have learned never to examine a dream character from a subjective point of view, however bizarre the picture might be, without first making absolutely sure that there is not at least some objective truth in it.

"SEEING THROUGH" PEOPLE

One of the simplest examples that comes to mind is the case of Mrs. B., whom I met on holiday last year. We were talking about the widespread use of drugs, pills, and medicines in modern society and deploring the psychological dependence on them of regular users. Mrs. B. agreed with me wholeheartedly that it was best to keep away from them altogether if possible, adding that she never touched the things. That night, I dreamed that Mrs.

171

B. was standing in her bathroom before a shelf full of bottles, swallowing pills by the dozen. I woke up quite convinced that she had committed suicide, and was greatly relieved to find both Mr. and Mrs. B. eating breakfast as normal. Later in the day, I related my dream to Mr. B., who laughed and said, "It's funny you should dream that. I keep telling her that if she takes any more pills and things, she'll make herself ill, but she takes no notice. She's a real hypochondriac—always something wrong with her." I am still not sure how I knew this. It is possible that something failed to ring true as she talked to me— her tone of voice, the slight facial tic, the nervous fidgeting—or that I had actually seen her taking something during the day. Anyway, it is probable that the two conflicting pieces of information met in my brain to form a puzzle which was later nicely dramatized in my dream.

A similar dream occurred at a time when I was participating in a psychodynamic group. In the dream, the group members and I were on some kind of journey and we decided to stay overnight at a rather sleazy, cheap-looking hotel. One of the girls, Susan, a fairly well-known left-wing activist who was engaged to a Communist reporter, objected strongly to the hotel and said she was going to stay at the very expensive hotel over the road. We discussed my dream at the next meeting at which Susan was absent, and everyone expressed surprise that I should have chosen her of all the group members to play this role. The following week, I took her on one side after the meeting and told her my dream. At first she looked surprised and slightly shocked, then she laughed and said, "So you've seen through me at last. That's exactly what I would have done. In fact, I got into trouble for something similar only the other day with my boyfriend." At a subconscious level, I must have picked up hints that Susan's involvement in left-wing politics was not as wholehearted as she had tried to maintain. In our particular group, this was not a very important issue, but had we all belonged to the Communist Party, the dream information would have been of the greatest interest!

A much more serious example of seeing through people

172

in dreams occurred some years ago when my husband dreamed that a new business colleague had invited him to dinner and served, vegetables that were full of worms. My husband felt this was the dream's way of saying that his colleague was untrustworthy, so he checked his suspicion and found it correct. He therefore canceled the deal he was about to make, which could ultimately have lost him a lot of money. This is a clear case of the necessity of checking on the accuracy of the dream perception before taking action, as the whole thing could have been pure fantasy on my husband's part.

Equally, the dream might have been misleading if taken literally, even if it had been based on a correct perception. A good example of this was provided by one of my dream-group members, Lisa, who dreamed that the nanny she had employed to look after her baby screamed at her, "I hate your baby. I hate all babies. I'm only doing this for the money." Lisa was horrified because although the nanny was not the most efficient person in the world there was no apparent reason to consider her vicious. Nevertheless, Lisa took notice of her dream and kept the nanny under close scrutiny. Then she had another dream in which a ten-pound note was stolen from her bag. On waking, she discovered that she had left her bag downstairs overnight and that a ten-pound note was in fact missing from it. Lisa jumped to the obvious conclusion and reported the matter to the local police. They accordingly planted money in the house, stained with a special dye that rubbed off onto the hands of anyone touching it. The money duly disappeared and Lisa called in the police. The nanny's hands were clear, but the cleaner's hands were stained bright red and blue and the missing money found on her person.

Of course, Lisa felt terrible about this and the group discussed the possible reasons for the dreams. The first dream remained a mystery, and eventually had to be tackled along Gestalt lines, with Lisa playing the roles of the nanny and the baby, but it failed to tell us anything about the objective situation. The second dream, however, seemed fairly clear in that Lisa knew at the subconscious level about the ten-pound note which she had left in her bag downstairs. This must have aroused anxiety before she went to sleep, hence the dream of its being stolen. As she already had doubts about the nanny's integrity on account of the first dream, what was more natural than that her sleeping mind should weave a story combining the two fears? It seemed rather uncanny, however, that the dream should have been so correct about the money's actually being stolen, and a possible solution presented itself the following day when the cleaner asked the court to take into account several other smaller thefts she had committed in Lisa's home. It is possible that Lisa had received subliminal perceptions about her money's being stolen over a period of time and therefore one part of her expected further thefts to take place. She could quite easily have missed a pound or two without realizing it consciously, but ten pounds was a different matter altogether. The moral of this tale is, of course, to take dreams seriously but to check thoroughly on all objective interpretations before taking action of any kind. The subconscious mind may have considerable powers of detection, but like any other detective it can make mistakes.

"PRECOGNITIVE" DREAMS

The dreams which most frequently lead to sensational articles in the press are those which appear to predict the future. In the technical terminology of psychical research, any dream which seems to indicate that the human mind has foreknowledge would be called "precognitive," as distinguished from cases of "clairvoyance," the apparent faculty of being able to see things or events that *already exist* without the knowledge's passing through ordinary sense channels.

It is not my intention to comment here on those dreams which appear to have foreseen some major public catastrophe like the sinking of the *Titanic* or the assassination of President Kennedy, except to say that some of the well-authenticated stories do seem very strange, even allowing for the fact that on any given night there are probably thousands of people dreaming about shipwrecks, dying presidents, and so on. The only predictive dreams of which I have had any direct experience have been of a much more personal kind, and my conclusion is that they too can usually be explained as the result of subconscious "detective work," although like the apparently clairvoyant dreams, they can often seem quite uncanny at the time.

I recently experienced a case of the most straightforward kind of "precognitive" dream in which my front tooth fell out with a clatter onto my plate as I dined with a distinguished body of people in a restaurant. During the course of the next day, I related this dream to my Freudian analyst, who immediately plunged deeply into the complexities of castration anxiety and the loss of my fantasy penis. That night, at a wine and cheese party, as I dug my teeth into a piece of cheese the cap of my front tooth came loose and fell down onto my plate! At first, I was rather disturbed by my apparently precognitive powers, until I realized that I had known perfectly well for some time that the cap was not as firm as it should have been and that I ought to have visited the dentist long ago. In fact, this was simply a case of a "warning" dream's coming true before I had time to heed it. Had it occurred a week earlier, I should probably have made an appointment with my dentist and there would have been no precognition.

A much more distressing example of apparent precognition was told to my dream group by Sally, who dreamed she was being presented to a Persian king in the grounds of his palace. As they talked, a group of happy, laughing young girls came into the garden, followed by a rather sad-looking, middle-aged woman who she thought must be the king's chief wife. This woman was obviously in charge of the harem and was sad, Sally felt, because the king no longer wanted her sexually and had relegated her to the role of household organizer. One of the girls came up to Sally and said, "Don't you recognize me? We were together in a previous incarnation."

Sally woke up very depressed, as she felt instinctively that the king represented her husband and that she was the chief wife. Associating to the image of "Persian king," she said she had a suspicion that her husband had more than a trace of the "overlord" in him, in spite of his overt kindness and consideration. In addition, the "Persian garden" reminded her of the book *The Perfumed Garden*, a manual of Eastern sexual techniques—a garden to which, in the dream, she was a mere visitor and observer. She explained that over the past few years she and her husband had grown apart sexually, while she devoted more and more of her time and energy to the house and family. The laughing young girl's reference to a previous incarnation reminded her of the early years of their marriage when she and her husband had been very sexually involved and joyously irresponsible. While she knew that her husband, who was in the film industry, came into contact with many pretty young girls, she rejected any suggestion of his having affairs with them. "He's just not the type," she said. "He's far too inhibited." The group concluded that the dream must have mirrored her feelings of anxiety about the state of her marriage and advised her to try and change the situation. It was too late, however, as a few months later her husband introduced a young girl into the household, saying that she needed a temporary home until she found somewhere to live. There thus began a long series of affairs with various girls he brought home from time to time, while Sally cooked, cleaned, and looked after them all.

The dream was uncanny in the accuracy of its prediction, but it seems clear to me that somewhere along the line Sally must have had some pretty penetrating insight into her husband's character—and indeed her own. Part of her mind knew that she did not really want to resume an energetic sexual relationship with her husband, and while her conscious mind was reassuring her that he was too inhibited to have affairs with other women, her subconscious mind knew otherwise. The result was that she had probably begun to work out, below the surface of consciousness, a solution whereby they could continue to live together, which her sleeping mind had dramatized in the form of a dream. Of course, Sally was very upset at first when her solution "came true" but once she became used to the new situation, she seemed reasonably content with the arrangement as long as the neighbors did not know. The group warned her that one day her husband might find a girl he really wanted to marry and leave her, in spite of her devoted work as mother-housekeeper, but she refused to believe this as it was not part of her dream. We all hoped she would have another one to convince her, since we felt she was living in a totally unreal situation.

Sally's dream reminded another group member, George, of several "precognitive" dreams he had experienced a few years previously. At the time, he believed himself to be very happily married and was decidedly amused to dream of holding divorce papers, saying, "I shall marry someone more mature next time." A little later, he dreamed he was getting divorced to marry an old flame, and in yet another dream he was trying to telephone a girlfriend but was being impeded by his wife on the telephone extension. These latter dreams shocked him immensely as he loved his wife and had never once been unfaithful to her in nine years of marriage, nor even seriously considered doing so. Three years later, however, they had divorced and were both happily remarried. Looking back on the dreams, George said it now seemed perfectly obvious that he and his first wife were quite unsuited to each other and he could not understand why they married in the first place. In this case, as with Sally, the "predictive" dreams simply showed that George was already aware at the back of his mind that all was far from well with his marriage, but his vested interest in it had prevented him from recognizing this.*

* When I have related this incident at public lectures and seminars, the objection has often been raised that "predictive" dreams of this nature could be cases of self-fulfilling prophecies, in that a dream of divorce could occur simply as a natural expression of worry in any marriage but might serve to plant a seed of destruction in the mind of a suggestible person. It has even been put to me that my principle of taking dreams seriously might actually encourage such destructive suggestions. I believe this grossly overrates the power of suggestion, and I have found that subsequent discussion with the questioner almost always reveals that he himself is uneasily

There was, however, a small circumstantial detail in George's first divorce dream that was not so simply explained. It ended with the divorce solicitor's taking the papers back and saying, "It's all right, you won't actually need them this time." When a year later George's wife first shattered him by leaving with another man, he had naturally wondered if his divorce dreams were coming true, but there had actually been a brief reconciliation before they finally decided to go their separate ways.

A third case of dreams "predicting" the course of a relationship was reported by a professional colleague of mine who some years ago fell in love with a man with whom she worked, just before she was unexpectedly sent to America for six months. There had been no sexual involvement, and when she began dreaming of going to bed with him, she dismissed it as wish fulfillment. In one, she was very disappointed when he telephoned to say he "could not make it" to her flat that day; in another, he was naked but turned away from her so that she could not see his penis; and in yet another, she noticed that he had only one testicle. In the final dream of the series, which occurred just before she came home, she dreamed they were sitting together in the cinema when he suddenly got up and moved to the row in front, saying that he was more comfortable there. However, she put these ambivalent dreams out of her mind when, on her return home, he met her at the airport and firmly swept her off to live with him. For several months

aware of cracks in his own marriage and is trying hard to behave as if they weren't there. Of course, I should never *encourage* anyone to break up a relationship, or indeed take any drastic decision, on the basis of dreams. I merely insist that the dreamer take responsibility for his dreams and, if necessary, face up to the truth of negative feelings revealed by them. If a marriage is suffering from strain, then the only real hope of saving it is to confront the situation openly and honestly. If it is better that it break up, then I believe a quick break is better than a long, painful struggle so that both partners have a fair chance of starting new lives. For my views on the possible use of dream power in the family, see Chapter 11.

they enjoyed a reasonably happy affair, until the odd occasions on which he turned away from her in bed saying he "could not make it" became too frequent to be ignored. Eventually, it became clear that he was becoming impotent through strong feelings of aversion to women generally, which he had always known about but had tried hard to overcome with her. Her dreams had picked up these feelings which he had tried to hide, and the final "prediction" came true when he left their flat for another one of his own in the same district, a move which heralded the end of their affair.

My most recent "precognitive" dream was in a lighter vein. I dreamed I was giving a lecture to a spiritualist meeting, but instead of being at the front of the hall I was reading my lecture (not my usual habit) from a chair at the back of the hall. At the end, they all clapped politely without even turning around to look at me. I was worried because it had been so short but consoled myself with the thought that there would be lots of time for questions. At this point the chairwoman rose, gave out a few notices, and everyone started to go home. I noticed that Rosalind Heywood, one of Britain's foremost writers on psychical research, came forward, shook hands with the chairwoman, and left. I was very upset in the dream, as I felt she must have received a special invitation to the meeting (as far as I knew, dreaming was not her major interest) and would go away disappointed.

This dream took place when I was on holiday in Cyprus, and I was at a loss to understand it, as my mind was very far removed from work lectures. I forgot all about it until six weeks later when I was due to give a lecture on dreams for an organization concerned with spiritual and psychological studies. My husband and I had been invited to dine with the secretary and one or two other members before the meeting, and as we drove to the restaurant, I suddenly remembered my dream. "Heavens," I said, "do you realize I'm going to give a lecture to a sort of 'spiritualist' meeting just like my dream in Cyprus? If Rosalind Heywood is there, I shall turn around and go home, because something is sure to go wrong." As we entered the

179

restaurant, Rosalind and her husband greeted us warmly and said how much they were looking forward to hearing my views on dreams! I was speechless for a moment and then told them about the dream. They laughed and said, uncanny though it was meeting Rosalind at dinner, they were sure that the rest of the dream was not precognitive, since they could not see how anything would go wrong at this stage. After dinner, I took my place at the speaker's table at the front of the hall, relieved to find that it was not at the back as in my dream! I reached into my briefcase for my notes, and to my horror found they were not there. I realized that I must have left them at home, and while I could perfectly well give a general lecture on dreams without notes, my talk would be greatly impoverished if I could not refer in detail to the examples I had collected. There was only one thing to do. While my husband rushed home in a taxi for the forgotten papers, I gave the first part of the lecture and embellished it by telling this particular dream, giving as rational an explanation as I could muster of what had occurred.

In the first place, I was forced to admit that I had been decidedly uneasy about giving the lecture, as I felt my views on dreams were too down-to-earth for the taste of people who belonged to a society for *spiritual* and psychological studies. This anxiety had clearly led to the dream in Cyprus, even though I was not consciously worrying about it at the time. Had I taken the dream seriously, I might have seen it as a warning that part of me would try to dissociate itself from the meeting, in which case I would have taken extra care to see that I did not "leave part of myself" at home. While agreeing with me on this general interpretation, the audience was quick to point out that I could have had no special reason for knowing that Mrs. Heywood would even be at the lecture, let alone the dinner. I accepted this, and professed myself convinced that she had been in touch with me telepathically. I suggested that she had deliberately used her paranormal powers to arrange the whole thing in order to shock me into a less skeptical attitude toward ESP!

While I certainly would not wish to assert dogmatically

180

that the mind has no paranormal powers, what I am concerned to argue is that it *does* have considerable powers both of "detection" and "prediction" which are not paranormal at all. If dreams or parts of dreams come true, then it is likely that the truth they contain involves perceptions and possibilities which have been passed over by the conscious mind in waking life. Dreams also throw up feelings we find difficult to articulate, representing them in clear picture form, which when properly understood may be "predictive" in the sense of indicating the probable outcome of certain life situations. Dreams of this kind, wrote Jung, "are no more prophetic than a medical diagnosis or a weather forecast. They are merely an anticipatory combination of probabilities which may coincide with the actual behavior of things but need not necessarily agree in every detail. Only in the latter case can we speak of 'prophecy.'" Such "prospective" dreams, as Jung called them, are particularly useful in all forms of therapy as they indicate how the patient feels about the therapist and treatment at any given moment, and hint at future progress or failure in the consulting room.

"PROSPECTIVE" DREAMS IN THERAPY

Jung himself quotes one particularly striking case of a woman whose dreams expressed the difficulties she would encounter with three analysts to whom she went for treatment. After beginning treatment with the first, she dreamed she had to cross the barrier to the next country but could not find it and no one would help her. The analyst realized that this dream expressed a "vote of no confidence" in him and so he referred her to a colleague. Again she dreamed she must cross the frontier. After a long search, she noticed a small light far away and thought it must be the customs house. To reach it she had to travel through a dark wood in which she lost her way, and woke up in terror as someone who seemed to be traveling with her suddenly clung to her like a madman. Jung believed this indicated a feeling that she would in some way be overwhelmed by the analyst, and once again the analysis had to be broken off because she made no progress. Finally, she came to Jung as a patient. This time, she dreamed she had already crossed the frontier and found herself in a Swiss customs house. She believed she had nothing to declare but the customs official dived into her bag and pulled out two large mattresses.

Jung interpreted this dream as an indication that she trusted him and that the analysis would be successful. He saw "crossing the frontier" as a sign of her growing will to health, and the mattresses as the marriage she finally contracted after overcoming her sexual problems in therapy. All three dreams, according to Jung, anticipated the difficulties and eventual outcome of all three attempts at therapy.

It is now generally accepted by analysts of all schools that the first dream of a patient in therapy is likely to give an indication of the future course of the treatment. In my own case, this was certainly true. After the first few sessions of my Freudian training analysis, I dreamed of having a fierce quarrel with my mother because she insisted on employing a builder whom I knew to be a clumsy workman, hammering things together in a shoddy fashion so that they fell to pieces as soon as I came to use them. He also did jobs no one asked him to do, threw away furniture of which I was very fond, and replaced it with his own, which I hated. In the dream, my mother took not the slightest notice of my warnings, and I woke up extremely upset.

Of course, I had no difficulty in recognizing the "bad builder" as my analyst, and he interpreted the dream as a sign that I intended to resist analysis by discrediting him in advance. This I accepted as a possibility, and for the first year I took special care to go along with his interpretations and ideas, although I often felt he might be wrong. For example, he insisted that my work (which I loved) was no more than a substitute penis, and that my true fulfillment lay in devoting myself to husband and family. Later in the analysis, when my husband actually faced me with the choice between home and career, I had been so brainwashed that I chose the former in a desperate attempt to become what he called a "real woman." This turned out to be a living death for me, as my "coffin dream" on page 114 so clearly predicted. Needless to say, my analyst saw my choice as the outcome of a successful analysis, whereby I had gained insight into my deepest needs, despite the fact that I felt depressed, frustrated, and totally alienated. It was only after I had terminated the analysis (which I did in order to comply with my husband's wishes) that I found life so impossible that I had to resume work, after which the marriage broke up and I found a much happier mode of life.

Looking back, it is clear that my dream had predicted the course of the analysis with astonishing accuracy. My analyst had insisted on doing a job I had not asked him to do by treating my career as a symptom, in spite of the fact that I had gone to him not because I was ill, but for training. He had also used his Freudian theory like a hammer, trying to refurnish my life with his own (and Freud's) values about what a "real woman" should be, although this did violence to my whole nature. Associating to my mother in the dream, I am now reminded that on a number of occasions in my childhood she had threatened to take me to a "psychiatrist," so that I might be cured of my willfulness in refusing, among other things, to help her in the house while my brother went out to play. In depicting her as the "bad builder's" advocate, my dream had forecast very neatly how my analyst would ally himself with the voice of my mother that wanted to fit me to society's norms by training me to be a nice little housewife.

I was reluctant to believe, however, that Freudian analysis had nothing to offer me, and indeed I had gained many valuable insights from it, so I tried again later on with another analyst. Alas, my first dream after a few sessions found me lying on a couch so small that my head stuck right out of the window. Looking around, I saw that the garden was a neat little cemetery, and I knew that each grave contained the head of a woman which had been cut off to make her fit the couch.

In spite of this clear warning, I persisted for many

months, but eventually had to leave after being made ill by the analyst's constant Procrustean efforts to fit me to a theory in which women are expected to sacrifice their individuality and initiative to the service of men. I still felt something of a failure at quitting analysis, but could no longer ignore the inner voice that told me to believe in myself. At the time, I did not realize that the next few years would see a swing of public opinion away from Freudian analysis, expecially for women, which would lead people to congratulate me on my lucky escape. "The 'cured' patient," writes Eva Figes in her recently published book *Patriarchal Attitudes,* "is actually brainwashed, a walking automaton, as good as dead. The corners have been knocked off and woman accepts her own castration, acknowledges herself inferior, ceases to envy the penis and accepts the passive role of femininity. Sadly, man recognises that the ideal, submissive woman he has created for himself is somehow not quite what he wanted." Miss Figes adds (without the benefi. of my "couch dream"), "Freud's basic view was that every woman was a square peg trying to fit into a round hole. It did not occur to him that it might be less destructive to change the shape of the holes rather than to knock all the corners off."

The modern movement of Gestalt therapy is explicitly anti-Freudian in this respect. Although it derives many insights from Freud, its basic principle is that none of us is here to live up to the expectations of others or adjust to society and that the fundamental right of all human beings—men, women, parents, children, therapists, and patients—is to be ourselves, a sentiment which Freudian pays lip service to but rarely carries out in practice. Perls is firm on two points here. In the first place, he argues, it is difficult to know exactly what we are supposed to adjust to in our present constantly changing society, and second, he sees the *need* to adjust as a neurotic symptom to be overcome. We only adjust, he says, when our hankering after security prevents us from standing on our own feet and intelligence, and from taking risks. "I believe we are living in an insane society," he writes, "and that you only have the choice either to participate in this collective psychosis or to take risks and become healthy. . . . If you are centered in yourself, then you don't adjust any more."

Significantly, when I started my training in Gestalt therapy, I dreamed I let an eagle out of a cage and woke up with an immense feeling of relief and joy. The group leader, who was from California, told me later that the Navajo Indians believe in three spirits inhabiting the San Francisco Mountains—the wind, the lightning, and the birds. The eagle is to them a particularly powerful spirit which must never be caged, and they would have interpreted my dream as a very propitious omen for the future.

An equally propitious dream occurred when I began an exploratory Jungian analysis. I dreamed that I had been left a large, old country house, and I wondered whether to sell it or spend a great deal of time and money renovating it. I knew I should prefer it ultimately to a smaller, modern, labor-saving house. Starting to explore, I entered a room in which hunks of meat were hanging on hooks and I had more than a suspicion that they were maggoty. I shuddered and turned to go when I heard something scuttle across the floor and I felt I had disturbed something that had lain dormant for a long time. As I looked to see what it was, the room became lighter and larger, and I woke up with the feeling that I would clean out the house and live in it. This dream indicated that I felt analysis would expand rather than diminish me, a prognosis which turned out to be correct.

CONCLUSION

The essential first step in dream interpretation is to check for possible truth about the external world, not only because it is valuable in itself, but also because the process of checking makes all the difference to the way we understand any other messages the dream may contain about our inner subjective problems. For example, if I dream of the queen's coming to tea and finding a dirty hairbrush, it may tell me something about my feelings for my mother, but any analysis at this level is likely to go quite differently according to whether or not I have a dirty hairbrush in real life. If I do, it is sensible to assume that the dream expresses a worry about untidiness and dirty habits, and it is probably quite unnecessary to get led away into associations of hairbrushes with pubic hair, or whatever. If, on the other hand, my hairbrush is immaculately clean, such associations are the only way to discover the meaning of the dream.

Most of the dreams I have described in this chapter have expressed their "objective truth" fairly directly, but Sally's dream of the Persian harem and the "prospective" therapy dreams show how perceptions can be presented by the dreaming mind in symbolic form. However, I would suggest that unless the symbolism in a dream gives a fairly immediate meaning by association, the task of checking for objective messages may be too difficult to be practicable. For example, a dream of a lion running away with a deer *might* show that my mind had somewhere perceived that my husband was being unfaithful, but so many alternatives interpretations are possible that it would be hard to settle on this one for objective checking unless its meaning sprang immediately to mind. On the other hand, whenever a dream refers to real people, things, relationships, or situations in the external world, a check for possible objective truth is simple and in my view essential. Even if the message is a relatively trivial one, it is still fascinating to learn about the way our conscious minds miss things in waking life and later throw them up in the form of a dream.

If the dream does turn out to have a significant objective message, practical action will depend upon the circumstances. In the case of "reminder" and "warning" dreams, the implications are immediately obvious. With dreams that seem to contain "clairvoyant" perceptions or to "see through" people, careful checking is essential before one takes any action at all, as we saw in Lisa's dream of the stolen money. If the dream concerns an intimate personal relationship, the sensible thing is usually to discuss it with the person involved, but in less intimate situations, like that of my husband's business colleague or Lisa's nanny, it is best to treat the dream as a possible warning and check up on it by other means.

With dreams that seem to predict a future course of events, the problem is more difficult, because we may feel we ought to try to prevent things' going the predicted way, as I did in persisting with my Freudian analysis, and my colleague did in continuing her affair in the hope of curing her lover of his aversion to women. There can clearly be no hard-and-fast rule here, but there is a lot of evidence to suggest that the unconscious is often wiser than the conscious mind in matters of this sort, even if its wisdom consists only in making us aware of the forces we shall be up against if we persist with our conscious plans.

Psychotherapists and analysts in particular should beware of their professional habit of treating all their patients' communications, including dreams, as mere "projections" of the personality, containing no objective truth. For example, if a patient dreams of his analyst as a murderer, he may indeed be projecting onto him the image of his father, but the dream may equally well be telling the analyst that he is doing violence to the patient's essential self, perhaps by insisting on dogmatic interpretations instead of "listening with the third ear."

When, and only when, we have explored a dream thoroughly for signs of objective truth and checked on it, should we take it as a mirror reflecting our subjective attitudes toward life. Often, of course, the line between "objective" and "subjective" meanings is a hazy one. For example, my "singing psychoanalyst" dream undoubtedly showed that I had picked up *hints* about my friend's true nature, although it had greatly exaggerated them. The meaning of the dream, however, would have been quite different had it contained no truth at all or been way off the mark, in which case I should have wanted to know why I saw him in that particular light. It would then have been classified as a "looking glass" dream, which differs from dreams that "look outward" in that they draw more energy from the dreamer's personality than from the environment. Such dreams, which are the subject of the next chapter, tell us more about ourselves than about the people and situations they depict. As we shall see, however, many dreams can be interpreted on more than one level, especially the longer ones containing several episodes.

CHAPTER 9

THROUGH THE LOOKING GLASS

When Alice went through the looking glass, she found some familiar things which were straight reflections of the ordinary world, but a great many other things that were "as different as possible." When our dreams distort reality, as they do most of the time, then the distortions come from our own minds and can tell us a great deal about ourselves. "A skillful man," wrote Emerson, "reads his dreams for his self-knowledge," and in this chapter I shall consider how to read them in order to learn about the way our inner attitudes and prejudices—many of them consisting of "programs" laid down in childhood—are influencing the specific situations in our lives at the time of dreaming. In the next chapter I shall consider how dreams can help us understand and deal with our deeper inner problems.

The basic principle I shall be following in this chapter is that of looking at the dream as a picture and trying to relate that picture to the dreamer's immediate circumstances. I shall concentrate on four of the most important kinds of dream image—people, animals, houses, and vehicles—and in each case I shall show some of the things we may learn from them, both when they carry an obvious reference to the dreamer's current life situation, and when, in the absence of such a reference, they have to be treated as symbols whose meaning is to be sought through associations. My illustrations, derived mainly from my own dream-study group, will incidentally bring in many other kinds of dream symbolism, so that by the end of the chapter the reader should have a good overall idea of how to interpret what he sees in the looking-glass world of his own dreams.

LOOKING-GLASS PEOPLE

Intimates

Human characters play the leading parts in the vast majority of dreams, and if they are people who are very close to us in everyday life—husbands, wives, lovers, parents, or our own children—they are unlikely to represent anything other than themselves. In such cases, the meaning of the dream depends on what the character is doing, what we are doing to them, and the general situation in which they appear. The question to be asked in all cases is "What does the dream tell me about my present feelings or thoughts about this person?"

Sometimes, the meaning is very straightforward, as in the case of Joanna, a member of my dream-study group, who dreamed that her husband had been caught out resuming an affair with a girl he had slept with some months previously. In the dream she found herself creeping up to his bedside while he slept, intending to kill him with a hatchet. As she raised the hatchet to deliver the death blow, she paused, thinking that a quick death was too good for him, and decided to cut off his hand first so that he would wake up and realize just why he was being killed. This could have been a "looking outward" dream, based on the subliminal detection of furtiveness in her husband's behavior, but Joanna assured us that she had investigated the situation very carefully and was satisfied that her husband had remained totally faithful after the original affair had blown over. The dream, therefore, clearly indicated that for *her* the affair was not over and done with at all as she consciously believed.

Underneath her conscious decision to let bygones be bygones, she was nursing revengeful feelings which might well have caused serious trouble had she not been made aware of them by the dream. Associating to the details of the dream, Joanna was reminded of the proverb "Let sleeping dogs lie," and admitted that one part of her still saw her husband as a dog. At the conscious level, she was letting the sleeping dog lie by not recriminating him about the past, but her unconscious purpose in "burying the hatchet" was much more sinister: she meant to lull him into a false sense of security and then seek her revenge, perhaps by starting an affair of her own or doing something to damage his career. It was clear that her slow method of killing him in the dream meant she wanted him to listen to her expression of feelings about the whole affair so that he would fully understand how much he had hurt her.

The group suggested that in the first instance she should act out her dream revenge as a psychodrama, beating a large cushion with a tennis racket in the middle of the room and giving full vent to her feelings. Afterward, she told her husband about the whole thing, and they decided to establish a new kind of relationship based on greater awareness of the tensions between them, which they had hitherto been suppressing in the interests of surface harmony.

Most dreams are not as straightforward as this, however, and quite complex associations are necessary to reveal their meaning even when there is no difficulty in recognizing the main characters. For example, another group member, Brian, brought us a dream which worried him because at first sight it seemed, like Joanna's, to indicate a murderous wish inside himself directed in this case toward his eldest son. He dreamed that his son and several of his

191

school friends were lined up by some mysterious baddies to be killed by means of a death ray, while he himself was being forced to watch. One boy, the son of Brian's business partner, was chosen to be the first victim, and Brian awoke in horror as the boy lay writhing on the floor, while a voice said, "It's your son's turn next."

Brian knew all about the Freudian theory of unconscious hostility between fathers and sons but thought this was going too far for comfort, and in any case left many questions unanswered, such as why other boys were being killed and why this strange death ray had been chosen as the murder weapon. When we encouraged him to associate to the dream story, it became quite clear that Brian did see himself as a potential murderer, but only indirectly and not in the Freudian sense at all.

Brian's immediate association to "death ray" was a science-fiction play he had seen on television the previous night, about a ray which in small doses could turn a person into a genius, but if too much were given would turn him into a zombie. His colleague's son, said Brian, had just returned home from his first term at a leading private boarding school, and all his son's school friends were destined for a similar fate. Although Brian objected strongly to the private educational system on political grounds, he had allowed himself to be persuaded by his wife and colleagues that he too ought to give his son the benefit of small classes, better-qualified staff, and so on, even though he thought the system should be changed. He had accepted his wife's argument that his feelings of misgiving were attributable to the inverted snobbery of his own working-class status by going to a grammar school, rather than to any real political principle.

The dream, however, revealed a different story about the origin of Brian's misgivings. It showed that at the back of his mind he saw the whole process of middle-class private academic education as one which, for all its intellectual virtues in small doses, had the effect in larger doses of turning children into zombies, products of a competitive, conformist, and class-conscious society. He had noticed a change for the worse in his colleague's son after only one term of such "brainwashing" and felt himself indirectly responsible for the future collapse of his own son.

Skeletons in the Psyche—Intimates from the Past

When we dream of people with whom we have had very close relationships in the past, such as parents or siblings, they may represent themselves if we are still in active contact with them, but they may equally well be symbols for those parts of ourselves which have been taken over from them in earlier days. Their presence in a dream is usually sparked off by something in waking life which resembles and revives a similar situation in the past. For example, in my dreams of the bad builder quoted on page 182, the row I had with my mother for employing him against my wishes had no actual reference to the current relationship with my mother, whom I had not seen for several months. Its contemporary reference was to my analyst, who was symbolized in the dream as the bad builder intent on destroying my individuality in much the same way as my mother had demanded conformity in childhood. While the dream seems to be saying on the surface that I feel my mother would be delighted to have someone finish the task she had started, the truth is much more sinister. The row is actually between two conflicting parts of my own personality—the "good girl," based on my idea of the kind of person my mother wanted me to be, and the "rebel" who refuses to submit to manipulation. For years my "mother" was a constant visitor to my dreams, indicating that her influence still bugged me from within even though I had detached myself from her in the external world.

Psychoanalysts say that we "introject" parents and siblings, and indeed any intimate authority figures of childhood, into our psychic systems so that even though they may be away from us, or even dead, their voices still speak within us and influence our behavior. Eric, another group member from a working-class background, told us that his dead father visits him in dreams whenever he attempts to improve his position in the external world. On one occasion, when he was contemplating buying a house in a better district, he dreamed his father telephoned him from the Red Sea and asked his son to meet him there the following day. Eric interpreted "red" as warmth and passion, and "sea" as the emotions, which reminded him of his father's firm conviction that real earthy human emotions existed only within the framework of the working class and that all middle-class life was pretension. Although he was consciously convinced that this was far from true, Eric suffered much internal conflict before he could actually bring himself to make the desired move, as the father within still insisted that he would be cutting himself off from "real" life.

Sometimes the inner voices give us advice that is sensible, but much of the time they are rigid and stereotyped, and far harsher than the voices of our real parents ever were. These skeletons which lurk in the cupboards of the psyche are dealt with in the next chapter, where I shall show how it is possible to get to know and come to terms with them without recourse to psychoanalytic treatment.

Friends and Colleagues

When we dream of friends and colleagues with whom we are in fairly close contact in waking life, then the dream is likely to tell us how we are feeling about these people themselves. Of course, we should always check for objective truth first, as my husband did when he dreamed his colleague served him rotten vegetables at dinner (page 173). In this case, the dream was "outward looking" in that the colleague later proved to be untrustworthy, but had there been no truth in the dream's warning, my husband would have had to ask himself why he had had the dream. It could have been that the colleague wore a bow tie and his father had always warned him as a child to distrust men who wore bow ties, in which case he would have been able to recognize the true irrational origin of any feelings of hesitation he might experience later on.

194

Sometimes, however, the dreaming mind will use the figure of a friend or colleague to say something about another person altogether. For example, an acquaintance of mine who had left her husband and returned to her parents' home dreamed that her father's place at the dinner table was occupied by a former colleague, Dr. Jack Dominian, a Roman Catholic psychiatrist who had written a book on marriage breakdown. As she was no longer in contact with Dr. Dominian, the dream obviously referred to her father, under whose "dominion" she felt herself to be, particularly in connection with her marriage, which he thought she should keep going in spite of all the difficulties.

If we dream of a friend we have known in the past, but with whom we are not currently in contact, we can be pretty sure that the dream's message is not about this friend; it is more likely to be concerned with a present situation which evokes a response very similar to that of the past relationship with our friend. For example, one of our group members, Mark, dreamed he was being served a roast beef dinner by a girlfriend of his very early life but was anxious because he felt he ought to be eating at home with his parents. Since he had not seen this particular girl for over ten years, the group asked him to try and discover what she represented. He said she was a small, blond girl, just like his newly married wife, who had in fact served him roast beef the previous day.

It then became quite clear that his unconscious mind had not yet adjusted to the fact that he was now a married man and under no obligation to eat with his parents. Under the surface of his apparent devotion to his wife, he was thinking of her in the same way as he thought of his past girlfriend, as someone he used to slip out and see occasionally against the wishes of his parents, with whom he lived until the time of his marriage. The fact that he saw his marriage as just another illicit affair and still felt his real devotion lay with his mother was actually making life very uncomfortable for his wife, who constantly complained that he never listened to her and that her wishes were always subordinated to those of his parents. Until the dream, he had considered her outbursts quite unreasonable but now understood how she felt about his casual treatment of her. He determined to make it up to her, and we persuaded him to tell his wife about the dream so that together they could help the "baby Mark" to grow up.

A rather different kind of symbolism was illustrated by another group member, Celia, who had recently set up house with a man whose wife repeatedly found reasons for postponing any divorce action, although they had been separated for years and he had always treated her generously. Celia dreamed that she and her boyfriend bought a very pleasant house at bargain price from some old friends of hers whom she had not seen for many years. They showed her around the house and she was delighted at the lovely, large rooms with big windows until her friend said, "You will, of course, allow us to stay until 1982 when our lease expires." Celia then realized that she had bought the house without inquiring about sitting tenants who would expect her to keep the house in good order while they paid minimum rents. Worse still, she thought, there are probably no decent rooms left for us. Her associations to the dream revealed that the surname of her friends was Law, which reminded her immediately of divorce. 1982 was the year in which her boyfriend's youngest child would be through university, so the dream showed that at the back of her mind she felt hopeless about being able to marry before then. In fact, she recalled that in the early days of her boyfriend's separation, his wife had upbraided him for leaving before the children were off their hands. Moreover, the dream exposed her fear that she herself would be working all those years to help keep his wife and children in the manner to which they had become accustomed.

In this case, the dream friends symbolized not people but an institution, "the Law," and I have come across many examples of this kind of symbolism where the figure of a friend is used to represent some general principle, situation, or way of life with which the dreamer is currently concerned. In such cases, the dream's meaning may be discovered if one looks at the friend's name, as in Celia's dream, but it may also be indicated by something he stands for in the dreamer's life, as in the case of the following dream of one of my colleagues who was proposing to give up his secure, lucrative job in advertising to become a free-lance writer.

He dreamed of leaving a picnic to go on a journey when it began to rain. He knew in the dream that shelter could probably be found by climbing onto a cliff top, which meant negotiating a rather steep, narrow path around an almost spiral bend, but he felt very nervous about his ability to do this without falling when the path became wet and slippery. He gritted his teeth, determined not to show his fear, and asked one of his companions who had already reached the cliff top to help him by taking the bag he was carrying so that he would find it easier to keep his balance. Looking up, he saw that the companion was his friend, dramatist James Brabazon. The dream was a beautiful pictorial expression of my colleague's current anxiety about his ability to negotiate the transition to a new way of life, and when I asked him what James Brabazon was doing in the dream, he replied that this was a man who had, in a waking life, risked the transition from a secure administrative job to free-lance work and survived.

Finally, friends and colleagues in dreams can sometimes symbolize parts of the dreamer's personality, just as parents and siblings can, and such dreams almost always merit further analysis on "inward-looking" lines, once their reference to the dreamer's immediate situation had been thoroughly explored. Martin, a colleague of my second husband who at the time was involved in marketing a new electronic device, dreamed he was going to demonstrate the device in Russia and was smuggling my husband over the border in a suitcase to do the demonstration. As they were passing the customs guards on the way back, Martin was alarmed to see movements inside the suitcase which would arouse the guards' suspicions.

Dreams often use the image of something secreted in a

suitcase or box to depict a part of the dreamer's personality which is being concealed or kept down, and in this instance it seemed clear that Martin felt some hidden part of himself stirring—something represented by my husband—of which he feared those in authority (the guards) would disapprove. He thought of my husband as someone who was always appearing on television or in the press, broadcasting and writing, and my guess was that Martin felt he himself had powers as a public performer which the firm was at that time not allowing him to use. Our advice to Martin was not only to reexamine his role in the firm, but also to look at his other dreams for clues about the underlying forces in his personality which had made him take a secure, routine job in industry instead of one which would give expression to his unused talents.

Public Figures, Historical Characters, and People from Fiction

When we dream of people we know only as public figures, such as royalty or film stars, they obviously cannot stand for themselves at all; as Hall puts it, dreams are personal documents which do not concern themselves with our attitude toward public affairs. The same applies to dreams of fictional or historical characters. All figures of this type must be examined by means of association to see whether they are being used by the dream to "say something" about real people in the dreamer's life; about situations, principles, or institutions with which the dreamer is concerned (like the "Law"); or about parts of the dreamer's personality. The general principle of interpretation is the same as when figures of parents, siblings, friends, or colleagues symbolize something other than themselves: always ask why the dreamer has chosen this particular symbol rather than another. The answer may lie in the name, in associations with the dreamer's past, or in some outstanding quality which he represents in the dreamer's mind.

When my first husband and I had become reconciled after our initial marriage breakup, he dreamed of looking across a desolate piece of wasteland on which was being erected a church of modern design. It was built of gray blocks of concrete, which he found displeasing as he loved the gold and splendor of old churches and cathedrals. A notice said it was being erected by the "ex-Mrs. Armstrong-Jones," and he felt disgusted that she was doing it for her own glory and not for the glory of God.

He had no associations to Princess Margaret's mother-in-law, but remarked that his patients (he is an osteopath) often commented on his beautiful *strong arms*. So, if he was Mr. Armstrong-Jones, then obviously I was his wife. In choosing the ex-Mrs. Armstrong-Jones to symbolize me in the dream, his mind had chosen a very neat way of expressing the fact that he saw me as his *ex*-wife, even though we were reconciled. The horrid concrete church he associated with my psychology, which he found arid and bleak. In the early days of our marriage we had engaged in many forms of religious activity, including Freemasonry, which is rich in color, symbols, and drama, and his dream depicted clearly how he felt I had replaced all this with the new, modern "religion" of academic psychology.

On talking this over with him, I admitted that I had tended to become scornful of our old ways of thinking and had more than once used my psychological knowledge to "put down" what I considered to be his un-thought-out philosophies. I believe this factor may have contributed more than a little to our breakup, and the dream was my husband's very ingenious way of telling me so. We dismissed the idea of the *ex*-wife as a hangover from the past, but the dream may well have been prospective in that I really did become the "ex-Mrs. Armstrong-Jones" a few years later.

Another dream depicting a public figure, this time representing not a person but an institution, was reported by one of my group members, Jeremy. In the dream, he was watching a military procession led by the Duke of Norfolk down the Mall, and it seemed to be wartime because guns were firing and explosions could be heard all around. His girlfriend, who was standing by his side, poured scorn on the whole occasion and said how stupid the whole thing was. Suddenly a shot rang out and a young soldier in the procession fell down dead. Jeremy said, "If he's anything of a man, he'll go back and get him," which of course the Duke did, and carrying the soldier in his arms, he continued to lead the procession as though nothing had happened.

Jeremy had just become engaged to his highly unconventional, rather hippie girlfriend, who wanted him to leave his civil-service job in order to travel. She was also very scornful of his being a member of the Church of England, as she considered this the height of stuffiness. Although Jeremy was decidedly alarmed by her unconventionality, one part of him was also drawn to it. He said the Duke of Norfolk meant to him the Establishment, since he knew the Duke was a Roman Catholic, an official of England's most famous cricket club, and the organizer of the ceremonial at the coronation. The dream's message to Jeremy was clear; he felt his own Establishment tendencies to be "under fire," and also that his present feelings about it were much more equivocal than they used to be. While he undoubtedly saw the Establishment as having a certain dignity and courage, he also recognized it as inflexible and prepared to sacrifice the lives of those who served it in the name of ceremonial order.

Freud held that royal figures in dreams were almost always symbols of the dreamer's parents, or siblings, but I do not find it very interesting to assume, as he did, that such symbols serve merely to express the wishes or conflicts of infancy. If, of course, we have an immediate, direct relationship with a parent or sibling at the time when an appropriate royal personage appears in a dream, then the dream is likely to be saying something about that particular relationship—for example, that my mother is trying to "queen it" over my life. If there is no such direct relationship with parents or siblings in present experience, nor any other actual person or situation for which a royal figure might stand (as the Duke of Norfolk did in Jeremy's dream), then I should want to look for the meaning of a royal dream-figure in some aspect of the dreamer's personality which he or she feels to be royal.

At the time when my first husband had finished his professional studies and we started to be drawn into fairly high social life, I dreamed of being at a party with Princess Anne. To my horror, I found myself conversing with her about politics, religion, and sex, the three things I knew were taboo at formal occasions. She seemed quite interested, but the woman standing by her, who I thought must be her chaperone, looked very shocked and made disapproving noises. The dream expressed my conflict between behaving like my mother's daughter—the proper, well-trained, dignified, and "royal" girl represented by Princess Anne—and my much more unconventional self, which positively enjoyed shocking people. A dream of this kind is likely to yield further useful information if analyzed on "inward-looking" lines, and in the next chapter I pursue my own problem of "internal royalty" in some detail.

Exactly the same principles of interpretation apply to historical and fictional characters in dreams. When they appear we must ask whether they refer to some other person in our present life, an institution, or a part of ourselves. For example, in one dream I was watching the play *Hamlet* when it was announced that the girl who had been playing Ophelia had suddenly been taken ill. They asked for a volunteer from the audience to take her place, and I offered my services since I thought it was a small part and not very demanding. As I stood in the wings awaiting my cue, I suddenly realized I did not know a single line and fled in panic.

The dream occurred at the time I had given up my work to devote myself totally to home and family, and showed clearly that I felt it a role I was quite unable to play. I just did not know how to the play the "little woman," constantly subject to weakness and nervous breakdowns, and the dream was prospective in that eventually I gave it up in despair. Whenever we have dreams like this, or similar ones like forgetting lines onstage, we can be sure there is some role in our present life which we are either unable or unwilling to play.

Strangers or anonymous figures are obviously symbolic if they play a significant part in a dream, and their meaning has to be discovered in the same way as those of the dream characters described in the previous sections. The figures may stand for actual people, for situations or institutions, or for parts of oneself, and the interpretation turns on whatever is expressed by the character's quality or name.

When I first met my second husband he was well known as a presenter of Christianity in modern scientific terms on radio and television. His basic belief was in the divine power of Love, and he interpreted the doctrine of the Trinity as a revelation that all love involved three aspects—giving and receiving between lover and beloved, and the overflowing of their relationship to others. Shortly after we had begun our affair, I dreamed of being in bed with a stranger whose name was Christian and a former colleague of mine called Miss Locke. Christian started to make love to me and then suddenly stopped, saying, "Excuse me, I'd better make love to Miss Locke first because she's getting married in a fortnight." I accepted this in the dream on the grounds that if Miss Locke were really going to be married in a fortnight, I had nothing to lose by being magnanimous. Unfortunately he showed no signs of returning to me, and I awoke in distress.

The dream contained two kinds of "looking-glass people." Miss Locke was a real person who was indeed getting married in a fortnight, but I had no special relationship of any kind with her. When I associated to her name, however, I was reminded of the time many years earlier when a young Swiss boy had rowed me across the Lake of Lucerne, and solemnly pronounced that one woman was very much like another in bed. *"Loch ist loch, und fertig,"* he said, which translated means, "A hole is a hole and that's all there is to it." Obviously then, Miss Locke represented "women" in my mind is a specially sexual context. Associating to Christian, I was easily led to the Christian aspect of my new boyfriend: the dream revealed that I had an underlying suspicion that the overflowing of the Trinity in his theology might possibly mean that he would overflow to other women!

Dreamers usually have little difficulty in recognizing the underlying identity of strange dream figures if they symbolize actual people. My colleague who dreamed of a man in chain mail (page 135) knew at once that he represented her husband, while Sally had no difficulty in identifying the Persian king as her husband once she had recognized the chief wife as an aspect of herself (page 175). In a similar way, strangers in dreams can often be readily associated with parents or siblings who have become parts of ourselves by introjection. For example, Peter, one of my group members, dreamed,

I was coming back from America and was vaguely aware that two fellow passengers on the boat were a rather natty "City Gent" type and a turbaned Indian who worked for a tea company. I gathered that the City Gent believed the Indian was some kind of competitor, following him around to gain information, although I felt there was no truth in this. As we got off the boat and lined up for taxis, the City Gent suddenly turned on the Indian whipped out a knife, and cut off his hands, before leaping into a taxi and disappearing. My impression was that this had been a ruthless stroke designed to stop the Indian from following him any longer. I was horrified, although the Indian did not seem so much hurt as flummoxed at losing his hands, and seemed to be worrying about how he would carry his bags in the future. I mentally followed the City Gent and asked why he had done it, especially as he had no proof that the Indian was following him at all. He replied that in this harsh commercial world there was no time for scruples or even doubts, and the only way to survive was to take quick, ruthless action.

Peter could not associate either the Indian or the City Gent with anyone in his life at the time. The nearest he could get was a feeling that the Indian seemed rather like his long-suffering father, who had been dead for several years. His father, he said, despised all capitalists but particularly those who made money simply by financial manipulation in the City. Peter added that he had always felt rather guilty about admitting to his father that he owned a few shares, and this reminded him that he had sold some shares the previous day to raise money for a much-needed holiday abroad.

This made it clear that the City Gent in the dream was the driving, ambitious side of Peter himself, which felt itself constantly dogged and threatened by the introjected figure of his father. This interpretation was corroborated by the fact that both characters had been with Peter on his dream voyage from America, the land of affluence. By representing his father as an Indian the dream showed that it was not so much the old man's personal needs which nagged at Peter (he had not been really poor for many years before his death), but his constant preaching about the wickedness of anyone allowing himself luxuries when there were still millions starving in India.

Associating to the Indian's hands, Peter was reminded first of the waving hands of beggars in Eastern cities, and then of the fact that the cutting off of the hands was the ancient punishment for theft. So the dream revealed that beneath Peter's apparently calm and easygoing exterior lay a serious split of personality. Whenever he made any money or even spent a little on himself, he was nagged by a terrible sense of guilt, which he dealt with by retreating inwardly into the equally extreme opposite stance of the "ruthless capitalist" who cut off all appeals from the needy as being demands akin to theft.

This kind of inner split is quite common in our present society, where many people have become better off than their parents. Their personal guilt is very often reinforced, as Peter s was, by the absorption in childhood of so-called Christian teaching which urges constant self-sacrifice, makes a virtue of poverty, and condemns any self-concern as wicked selfishness. Such inner splits can ruin peoples' lives, the greatest danger being that they may go on for years behaving in an apparently kindly, generous, and self-sacrificing manner, and then suddenly produce a ruthless "cutoff" of some kind, which is far more hurtful to those around them than a sensible, middle-of-the-road "self-ishness" would have been.

Anonymous children in dreams can represent un-developed parts of ourselves, or parts of ourselves that have remained stuck with the conflicts of childhood, but they can also represent aspects of our total life situation where some new state of life is seen as a growing thing. In my own dream of the "Masonic birth," described on page 112, I interpreted the handing over of the baby to the Worshipful Master as my new state of marriage, which I was dedicating to God. An equally vivid piece of baby symbolism occurred in a dream my second husband had soon after we met, when we decided that the only sensible basis for an intimate relationship was one of complete honesty and openness about our feelings, hopes, fears, needs, and so on, instead of the usual indulgence in "game playing." He dreamed his stepmother had presented him with a baby that had been born with the top of its skull missing, so that its brain was completely exposed. He was horrified and asked his stepmother why she had allowed it to be born and what sort of life she expected it to have. She replied in her wise country-woman's voice, "As good a life as yours," and he woke up feeling almost reassured.

He recognized the dream as an expression of both the challenge and the apprehension he felt at the prospect of a radically new way of life without defenses. He referred it particularly to the challenge and apprehension he felt about being completely open on the subject of his religious beliefs, making clear to people what he really believed in-stead of allowing his audiences to think that his scientific arguments supported whatever beliefs they themselves wanted to hold. In a way, the dream was prospective in that the "baby" is still alive, well, and kicking, just as his stepmother had predicted.

LOOKING-GLASS ANIMALS, INSECTS, AND OTHER CREATURES

Alice glanced nervously along the table, as she walked up the large hall, and noticed that there were about fifty guests, of all kinds: some were animals, some birds, and there were even a few flowers among them. "I'm glad they've come without waiting to be asked," she thought: "I should never have known who were the right people to invite!"

Unlike Alice, we must take full responsibility for the creatures we invite into our dreams. Usually they are symbolic, but may have a direct meaning if we are intimately concerned about a real animal in waking life. For example, a friend of mine dreamed that her dog was killed on the busy main road at the bottom of their garden, just one week before it met its death beneath a passing truck there. The dream clearly indicated my friend's anxiety about this possibility and would be classed as a "warning dream."

One of my dream-research subjects produced a vivid dream of fishing the dead body of her dog out of the river, and in this case there was little doubt that the dream referred to her own real dog. She was finding the animal a burden but did not want to have it destroyed because her son was fond of it. The dream expressed a straight wish that the dog would have an accident and relieve her of the responsibility for its death. Such realistic dreams of animals are rare in my experience, however, and are likely to occur when an animal plays as intimate a part in the dreamer's life as a husband or a child.

Most dream animals are symbolic and, like Alice's looking-glass animals and insects, they often undergo strange transformations. "This was anything but a regular bee," Alice discovered as she watched the creature bustling about among the flowers: "in fact, it was an elephant." Ruth, a group member, dreamed that a hippopotamus was chasing her through the house, bumping into things and causing havoc. She suddenly realized that all it wanted was food, and so she fed it with bread until there was no more left. She dashed out to buy more and continued feeding it. At last it went away, but she knew it would be back for more when it became hungry again. It did return, and when the bread ran out it turned into a leopard and pursued her angrily.

Associating to "hippopotamus," she said that feeding it reminded her of her husband, who always seemed to be hungry. Whenever they went out and friends offered him food, he would always accept even though he had just eaten an enormous meal at home. Ruth knew this was not normal hunger and assumed that it must be some kind of comfort substitute. The dream depicted her husband as an unsatisfied hippopotamus, with the more sinister implication that this creature would turn into a man-eating leopard if the "food" ran out. Ruth interpreted the dream as warning her of a hidden vicious streak in her husband's nature which might turn and rend her if she failed to pander to his neurotic needs.

Another group member, Sonya, dreamed of lying in bed with a big black dog sleeping peacefully beside her. She wanted to pat it in a gesture of affection, but knew that she ought not to awaken it. She could not resist, however, whereupon it woke up, seized her knee between its teeth, and started to eat her. Associating to the dog, she said that her boyfriend became very upset from time to time because she had the habit of patting him on the head like a "good dog" whenever he did something to please her. He said he found the gesture castrating and demeaning. Sonya's dream clearly showed her subconscious fear that he was not as docile as she had hitherto assumed and might one day retaliate in a way which could hurt her.

When people are depicted as animals in dreams, it is usually because the dreamer's mind feels something about that person which is expressed by the appropriate animal quality. Thus, it may tell us that we see someone as a dog or a bitch, a lapdog or an Alsation, a sheep (in analysis I had several dreams in which I was a lamb being led to the slaughter), a snake-in-the-grass, a rat, a mouse, an ape, or a lion. In all cases, of course, it is important to consider whether or not the dream contains any "outward-looking" component—whether it represents an accurate detection of some characteristic of the person which the dreamer's waking mind has passed over—or whether it expresses some wholly subjective feeling.

The introjected personalities of parent or siblings can also sometimes appear in dreams as animals. The very first dream I had when I began dream-catching experiments on myself (waking myself up at intervals during the night by means of an alarm clock) was of finding myself back in my childhood home, in which a drugged or sleeping lion lay in the basement. Something had disturbed this beast, and now it was prowling around the house. I telephoned the zoo—the number was Z 7000 in the dream—but instead of requesting them to come and catch the lion, I found myself asking its name.

Associating to the dream, I remembered that my brother was astrologically a Leo, and I interpreted the dream in terms of a dormant, introjected brother inside me being brought to life. My hunch was corroborated in no uncertain terms over the course of the following few weeks when my brother appeared in many of my dreams in a specifically sexual context which came as a considerable surprise to me in spite of my theoretical knowledge of Freud. Animals in dreams often represent sexual impulses directly and our choice of animal indicates how we conceive of these impulses. My choice of lion, therefore, represented a very neat condensation. It showed that ever since my childhood relationship with my brother I had felt my sexual impulses to be dangerously powerful—and had for this reason "put the dangerous beast in me to sleep," never allowing my feelings to go fully, in spite of a sex life that on the surface had seemed perfectly satisfactory.

Now, something (I suspect the dream-catching experiments themselves) had aroused the slumbering animal, and I was much concerned with how to control it, as demonstrated by my dialing the mystic number seven and attempting to name the beast, which is the magical way of gaining power over something. The whole thing was, of course, a classical "Freudian" problem, but over the next few years, I gained most help not from analysis but from working with other dreams by the Gestalt technique, as I shall be describing in the next chapter.

Dream animals, like dream people, can sometimes symbolize situations, principles, or institutions. In a Gestalt therapy group I attended recently, one member reported a dream in which he discovered an elephant wandering around in the loft at the top of his house. While he was wondering who on earth could have let this animal in, it lumbered slowly over to the back wall of the loft and proceeded to shit all over it. He was horrified, and noticed that the back wall was already piled high with elephant dung so that a small window there was completely blocked.

I was fascinated by the obvious Freudian and Jungian possibilities, but the group leader had other ideas. He asked the boy to act out the dream, and during the course of this it became clear that "elephant shit" had a very unique meaning within the context of Gestalt therapy. The boy recalled that Perls distinguished three classes of what he called "verbiage production"—chickenshit, which is small talk like "good morning, how are you today" and "nice weather we've had lately"; bullshit, which consists of rationalization and excuses, such as "I can't love anybody because my mother didn't love me when I was little"; and elephantshit, which is philosophizing and intellectualizing about meanings and theories instead of experiencing them. This dream was telling him in no uncertain terms that his efforts to "see the light" were being blocked by his talking around his problems in abstract terms instead of actually working with them in some constructive fashion.

Another instance of animals' symbolizing a principle or institution, in this case similar to Alice's looking-glass experience of the bees that were elephants, was reported by my colleague who dropped out of his job to take up freelance work. Sometime before making his decision, he had this dream.

We lived in a land where people lived in symbiosis with insects which grew up into elephantlike animals. They started off as small sluglike octopi with slimy tentacles, with which they attached themselves to peoples' skins. Everyone accepted them without demur, because when the things grew up, they would act as transport for people. They looked like silly, big, benevolent fat slobs, and they would pick people up with their tentacles and take them wherever they wanted to go. I woke up screaming because I suddenly realized that I was covered wih these things, which were crawling all over me. They weren't dangerous—just revolting. The people just sighed and were quite happy to remove them, as if to say, "Oh well, it's natural for some people to rebel, we suppose, but it's a good job that we don't all do it." They weren't worried, as there were still lots of people left who could carry these creatures around.

The dream showed exactly how he had come to feel about the commercial world—you let it feed on your body in the early years so that it would eventually carry you around when you retired. All his life he had allowed this "security bug" to crawl over him, but at the time of the dream found it so repugnant that he had to beg for mercy.

LOOKING-GLASS HOUSES

Your house is your larger body.
It grows in the sun and sleeps in the stillness of the night; and it is not dreamless. Does not your house dream? and dreaming, leave the city for grove or hilltop?

Houses are extensions of ourselves—our larger bodies, as Kahlil Gibran describes them in *The Prophet*, and most dream houses say something about our lives and relationships rather than about actual buildings of bricks and mortar. However, when we are from time to time preoccupied with house buying or house building in waking life, our dreams can throw up messages about our worries concerning these houses. Two good examples were given to our group by Joseph, another young man of working-class origin who had recently married a bank manager's daughter and who was living with his wife's parents until they found a suitable house of their own.

In the first dream, Joseph and his wife were house hunting, but every house they looked at seemed to be in a state of ruin. His wife thought they might pick one up cheaply and renovate it, but Joseph felt they were all so much in need of repair that this would be quite beyond their means, even though his father-in-law had promised them a bank loan. They then found one which looked suitable, but it turned out on further inspection to have its ground floor completely gutted, and anyway it was situated on the main motorway to London. So, they gave up and caught the train home, but instead of stopping at Finsbury Park station as it normally did, the train carried them right on to Kings Cross terminus in central London.

Challenged with the principle that we are the authors of our dreams, Joseph admitted that he was responsible for making his dream houses useless, adding that he knew he was reluctant to make a purchase in waking life. The dream clearly depicted the reason for this reluctance: his family had never owned any property and in contemplating buying a house, he was convinced that he was "going beyond his station" in life.

A short time after the dream, they actually found an old, rather dilapidated house in a good area and agreed to purchase it. Because of its condition, the asking price was not high, and they were both reasonably pleased with their bargain. Joseph's next dream, however, revealed his true feelings about the deal. In it, he was chatting in a bar to his office manager, who told him that he had overheard two men discussing how some idiot had been conned into buying a house in X. Road for twice its value, as it had some terrible defect the customer had not noticed. As Joseph's new house was in X. Road, he jumped to the conclusion that he was the idiot in question, and he woke up relieved to think that he had been warned just in time.

Of course, Joseph checked on the dream and arranged for an extra-thorough survey to be carried out on the house. Nothing terrible was discovered and they bought it; they have in fact lived in it for over a year now and are extremely pleased with it. Joseph admitted that he must have

211

been hoping for a last-minute reprieve from the anxiety-making commitment without losing face with his wife. He remarked that the office manager in the dream resembled his dead father, who had always been horrified at the thought of buying anything as expensive as a house, and had always warned Joseph about the sharks waiting to pounce on innocent people. Joseph recognized that it was his father's voice inside him which was responsible for his anxiety. The dream had cleverly depicted the voice as that of his office manager, to whom he was prepared to listen, instead of that of his father, whose values he had consciously rejected long ago.

I have not come across any cases of houses symbolizing other people, although the possibility is brilliantly suggested by James Thurber's famous cartoon entitled "Home"—a horrible picture of a little man approaching a suburban villa which at the rear flows out into a predatory woman waiting to gobble him up. I have, however, frequently found dreams using houses to say something about how the dreamer sees the life-style of someone with whom he is involved. For example, after my marriage breakup I had several dreams in which my ex-husband's house had grown much bigger and grander, with all kinds of new luxury furnishings. These dreams gave vivid expression to my feeling that my freedom had been obtained at the price of being excluded from any share in the growing affluence of a successful man.

Dreams also very often use houses to say something of this kind about the dreamer's own life style. My "two houses" dream, described on page 139, in which I was faced with the choice between a house on the top of a hill and a cottage on the beach, was at one level an expression of a conflict between two possible life styles, a career or a home, although it had a deeper, "inward-looking" significance as well.

Because we live in houses with people, a house can often provide a useful dream picture of a marriage or a family relationship. Joanna, whose dream of murdering her husband with a hatchet was described on page 190, had another dream during the same period of marital unrest. In it she found herself living in a churchlike castle which she was trying to renovate without success, as something always happened to thwart her efforts. At one point in the dream, her au pair entered and asked if she should clean the gold and silver. Joanna told her not to bother as, looking around, she noticed the masonry beginning to crumble. She woke up frantic with anxiety as the whole building tumbled in ruins around her.

This dream portrayed Joanna's ambivalent feelings about whether or not to save the marriage, although her conscious waking mind had already forgiven her husband his infidelity. Her unconscious mind, however, had quite different ideas and was intent on bringing the relationship to an end and, as her other dream showed, on murdering her husband to boot. Joanna was naturally very upset by these hidden feelings, especially as she believed the dream was also trying to tell her that her marriage contained many precious things, as symbolized by the gold and silver, and moreover was of religious significance, as shown by the churchlike appearance of the castle. So far, her story has a happy ending because she was able to work with these dreams and come to terms with her fears, particularly by enlisting her husband's help.

Another story of dreams' saving a relationship was given by one of my dream-research subjects, whose dream of being crucified between his wife and his boss was described on page 136. A short time after the crucifixion dream, he had another in which he arrived home from work one night only to find that his house had been razed to the ground in his absence. The neighbors told him that the workmen from the Council had come to pull it down early that morning, but no one knew where his wife was. He interpreted the dream not as a wish that the relationship with his wife should end, but as a fear that she might one day suddenly leave him without a word if he continued to spend so much time away from home. This dream upset him so much that soon afterward he changed his job for a less exacting one.

A very common dream experience is that of going back to the house of one's childhood. Hall suggests that this can

213

indicate a desire to expand one's life space, since in childhood even an ordinary house looks very spacious because the child is so small. This may be so, but my experience also suggests that dreams of childhood houses, like dreams of friends or relatives from earlier life, usually indicate that something in the dreamer's current situation is reminding him of an earlier situation. My dream of the lion, for instance, was set in my childhood home, indicating that my dormant sexual impulses were beginning to stir at the time of the dream, just as they had been brought to life by my brother many long years before.

George, whose "divorce" dream was described on page 177, dreamed he was back in the home of his childhood, and his wife and mother were baking an anniversary cake in the kitchen. His wife presented this to him with a great flourish and he thanked her politely. His mind, however, was on the walls of the rooms, which were literally running with damp and cracking in various places. He pointed this out to his mother, who dismissed it, saying that it would clear up in time and that he really ought to buy it on a twenty-one-year lease. This was one of his first dreams showing that he felt all was not well with his marriage (the house), and it added the message that his "mother within" was urging him to take over the same kind of "house" he lived in as a child—a relationship which covered up a rather desperate situation with surface politeness and family ritual. George said that twenty-one years was the normal length of time one lived at home before becoming independent of parental authority. The dream portrayed him taking the same role as his mother inside, which assured him that any temporary discord would "clear up" before long.

Sometimes, a dream makes a point about a relationship or a situation by putting the dreamer in a house with a certain view or prospect. During my Freudian analysis I dreamed that I looked out of the consulting-room window and saw row upon row of uniformly gray, square houses, quite unlike the view from my analyst's real-life window. This was a very clear indication of my feeling that my prospects in analysis were bleak—and not just bleak, but bleak in a particular way in offering a view of life which was "square" and conformist.

Freud held that houses often symbolized the body, and parts of houses the various limbs and organs of the body. For example, pillars and columns may represent the legs as they do in the Song of Solomon: "His legs are as pillars of marble set upon sockets of fine gold"; gateways stand for body orifices; balconies and verandahs for breasts; water pipes for the urinary apparatus; and so on. Freud quotes the case of a woman who dreamed that a policeman accompanied by two tramps ascended some steps to a church, in front of which was a path which led up to a hill. On both sides of the path there grew grass and brushwood, which became thicker and thicker until at the top of the hill it turned into a wood. He interpreted the church as the vagina, the policemen and tramps as the penis and testicles, the hill as the mons veneris, the wood as pubic hair, and the ascent of the steps as intercourse. While this kind of interpretation may possibly be useful for some people in analysis, it has little place in our work and I believe we would miss many fruitful insights by employing it. It can even do violence to a person, as we saw in Chapter 6, by ignoring the wider implications of a dream. Pillars may well stand for "strength," gateways for a new start in life, balconies for "lording it over" the common run of humanity, and leaking water pipes as loss of emotional control, while the symbolism of churches, prisons, barracks, and so on seems quite obvious.

However, in all cases, the dreamer's own associations are vital for interpretation. An empty attic in a dream may mean for one person a literal lack of brainpower (empty-headedness), while for another it may represent the discovery of unexplored higher spiritual areas of life. Dry rot in the basement may mean dried-up sexuality to one dreamer, while to another it may be a warning not to neglect the unconscious side of life. Structural defects in a house may reflect either a feeling of physical disintegration or pathological attributes of the personality.

Several people in my groups have had dreams in which a house in undergoing alterations or having extensions built; this usually indicates a personality change in the direction of expanded consciousness, often accompanied by improved bodily health.

In my experience, the dream house is truly the "*larger body*," symbolizing our relationships, life situation, and psychic space, a concept I shall discuss in more detail in the next chapter.

LOOKING-GLASS VEHICLES

Vehicles can sometimes have a literal meaning in dreams, just like animals and houses, if the dreamer's waking mind happens to be preoccupied with a vehicle. When my car started showing signs of old age and losing its parts, I dreamed constantly of breakdowns and accidents until I exchanged it for a new one.

Similarly, vehicle language can be used to describe people; for example, we speak of the "Mini mentality," the "jet set," and the "slow coach." Vehicles may also represent a life style in dreams. When Janet, one of our younger group members, left home to share a flat with friends, she dreamed of walking along the street quite naked except for a couple of hippie bells which hung from a ribbon round her neck. She wondered whether the people in the street would be shocked, but to her relief, they hardly seemed to notice. When she reached her car, she found that it had turned into an enormous van, complete with kitchen and bathroom, and it occurred to her that she and her friends could live in it, or at least use it for extended holidays abroad. The dream depicted her change from a rather restricted background to a more mobile kind of life, full of movement and space. Her nudity symbolized her intention to live as open and uninhibited a life as possible without shocking too many people, and she associated the hippie

216

bells with what was for her a more authentic life style than the one she had been living at home.

Vehicles often indicate the *direction* in which a relationship is going. Eric reported the following dream just after his wife had found out about an affair he was having with a German girl and insisted that it stop:

> I boarded a tram to my parents' home and found that it was going in the wrong direction. I was confused about the unfamiliar buildings, and a foreign girl student came and sat beside me and tried to tell where I was, deprecating the fact that a foreigner should have to help a local. I then got off the tram at the crossroads and found I was with my wife. An ambulance and police car were standing in the middle of the crossroads, as there had been an accident. An old lady dressed in black leather and wearing a Salvation Army hat was lying in the middle of the road, and as we passed, my wife patted her on the head in a gesture of sympathy. We tried to cross the road, but there was a constant stream of traffic going in both directions. The whole thing seemed very dangerous to me.

The dream took Eric back to his premarriage days when he lived at home with his parents, indicating that there was something in his present situation which resembled the earlier one. Eric saw the tram as his marriage which he felt was going in the wrong direction, being almost wholly geared toward professional success rather than to a cozy home life similar to the one he had enjoyed when he was single. His German girlfriend, he said, had promised to provide him with these comforts if he married her and had criticized his wife on several occasions for failing to fulfill his needs in this direction.

Crossroads in dreams are a common symbol for decision making, and the dream clearly depicted Eric's resolve to terminate the "ride" with his girlfriend and renew relations with his wife. He realized, however, that this would "hurt" his girlfriend, who was represented in the dream by the old lady who had met with an accident. He was already seeing her in his mind as an "old flame" who used to wear leather clothes and had tried to "save" him. His wife knew about the relationship and had more than once tried to persuade Eric to give her up, reassuring him that the girl would soon recover from her hurt. But the dream showed a deeper concern in Eric's mind: even if he terminated the relationship, would he and his wife manage to make the "dangerous crossing" toward a more satisfactory way of life?

Eric admitted that in a way he was glad his wife had intervened, as although he liked the girl, he was far from sure that he wanted to marry her. This brought to mind another dream he had previously had in which his car stalled before it reached the crossroads, indicating his reluctance to make the decision for himself.

In dreams of vehicles, it is important to note whether the dreamer is the driver, the passenger, the owner, and so on. While her husband was away on business, Marion dreamed she had answered an advertisement for a co-driver in the Monte Carlo rally. She was accepted, but when the man arrived to pick her up, she suddenly realized she could not drive. This did not appear to upset him and he told her to get in the car. She had on a tight green dress most unsuitable for a long drive, and she knew that her role was to have an affair with him during the course of the journey. The dream clearly depicted her desire to take a lover while her husband was away, but the fact that she was merely a passenger and not the driver meant that although she might initiate the relationship, the man would actually do the driving (make love to her) so that she could repudiate responsibility at a later date. It is an interesting fact that people with passive personalities prefer to be passengers rather than drivers of vehicles in waking life.

Most of us have had dreams in which we miss, or almost miss, the bus or train, and these usually represent quite straightforward fears that we shall miss out on something in our present lives. A good example was given by a friend of mine who was in analysis. She dreamed she climbed into a train just as it began to leave the station. Inside the carriage was a baby in a pram and a guard at the other end in a sort of box. A girl came running along the platform and jumped into the carriage just before it was too late, saying, "Thank goodness for that; it would have been terrible if the train had gone without me," and my friend realized that this must be the baby's mother. The guard had been watching all this very disinterestedly and had not attempted to help the girl at all. My friend identified him as her analyst, who was insisting that she continue her analysis, which had already lasted many years and seemed to have come to a dead end. She was forty-eight and desperately wanted to have a baby before it was too late. Staying in analysis, during which patients are not supposed to make major new decisions or changes in life style, meant for her "missing the train" as far as having a baby was concerned. The dream, in fact, turned out to be prospective, in that she did terminate the analysis, went back to Africa, and later wrote to me with the news that she was pregnant.

A vehicle may sometimes stand for an institution. For example, Joan dreamed soon after her baby was born that she was on a boat which was taking her family and all their possessions somewhere. The furniture was strapped onto the outside of the boat, and she was afraid it would be damaged if it got wet. Then suddenly the boat began to drift and people jumped off on all sides. Someone called to her to jump, but she held back, saying that she was still bleeding. Then she went to look for her baby but could not find it anywhere and feared it must have been washed overboard. She awoke desperate with grief.

The boat with the furniture and baby obviously symbolized marriage, in particular her own, which she felt had already started to "drift." The other people jumping off represented all the people in her life who had "abandoned ship," that is, who had separated or divorced, and whose voices inside were urging her to follow suit. This she could not do because she felt too vulnerable. In addition, she felt her baby might be washed overboard, or destroyed, by the drifting marriage.

Cars, trains, and airplanes as instruments of power can

represent the energy of the impulses, particularly the sexual impulses. A passage from Desmond Morris's book *The Human Zoo* illustrates this point nicely:

> sports cars . . . have always radiated bold, aggressive masculinity and have been considerably aided in this by their phallic qualities. Like a baboon's penis, they stick out in front, they are long, smooth and shiny, they thrust forward with great vigour and they are frequently bright red in color. A man sitting in his open sports car is like a piece of highly stylized phallic sculpture. His body has disappeared and all that can be seen are a tiny head and hands surmounting a long, glistening penis. . . . Even ordinary motor cars have their phallic qualities, and this may explain to some extent why male drivers become so aggressive and so eager to overtake one another, despite considerable risks and despite the fact that they all meet up again at the next set of traffic lights, or at best, only cut a few seconds off their journey.

The manner in which the driver controls his car may tell the dreamer how he sees his impulses. If he loses control, crashes with another vehicle, runs down a pedestrian, speeds through a red light, or plunges down a steep hill, it usually means that he feels himself overwhelmed by uncontrollable impulses. If he avoids having an accident by skillful manipulation of the vehicle, this indicates that he has brought the impulse under control. Dreams of motorbike, car, or airplane rallies and tournaments indicate a desire to display and demonstrate one's sexual prowess, while cars stalling, breaking down, or unable to reach top gear usually symbolize sexual difficulties. The extent to which we identify with our cars in waking life corroborates this point and is nicely illustrated by Tom Rush's song about the boy who likens himself to some old engine that has lost its driving wheel, after his car breaks down in Texas and prevents him from reaching the girl he longs to see.

Vehicles, however, do not always symbolize the energy of the impulses. When I first became a group leader, I dreamed of putting a Rolls-Royce into reverse gear. As it slid back toward a wall, I realized that my feet could not reach the contols, and I awaited the inevitable bump with trepidation. But the car gradually came to a halt of its own accord just before reaching the wall. The dream was depicting in beautiful picture language fears about my ability to control and run groups after my "reversal of roles" from patient to therapist. The fact that the car itself stopped before any damage occurred gave me added self-confidence about my abilities.

Freud believed that dreams of taking a train or other conveyance could be a premonition of death. I have not myself come across this in dreams, but the symbolism of a boat setting off down a river or a ship putting out to sea is often used in poetry to represent death. For example, Longfellow describes how Hiawatha, when his life's work is completed, launches his birch canoe upon the river and sets off into the dusk of evening.

> And the people from the margin
> Watched him floating, rising, sinking
> Till the birch canoe seemed lifted
> High into that sea of splendor
> Till it sank into the vapors
> Like the new moon slowly, slowly
> Sinking in the purple distance.

And Kahlil Gibran in *The Prophet*, from which I have already quoted, describes the death of the teacher in similar symbolic language. Here, by using a ship as the symbol of death, he also brings in the symbolism of the sea which is a favorite dream image of the "depths" of the unconscious mind and hence in Eastern philosophy represents the Great Mind underlying all creation, from which we came and to which we must someday return.

> Patient, over patient, is the captain of my ship.
> The wind blows, and restless are the sails:
> Even the rudder begs direction:
> Yet quietly my captain awaits my silence.
> And these my mariners, who have heard the choir of the

greater sea, they too have heard me patiently.
Now they shall wait no longer.
I am ready.
The stream has reached the sea, and once more the great
mother holds her son against her breast.

Poetry can teach us much about the strange symbolic
language of dreams, and I often wonder whether the poets
derive their inspiration directly—perhaps without knowing
it—from the depths of the dreaming mind.

THE LOOKING-GLASS SELF

To the Looking-glass world it was Alice that said
"I've a sceptre in hand, I've a crown on my head. . . ."

Not all of us, however, are fortunate or daring enough to
become royal in our dreams. In the vast majority of
dreams, we remain ourselves, and the meaning of the
dream lies in our relationship with the other characters, our
actions, and the things that happen to us. The dream self
varies from one dream to another as the looking-glass of
the night reflects hidden thoughts and feelings, as the examples in this chapter have shown. We may be a murderer
in one dream, a victim in another; sometimes we play an
active, vigorous role, at other times we are passive spec-
tators; often we are happy, but more often we are anxious,
troubled, and fearful. In each case, the dream tells us how
we have been seeing ourselves without realizing it in some
current life situation.

If we do become something other than the normal "I,"
as Alice did, then the dream is probably showing us that
we have become almost totally identified with the role in
question, at least in some situations. Such dreams are rare,
but I have myself gained valuable insight from some cases
of this kind—for example, when I appeared as a lamb
being led to the slaughter, one or two dreams in which I
have been a man, and a few others in which, like Alice, I
was a queen. When one of my group dreamed of herself as

her grandmother's ghost we were able to detect in her life both a sense of being unreal and a mere long-standing feeling that she was in some way just a "shade" of her grandmother. Dreams of this kind often prove to be part of a series with other dreams in which the sheep, men, queens, ghosts, and so on appear as other characters—parts of the "not-I." Such dreams almost always merit further analysis, along inward-looking lines, by the methods I shall describe in the next chapter.

In fact, whenever dream characters or themes recur, they reflect deeper problems underlying those which concern specific external events or situations. In these more special dreams, the probability is that *all* the dream images are parts of ourselves, and it is always interesting to discover with which aspects we identify and which aspects we project onto the other dream characters as the "not-I." The meaning of these dreams becomes fully clear only when we allow the characters to encounter the "I" in open dialogue and to "speak for themselves," as recommended by Jung and worked out in more detail by Perls. As I hope to show, the experience of doing so sometimes brings such a flood of new meaning that I am reminded of St. Paul's famous words: "For now we see through a glass, darkly, but then face to face: now I know in part; but then shall I know even as also I am known."

CHAPTER 10

LOOKING INWARD

"As I cannot change what is outside me," wrote the German philosopher Fichte, "let me try instead to change what is within." In the nineteenth century, the great age of willpower and expanding technology, this might have seemed to most people a failure of nerve. Today the influence of psychoanalysis throughout our culture has swung the pendulum in the opposite direction, so much so that many people have been led to underrate the extent to which things in the external world *can* be changed. In the preceding two chapters, I have tried to show the ways in which dreams can help us do just this, either by bringing to our attention experiences we have passed over in waking life, or by making us aware of how our inner attitudes and prejudices are shaping our reactions to specific people and situations.

By taking note of such messages in our dreams we can avoid many pitfalls and deal more effectively with day-to-day problems. At the same time, however, it is always necessary to consider the extent to which these problems challenge us to look inward to discover the inner weaknesses, imbalances, and conflicts that are making our lives less fulfilled than they might be. In this chapter I shall consider how dreams can help us not only to understand these inner problems but also to discover the hidden resources of psychic energy without which any effort to "change what is within" will be futile.

The method of looking at a dream as a picture makes us aware of these inner problems, as I showed in the previous chapter. By associating to some dream images, we can often discover how our lives are still being ruled by "skeletons" in the psyche—the voices of parents, siblings, or other powerful figures from our early years who go on dictating to us in ways that are quite inappropriate to our adult personalities. Other dream images show us facets of character we are neglecting, or impulses we are suppressing because the inner voices tell us they are shameful or dangerous. To discover the underlying roots of problems like these, however, and to unearth the energy needed for inner change and growth, my experience is that it is usually necessary to go behind the immediate dream-pictures, not by assuming some disguised latent content as Freud did, but by letting the dream images speak for themselves, as described in the second half of Chapter 7.

The technique is based on the assumption that *all dream images are parts of ourselves* which we have disowned because we find them a threat to the conscious image we have of ourselves. So we push them outside our "ego boundary," the sphere of conscious awareness, and say, "That's not me." Many people in our culture disown the weak, vulnerable side of themselves, which they consider "unmanly," while others push away the aggressive and sexual aspects of their personality because they are supposed to be "unchristian." But although the ego repudiates these unwanted qualities, they still remain within our total psychic space and are part of us. In Jung's terms, they form our "shadow" selves, and he even pressed the principle to the point of suggesting that beneath their murderous exteriors, the leaders of the Third Reich in Germany were teeming with tenderness and sentimentality.

One simple test to discover some of the disowned aspects of ourselves is to ask what we hate most of all in other people, for we are almost sure to find the very same thing simmering away in ourselves below the level of conscious awareness, just waiting for an opportunity to express itself. It invariably succeeds in this from time to time when the conscious mind is "off guard," and we say that the person has acted in a manner quite "out of character" with his normal behavior. Most people, says Perls, spend so much time and energy avoiding the things they fear in themselves that they have little left over for enjoying life. Only when we are willing to reclaim the alienated parts of our personality and the energy we have invested in keeping them down shall we really become "whole" people.

At this point, I advise readers who are serious about carrying out the experiment of "looking inward" at their dreams, to turn back to the second part of Chapter 7 (page 142) and quickly reread the section on Gestalt therapy, as I do not wish to repeat a full description here. I shall simply summarize the general rules involved, and I want to emphasize that I have merely *drawn on* Perls' insights for use in my dream work, so that what follows is not necessarily a picture of "orthodox" Gestalt therapy (if indeed there is any such thing). A reading list is available at the end of this book for those who wish to pursue the techniques of Gestalt therapy in further detail.

Sometimes a dream has so many characters or images in it that it is difficult to know where to start. I usually begin by letting the most obvious dream characters speak for themselves and encounter each other until two of them really come into conflict; then I know I have stumbled on something important. Usually, one character, nicknamed by Perls "topdog" and similar to Freud's notion of the superego, bullies, scolds, and lectures another character, who rapidly assumes the role of what Perls called "underdog"—an aspect of the personality of which we are ashamed and which we try hard to keep outside our ego boundary.

For example, in my dream of the two houses described on page 139, the two obvious dream images to start with were the house on the beach and the house on the hill. So I first asked the house on the beach to speak, and as soon as it mentioned that it contained a family which hated and feared the angry sea, I knew I had uncovered a conflict. Instead of inviting the house on the hill to speak next, I brought the family (which had not actually appeared in the dream itself) and the sea into an open encounter with each other and almost immediately found myself in the midst of a topdog/underdog battle, with the family berating the sea for not always being calm and placid. I soon discovered that in this particular conflict between stern control and free expression of emotion I had alienated the latter and must somehow reclaim it into my personality. The existential message of the dream became clear when the sea (my emotions) said, "I have a right to express myself," and once I had received the message, my task was then to see that I carried it out in my everyday life whenever possible.

Had I been acting out this dream in a group, the leader would probably have left it there, being satisfied with one existential message from the dream. However, I was not in a group and I was interested in the other dream characters, so I decided to continue the drama. I was particularly intrigued by the character of the "wind," which stirred up the sea and made it dance, and so I decided that I would invite it to speak for itself. In a way, this was the most interesting part of the dream, as I learned that in trying to stifle my emotions, I was in fact denying the very energy which gave me life. Very often a dream character or an image which is mentioned only indirectly, or is merely implied by the dream, turns out to have the most important message for the dreamer, as the examples in this chapter will show.

One of the great advantages of the Gestalt technique of acting out a dream and allowing the dream images to speak for themselves is that we become identified with the "aliens" in the psyche and actually experience their feelings instead of merely intellectualizing about them, as so often happens in psychoanalysis. When I spoke with the voice of the sea (my pent-up emotions), I literally wept with frustration because the voice of my topdog (the family in the beach house), would not allow me to dance over the full range of the beach (my life space). In other words, I *experienced* my frustration with all the intensity of a caged

227

beast, which is quite a different thing from a cold interpretation of one's problem by another person. You can doubt the truth of an interpretation, but you cannot argue when an experience comes from the depths of your own being.

The theme of having to choose between two houses was one that had recurred in dreams several times in my life, always at points when I felt my life space was being threatened. This provided a clear indication in advance that it sprang from a deep-rooted inner problem rather than from one particular set of circumstances in the external world. The Gestalt technique almost always yields dramatic results with recurrent dream themes and with dreams that throw up the same characters on many different occasions, particularly when these characters are mysterious, fictional, and not intimately involved in our everyday lives. In these cases, it is almost certain that these images and characters are parts of ourselves, drawing most of their energy from within the psyche, even though they may be sparked off by some external situation.

The following examples from my dream-study groups and my own dream life illustrate how I personally use the Gestalt techniques for "looking inward" and exposing what Perls called the "self-torture" games which sap so much of our psychic energy.

Very briefly, I feel that an understanding of the method will come mainly from following through the examples themselves, but here is a very brief guide to the main steps involved in using dreams to recover lost or alienated aspects of the personality:

1. Allow various dream images to speak for themselves until a topdog and an underdog emerge.

2. Their quarrel tells you the nature of the conflict or self-torture game underlying the dream.

3. The nature of the underdog gives you a clue about a particular hole in your personality—something that you are avoiding in waking life and that must be reclaimed.

4. Make underdog stand up to topdog and state his needs; this provides the existential message of the dream.

5. Retrieve the "buried treasure" and complete a Gestalt

(a "whole") by allowing it to take its rightful place in the personality.

Finally, I repeat that whereas a Gestalt therapist would not use the word "unconscious," preferring to speak of "alienation," I use the two interchangeably to denote aspects of the "inner unknown."

"SLOW AND STEADY WINS THE RACE"

Joseph's dream of house buying, described on page 210, is a good example of what the Gestalt technique can add to a "looking-glass" treatment of a dream. In this particular dream, Joseph's efforts to find a house with his wife were always frustrated, and they ended their journey home in a train which took them "beyond their station." Much of the dream's energy came from the external world as they were in fact house hunting at the time. Taken as a picture, the dream revealed very clearly that Joseph was reluctant to buy a house because people of his standing (or the standing he still felt himself to have beneath his adult self) were not in the habit of owning property. However, when he allowed some of the images in the dream to speak for themselves, another much deeper problem emerged.

First of all, Joseph retold the dream to the group in the present tense in order to experience it in the here-and-now. I then asked him to be the train and tell us why it went "beyond its station." He said,

> I went past Finsbury Park because I'm a *fast* train. I go straight to the terminus at Kings Cross without stopping at piddling little intermediate stations. If they'd really wanted to get out at Finsbury Park, they should have waited for the slow train, which stops at all stations. You can't take a fast train and then expect it to stop for you.

I then asked Joseph to be a slow train and talk to the fast train. Moving to the chair opposite, he said,

229

I'm what they call a slow train, and you've no right to despise me. You may be smarter, swishing through all those stations and showing off, but I'm more efficient in the long run because I cater for all those people who have to get off before Kings Cross. You don't stop to consider people. And if you go fast like that all the time, you'll come a cropper one of these days.

Joseph moved to the other chair and replied,

FAST TRAIN: Well, people seem to like me and I haven't had an accident yet. I admit you're useful to some people, but you're very dreary, plodding along like some puffing old elephant. This is the jet age, you know.

SLOW TRAIN: It may be the jet age, and it's just for that reason we ought to keep a bit of sanity in the world—it's just mad the way everyone rushes around. Remember Aesop's fable of the tortoise and the hare—slow and steady wins the race? The tortoise won because he kept plodding on, slow but sure, while the hare was so keen on racing that he fell into all kinds of pitfalls. He even went to sleep, which reminds me that *you* often get stuck in the tunnel outside the terminus, because it's such a crowded station, and then anyone who's on *me* will actually beat you to Kings Cross, like the tortoise. He who stops for people wins in the end.

FAST TRAIN: Well, you've got a point, but I still think there's a place for me somewhere.

Here was an interesting reversal of roles. Fast Train began by talking with the voice of Joseph's wife, to whom on the surface he felt slightly inferior, but as the dialogue continued Slow Train rapidly assumed the role of topdog, which moralized and lectured Fast Train underdog on the dangers of speed so that it could barely justify its existence. The part of Joseph which had got itself involved with this particular girl represented a desire for speed and flashiness quite out of keeping with his background, but inside him this voice was far weaker than that of his cautious side, which constantly harangued him with all the force of an

Aesop fable. Underdog usually manages to express himself in some roundabout manner, and in Joseph's case had done so by projecting outward onto his wife. Joseph was, in fact, saying to her, "You be fast and I'll be slow, and together we'll make a perfect unit." In this way, he evaded all responsibility for bringing about a change in his own personality.

When Joseph discussed this with the group, it transpired that this particular Aesop fable had been very much a part of his childhood, reinforcing his natural caution and the anxieties of his working-class background to the point where he would often make no decision at all for fear it might be too hasty. Joseph confessed that he never made up his mind about anything until the very last minute, just in case something unforeseen might occur to change things. He said he was reluctant to purchase a house at the present moment because he felt if he waited long enough, the "right" house, in perfect condition and at bargain price, might turn up, or better still, he might win the football pools, relieving him of the anxiety of borrowing money. On the other hand, he said, his wife might die or leave him, in which case buying a house would have been a complete waste of time! At the office, he said, he always submitted his work on or after the deadline, just in case his boss should cancel it in the meantime (as of course he occasionally did, thereby reinforcing Joseph's neurosis). He could never book a holiday or buy theater tickets in advance for fear that something might prevent his keeping the date. It was clear that "slow coach," the voice of his introjected parents, was crippling his own life and that of those around him by constantly reminding him that "Pride comes before a fall," "More haste, less speed," and so on.

These voices within the psyche are crafty because they function below the belt, as it were, causing us to react to situations in rigid stereotyped ways without knowing it. The way to combat them once they have become conscious is to feed back to them the opposite point of view; in Joseph's case, this might mean repeating such phrases as "A stitch in time saves nine" and "Never put off till tomorrow what you can do today." This is the method used by hypnotherapists whose treatment consists mainly of feeding in contrary suggestions to the relaxed mind. In the group, we encouraged Joseph to try standing up to "slow coach" by allowing Fast Train more of his energy. This was the result:

FAST TRAIN: Just a minute. You can't get away with this. I don't often get stuck in the tunnel, and I'm much more useful than you for people wanting to come straight through to the terminus. And, what's more, that fable of yours is stupid because it takes for granted that hares are always foolish creatures and they're not. If the hare had gone straight to its destination without stopping, as any *sensible* hare would, it would have beaten the tortoise hands down and had the rest of the day in which to enjoy itself. It's good to be able to go fast, because you can always slow down if necessary, but if you're always slow, it's very hard to speed up at all.

SLOW TRAIN: Er yes, I suppose you're right. Every case should be examined on its merits, I admit—and I do envy you sometimes.

This was a case of topdog's backing down as soon as he is challenged with real conviction, which Perls saw as one of the ways of bringing new balance into the personality. We suggested Joseph should try to remember this dialogue when confronted with decisions in the future and act rationally in accordance with the problem. Only in this way will he learn that quick decisions often bring positive results, not disastrous ones. This is the process which psychologists call positive reinforcement, now recognized as the basis of all successful learning. Hitherto, Joseph had hardly ever allowed himself to make a quick decision, and so had never given himself a chance to challenge the fantasy that they must inevitably result in disaster.

"ENERGY IS ETERNAL DELIGHT"

Joseph's dream and my "two houses" dream were both cases in which the total dream-story derived energy from

232

both the outer and the inner worlds in roughly equal amounts. Like Alice's looking-glass world, they contained some things that reflected the events of external life in a distorted, symbolic form, and others of a less obvious meaning which provided the basis for true existential messages about the dreamer's inner life when allowed to speak for themselves. From time to time, however, dreams occur which make no sense at all when looked at as pictures and defy interpretation even with the help of free associations. In these cases, the Gestalt technique is essential for getting any meaning at all, and in my experience it rarely fails to produce results.

Jack reported a dream to the group which seemed to make no sense to him when viewed as a picture, so he retold it in the present tense in preparation for Gestalt treatment, as follows:

I am in the south of France trying to make my way back to a place in Africa at which I have recently been staying, where enormous spiders get into bed with you, stand over the region of the solar plexus, and dig themselves in three times. It's a kind of ritual—when they've had three goes, they die, just like bees do after stinging you. There are always more spiders to take their place, and I can't imagine why I want to go back there to these horrid things but I feel compelled to take the first plane out tonight.

All Jack had been able to get out of this dream by means of association was that he loved the sunshine and the tropical climate of the south, although he had never actually been to Africa. He had always thought of Africa as the dark continent, a rather frightening, primitive place which both attracted and repelled him. He was not very keen on the insect and reptile life there, but he felt this would not actually prevent his going when an opportunity arose. He could find absolutely no association to the spider's ritual of digging into the solar plexus three times and then dying, apart from the fact that he had the idea that the solar plexus was the body's center of nervous

233

energy. In the dream the spiders were apparently drawn to this spot, but he did not know why, nor could he uncover the identity of the spiders with any degree of certainty. He supposed they might represent sex, as male spiders die after having fertilized the female, which then eats them. He could recall nothing of the previous day which could have sparked off this strange dream, and had no idea why it should have occurred that particular night.

I asked Jack to put "Africa" in the opposite chair and talk to it. He said:

I like your sunshine, space and wildlife. It will be a marvelous change to come to you after my gray, cramped life at home with all that mental work. I just don't seem to be able to move or feel my body here—I just sit at a desk all day long and go home so tired at night that I can't really enjoy myself. The only thing I'm not so keen on as far as you're concerned are those damned spiders.

So we asked Jack to talk to the spiders and find out what they thought they were up to. While Jack moved from one chair to the other as he took the parts of the spiders and himself, the following dialogue took place:

JACK: What the hell do you think you're doing spoiling people's holidays? We shan't be able to sleep if you crawl over us at night. Why can't you go back to the jungle where you belong and leave us alone?

SPIDERS: It's our nature to crawl over people. You attract us. If you lie still without moving, you won't even feel us.

JACK: But you're not natural somehow. I've never met spiders like you before. It's as though you're carrying out a special ritual over the solar plexus. You're up to something and I want to know what it is. You're not real spiders, you're phony.

SPIDERS: Oh, all right. We'll confess. You're right. We aren't real spiders. We're manufactured by the African government to suck out all your nervous energy while

234

you're asleep so you won't dissipate it on useless activities the next day. Here the fresh air makes you dance, swim, ride, and indulge in wasteful sexual activity. When we've taken three probes full of energy, our machinery stops and you think we've died, but nothing could be further from the truth. In the morning, the maid comes and sweeps us up and we are taken to Government House, where the energy is siphoned out of us to be used for running computers and so on. And then, the following night, we're back again for more. Very ingenious, don't you think, old chap?

JACK: I think it's quite outrageous. I come here for the express purpose of enjoying myself and you stop me before I even have a chance. Why do they do it in such an underhand way? I'm not stupid and I'd willingly give them a hand with their computers rather than have you bothering me.

We then asked Jack to find out why the government was behaving so unreasonably, and an "official" replied,

OFFICIAL: This is a very primitive country and I'm afraid you people just don't understand how dangerous it all is. Your way of life is so much better than ours —cleaner, cleverer, and more controlled. No progress can be made either mentally or spiritually if energy is dissipated in bodily pursuits. The reason we haven't got on is simply that the natives don't bother to store up energy as you people do; they send it out all over the surface of the body and spend all their time indulging the senses. We need people from the West to provide us with energy, which we then use in the process of civilization.

JACK: Why don't you ask us to help you instead of going to all this bother with the spiders?

OFFICIAL: Because, my dear chap, we need *all* your energy, and you would be willing to give us only some of it. Once you start to enjoy your bodies out here, you'll want to go on doing so, and we'd all be lost. We must have absolute control so that things don't get out of hand.

At this point, Jack was reminded how his father had been very keen on Eastern philosophy and had reiterated how important it was not to dissipate the vital energy of the body in sensual pursuits. He had shown his son pictures of Yogis who were supposed to have lived in the Himalayan mountains for several centuries, having learned the secret of eternal life in this way. Jack also remembered a favorite phrase quoted by his father from the biography of the famous Indian mystic Ramakrishna, who is reported to have said, "If a woman touches me, I fall ill. That part of my body aches as if stung by a horned fish"—an analogy not so very different from his own horror of the spider's sting.

Acting out the dream in this way and actually hearing himself repeat his father's words with conviction revealed to Jack how his life was being ruled by a rigid, morally sadistic despot inside, which prevented him from ever enjoying physical life to the full. On the surface, he rather prided himself on being sexually active, but when pressed by the group, he admitted to a sneaking feeling that full pleasure was somehow eluding him. He blamed his father for this, and said that he had been reminded of him the day before the dream on reading *The Marriage of Heaven and Hell* by Blake. I suddenly had a hunch this might have provided the stimulus for his dream, and handing him my Blake, I asked him to read it to us. He read:

> All Bibles or sacred codes have been the cause of the following errors;—
> 1) That man has two real existing principles, viz., a body and a soul.
> 2) That energy, called evil, is alone from the body; and that reason, called good, is alone from the soul.
> 3) That God will torment man in eternity for following his energies.
> But the following contraries to these are true:—
> 1) Man has no body distinct from his soul. For that called body is a portion of soul discerned by the five senses, the chief inlets of soul in this age.
> 2) Energy is the only life, and is from the body; and

236

reason is the bound or outward circumference of energy.
3) Energy is eternal delight.

Jack agreed that this was almost certainly the stimulus responsible for his mysterious nocturnal visit to "Africa," the land of the senses. Blake's lines had sparked off in him a deep underlying conflict about the proper use of the body's energies, for although he consciously disagreed with his father's philosophy, he could not quite get it out of his system. So we asked him to continue the dialogue, this time standing up to the "official," whereupon he shouted:

You're ruining my life, you bastards. Every time I try to enjoy myself, you make me feel guilty and spoil my fun. I have a right to enjoy my body and you're not going to stop me anymore.

I asked Jack to confront each group member in turn and repeat this last sentence until we all felt convinced he meant it. Then we all gathered around him, pretending we were the spiders, and dared him to fight his way out, which he did with considerable energy. The object of these exercises was not to provide in themselves an immediate transformation of Jack's capacity for feeling—we never change what is within as simply as that— but rather to give him the feel of his problem so that he would be on the alert for "spiders" (his father's spiritual prohibitions) whenever they crept out in the future to sap his energies at the first stirrings of bodily enjoyment. Hopefully, he will slowly learn to let himself go, and his increased pleasure should provide him with "positive reinforcement" for a more relaxed life style in which he is *free to choose* when he will indulge his bodily senses and when he will hold them back in the interests of other activities.

Jack's problem is a very common one in western society, as most of us are taught from childhood that our bodies are in some way shameful or dangerous and that their demands must be controlled. Freud himself believed that the "sublimation" of erotic energy into creative psychological pursuits was the only hope for a civilized society. This conflict between the free and joyful expression of erotic energy in sexual activity and its sublimation into "higher things" was beautifully illustrated at one of my dream demonstrations. The first volunteer was a quiet, rather shy psychiatrist, who reported having the following dream the previous night after attending an encounter group. "I discovered to my horror that I had committed bigamy. An arrogant Roman Catholic priest greeted me and shook me by the hand." As he conducted a dialogue with the "priest," a conflict very similar to Jack's emerged. In a slow, cold, merciless voice, the priest informed him that if he allowed his sexual energies free expression, he would be condemned to burn in hell forever. The conflict, we later discovered, had been sparked off by the fact that he had met a woman in an encounter group the previous evening, had kissed her, but had not experienced any sexual arousal. We suggested that this "moral victory" over the body had conjured up the figure of his "topdog" priest whose handshake could have been a form of congratulation.

As he enacted a further sequence of the dream, it became clear that he felt extremely frustrated by an inability to express himself artistically. We all felt that his creative energy was being needlessly dissipated in an abortive topdog/underdog struggle between sexual sublimation and expression and that if he could bring about some sort of compromise between them, he would discover new areas of artistic creativity within him. Allowing himself to become sexually aroused would not necessarily lead him into a life of promiscuity. The fear that relaxation of rigid sexual prohibition will lead immediately to orgies and the dissolution of society is a typical example of what Perls called a "catastrophic expectation," in terms of which our minds seem to work when we do not face up to things consciously. As Freud himself realized, our repressed impulses are often far more violent *because* they are repressed than they would be if they were allowed expression.

Moreover, those who actually do indulge in promiscuous behavior are by no means necessarily free from inner conflict. On the contrary, they are all too likely to be overprotesting against an inner repressive topdog whose finger constantly wags away inside, and the resultant conflict is just as likely to sap their creative energies as it does in the case of sexually inhibited people. Jack himself was a good example of this. On the surface, his sex life seemed to be completely free, and his topdog/underdog conflict in this area came to light only when his dream made it clear that he was still "bugged" by inner prohibitions. The way to health is not through puritanical denial of instinct or through reaction in the opposite direction, but through greater consciousness and a rational acceptance of the need for free expression on some occasions and restraint on others.

Even those of us who, like Jack, think we are "normal," can get quite a shock when we realize the extent to which we have been repressing physical energy out of fear or shame. This was brought home to me very vividly in a sensitivity-training group which was experimenting with "bioenergetic" exercises—exercises which have been specifically designed to release the energies that have become locked in our bodies because of emotional repressions imposed on us in childhood. As I carried out one particular exercise, which consisted of standing in a special position with knees bent and breathing deeply and rhythmically, I became conscious of the fact that my whole body started to vibrate with a flow of energy which I found distinctly pleasurable. After a time, as my body continued to "let go," I began to experience an inexplicable terror which brought the vibrations to a halt. I exclaimed, "What a shame!" to which the group leader immediately drew attention as a "Freudian" slip, saying that it was indeed a sense of shame which had prevented me from enjoying *full* bodily pleasure in the past. He promptly followed this up with a psychodrama exercise in which I acted the child responding to a reproachful mother, played by another member of the group. I discovered that my feelings of frustration and rage reached their peak whenever my "mother" uttered the words, "You should be *ashamed* of yourself"—a vivid flashback to my real childhood. Several years of psychoanalysis had not succeeded in giving me this

239

direct emotional insight, although we had talked endlessly around the problem.

Another thing I learned in the bioenergetic groups was that holding in the breath is a very common method of stopping any kind of body feeling, and this reminded me vividly of a fairly recurrent dream I used to have. In it, I would find myself lying on a bed or on the floor with a man on one side of me and a cage of small animals, usually white mice or rats, on the other side. These animals would escape from their cage and run all over my body. As it seemed imperative in the dream that they should not escape, I had to hold myself rigid and almost unbreathing until the man picked them off my body and replaced them in the cage. Sometimes the animals would actually settle on my chest or throat so that I was quite unable to breathe, and I would wake up choking. I had no difficulty at the time in associating the animals with sexual (animal) impulses which "overcame" me and which I felt obliged to control. I failed to realize, however, that my dream was trying to tell me in picture language exactly how I was controlling my body feelings in waking life—by holding my breath and becoming almost rigid. The bioenergetic exercise cured me of this, and the dreams ceased. But I could have learned the lesson many years earlier had I understood my dreams fully.

THE LADY IS FOR BURNING

An even more severe case of inner voices preventing enjoyment was brought to light in a remarkable three-episode dream by Peter, who had earlier reported the vivid dream described on page 209 about the City Gent cutting off an Indian's hands. Peter was somewhat of a puzzle to the group. He had been married for sixteen years, and declared himself totally devoted to his wife and children. Although he firmly believed that his was an indissoluble Christian marriage, he had insisted in the early days that both he and his wife should be free to have extra-marital relationships. Several years later, after the birth of his children, his wife left him, declaring she could stand his infidelities no longer. Eventually, Peter persuaded her to return on the promise that his affairs would cease, and since that time he had lavished money, care, and attention on her, providing her with every luxury except the one she really wanted— fidelity.

From this time, Peter's sexual affairs were kept from his wife, although he made no secret of them to his friends. She, in her turn, settled down to an almost totally inturned family life, refusing to engage in social engagements or entertain his colleagues, devoting her entire attention to a long and expensive psychoanalysis. In addition, she tried to persuade him that sexual activity for the over-forties was obscene, so that this side of their life became virtually nonexistent. Peter refused to listen to the group, who were convinced that his overprotested love for his wife was quite bogus; he insisted that his girlfriends meant no more to him than the satisfaction of his sexual needs, which were denied at home. Peter was the only one of us to be surprised when he fell in love with a girlfriend, left home, and asked his wife for a divorce.

The new arrangement, however, was far from a success as Peter was obviously still very much under his wife's thumb. When she insisted that he go home on weekends to look after the children, he went, leaving his girlfriend, Clare, alone in her flat; his wife demanded his total salary so that he was forced to live on Clare; and the divorce was not forthcoming. Not unnaturally Clare, who was also a member of our group, became upset and told him plainly that she had not left a comfortable setup with her husband to become a mere concubine, always taking second place in his life. She urged him to make his wife a reasonable allowance and insist on a divorce. It was at this point that Peter had his dream:

> My wife and I are preparing to go to a wedding conducted by Canon Smith, and I have the impression that it is his son's wedding. Somehow we can't get ready— neither of us can find the right clothes. By the time we get there, the wedding has already taken place

241

somewhere in the distance, and we meet a very upper-class girl, a cross between a peer's daughter I know and a very clever woman journalist, who tells us that she too has missed the wedding.

Then the scene changes, and I am in a bedroom with my wife. We are both sitting up in twin beds placed end to end facing each other. The upper-class girl comes in and starts to kiss me. I feel very sexy, but am worried about what my wife will think. As the girl moves aside, I see my wife's face contorted with horror and fear, and she is biting her wrist to stop herself screaming with rage and jealousy. I panic because I know that any expression of such intense jealousy is "against the law" and will incur some terrible punishment. I call out to her to stop, but it is too late.

Then I am whisked into another land and another time, where my wife is being condemned to the fire for her crime by a pagan king and queen sitting on thrones, only now she is no longer recognizable as my wife, nor is the crime jealousy. She is a ragged Indian squaw and her crime is to be a Christian. She has been condemned to be burned with her baby. I am the grand vizier of the pagan land, clad in a white robe, and I am pleading with the pagan monarchs to spare her, although I know this is a highly dangerous thing to do as they might suspect me of being a Christian, too. I prostrate myself before the queen in a vaguely sexual gesture, but the royal couple explain that there can be no exceptions as this is an immutable law that cannot be changed.

Looking at the dream as a picture and associating to it, Peter remembered that he himself had been married by Canon Smith sixteen years before, and at that time had been such a diligent church worker that people sometimes referred to him as the Canon's "favorite son." So it became apparent that the dream wedding was his own, which, at the back of his mind, he had resisted (he could not get ready), and indeed had never really gone through. This explained, at least in part, Peter's curious attitude toward his marriage. He had been able to extol the virtues of Christian

242

matrimony while remaining consistently unfaithful because he never felt truly married to his wife at all. At this subterranean level, he considered he had made a deal with his wife: he would keep her in comfort and devote himself to her children, provided she did not make any claim to his exclusive sexual attention. The dream showed how he felt his wife had broken her side of the bargain, thereby bringing down upon herself a "punishment"—the punishment of being burned right out of his life without warning at any moment he chose.

The third part of the dream seemed very strange and puzzling, however. Peter knew of Freud's view that kings and queens normally symbolize parents, but his pagan monarchs bore no resemblance whatsoever to his real mother and father, both now dead. Nor was his pampered wife anything like the poor martyred squaw. The group found it interesting that this dream contained a Red Indian woman about to be burned by a heartless pagan regime, while Peter's earlier dream had depicted a different kind of Indian having his hands cut off by a ruthless capitalist. It seemed obvious, as in the earlier dream, that all the dream characters were parts of himself, and so we asked the "pagan king" to explain why they had this law condemning Christians, and Peter, taking his part, replied:

We can't let this new religion contaminate our land. It has this absurd notion that we should spend our time looking after beggars and cripples, who are really too unfit to survive, instead of letting us, the healthy strong ones, get on with celebrating the glorious beauties and energies of physical nature. When we get old and decrepit, we kill ourselves painlessly. These Christians infect our society like a disease and spoil our enjoyment. They even try to tell us that sex is wrong unless it's tied up with marriage.

This speech revealed the pagan king as the absolute opposite of Peter's dead father, who had been decidedly puritanical about sex. In addition, he had preached Christian socialism and the duty of compassion toward the poor

243

and needy, declaring that no one had any right to a moment's enjoyment while there remained one suffering person in the world, and certainly not while there were starving millions in India. So the dream showed a part of Peter reacting violently against his father and setting up an inward substitute father who stood for diametrically opposite values—the survival of the fittest and death to the weak. In his real life, this showed itself in Peter's business success, his large house in a fashionable suburb, expensive private education for his children, unlimited spending money for his wife, and above all, sexual freedom. But on this last point, his wife had shown her weakness and she must die according to the law.

When we asked the "squaw" to speak in her own defense, we seemed for a time to come unstuck, as Peter declared that she was too confused and probably too stupid to understand what was going on. Then one of us had the inspiration of asking Peter to bo back to the previous dream episode in which he and his wife were in bed and tell her that he was leaving her ("burning her") for having broken their pact. "She" replied tearfully,

WIFE: How can you do this to a poor, helpless creature who has given you the best years of her life. Not content with humiliating me with your girlfriends, you're now going to desert your family. The least you can do is make it up to us in some way—you always called yourself a Christian, didn't you? Well now do your duty to the poor, miserable, and weak. Charity begins at home, you know.

PETER: But you're already better off than I am. I'm leaving you the house, the contents, the car, and giving you all my salary. What more do you want?

WIFE: But we've already been having all that. Oh, no (*voice becoming hard and threatening*), you'll have to do a great deal better than that. If you leave, you'll have to give us extra securities and luxuries to compensate for our misery and loneliness—say, a country cottage, a larger car (with a chauffeur), several holidays abroad each year, a yacht would be nice. . . . You know you

244

wanted all these things for yourself, and if you stayed with us, you might get them. We don't intend to be deprived just because some blonde has taken your fancy. You aren't entitled to a moment's happiness until you are sure that we have been compensated. So go and get working, both of you, and I'll let you know when I'm satisfied.

PETER: Isn't it a bit unreasonable . . .

WIFE: Unreasonable! I'm not unreasonable. Look, if by chance you suddenly came into a couple of million pounds, I'll settle for, say, 99 percent of it. You see, from now on, I'm entitled to the moon, but in my magnanimity I'll let you off that.

It rapidly became apparent that the "poor, helpless" wife within was nothing of the sort; she was in fact his bullying, moralizing, reproachful topdog, originally established by his father and later uncannily reinforced by the unrealistic demands of his real wife. This clarified many hitherto puzzling things about Peter's life. He had originally married his wife against the advice of Canon Smith and other friends, and had known all along that they were basically incompatible. His real inner motive for the marriage-that-never-was had been to find a suitable "Christian family" to which he could transfer his obligation to be continually unselfish, and so siphon back some of the results of his work to himself by building up an ostentatiously grand life. In this sense, his wife had been a very suitable match precisely because she demanded constant care and attention, was a chronic hypochondriac, and always thought of herself as poor in spite of Peter's salary, all of which allowed Peter to feel he was doing his quota of self-sacrifice without actually having to go to the much greater trouble of feeding the starving Indians. She was his private substitute for the Indians, and a very convenient one too, because in raising her standard of living, Peter was also able to raise his own without guilt.

The dream also revealed the root of Peter's strange neglect of Clare's ordinary human needs in spite of his being at one level very much in love with her. In his unconscious mind, she inhabited the forbidden pagan land of free sexual enjoyment, and as a self-sufficient pagan queen her function was to be worshiped, not looked after. By coming to live with her and daring to enjoy pagan pleasures while his "poor, helpless squaw" suffered "unspeakable deprivations," Peter found himself at an impasse: either he relinquished his pleasures (after all, pagans do not work night and day to fulfill their duty to Christians) or he burned his "Christian family" right out of his life. The dream sees him as the grand vizier, clad in a white robe (innocent of any decision that is made), prostrating himself before the pagan queen (Clare), begging her to save the Christians. The answer is "No," the decision is Clare's, and Peter is exonerated from any responsibility in the murder.

The session was a most dramatic one and made a considerable difference to both Peter and Clare. At one point, Clare turned to Peter and said, "But, love, I'm not asking you to burn your family, only to be sensible about finances and get a divorce." Of course, Peter's conscious mind knew this perfectly well, but his unconscious mind remained blocked in the "catastrophic conviction" that he had no right to happiness unless he gave all he had, and more, to the "Indians." We encouraged Peter to continue the dialogue with his inner wife and tell her that he had no intention of trying to meet her unrealistic demands. At first, "she" insisted on "her rights," but quickly backed down when Peter stood up to her and yelled, "If you don't shut up, you'll get your rights—the minimum legal rights you are entitled to and nothing more. I don't have to listen to your nonsense, nor do I have to live up to your stupid expectations." At this point, topdog was willing to begin to mitigate its demands and allow Peter to enjoy himself with a *reasonable* level of consideration for others. If he can continue to keep this new balance inside him, everyone will benefit, particularly Peter himself, whose inner split between "Christianity," which demanded total self-sacrifice, and "paganism," which demanded totally unnecessary levels of high living and sexual promiscuity, was spoiling his own life and the lives of everyone around him.

The process of becoming "centered," as Perls calls it, is

not easy. When one has functioned from two opposite ends of the pole for so long, it takes time to realize that there are possibilities in between. This realization slowly dawns when we deliberately change our behavior in the external world according to whatever insight we have received and discover that disaster does not overtake us. In Peter's case, this meant seeing his wife not as a ragged, martyred Christian squaw but as an ordinary divorced woman entitled to a reasonable amount of assistance. It also meant lifting Clare from her lonely, cold pedestal of pagan queen and treating her like a human being. Peter did both. Naturally, his wife recriminated him at first about the new arrangements but ceased to harangue him when she realized he was serious; as for Clare, she heaved a sigh of relief as she now understood how close she herself had come to the flames by showing any sign of weakness in "pagan land."

Peter's story has a hopeful sequel, as several months later he reported a further dream which seemed to indicate that a real inner change was taking place. In the dream his dead father appeared and upbraided him for living a life or orgiastic revelry with a popsy and neglecting his family responsibilities. This was itself interesting, in that Peter's "father," the original source of the problem, had now emerged in person as his oversized, ruthless "Christian" conscience, which nagged whenever Peter attempted to enjoy life. Now, probably for the first time ever, Peter was able to face his father *in the dream* and say, "You know it's not like that, Dad. The family is adequately provided for and my life with Clare is far from being an orgy. Nor is she a popsy; she's the person I love and want to share my life with, and I will not allow you to spoil things for us anymore." Peter woke up feeling as though he had won a battle, as indeed he had. In Gestalt terms, some of topdog's energy had been transmitted to underdog, thus restoring a measure of balance in the psychic system. If this exercise can be repeated whenever similar problems arise, Peter will eventually be able to find a place for both compassion and pleasure in his life.

Very often the acting out of a dream along Gestalt lines will actually bring out the energies that have been repressed from childhood, where an ordinary psychoanalytic interpretation gives only an intellectual insight into the problem, even though it successfully traces dream images back to the traumatic events originally responsible for the trouble. A good example of a Freudian dream interpretation which seemed undeniably correct yet was quite useless therapeutically was the one I described on page 107, in which my dream of waiting with mounting excitement for the queen to arrive at the rear entrance of Buckingham Palace in her car was readily and convincingly traced back to the experience of childhood enemas administered by my mother. I had no doubt that the interpretation was correct, particularly as it linked so neatly with many of my other dreams, including those in which my mother had a penis and my brother made love to me from behind, but I could find no resonance to this interpretation in my waking life. I did not recapture any sense of pleasure at the thought of an enema (I even tried the experiment of giving myself one, and found it horrible!), nor was I in the slightest bit attracted by lesbianism or sex *a tergo*. Neither did I suffer from any of the well-known anal-neurotic symptoms, such as compulsive orderliness and parsimony, though I must admit to being rather stubborn at times. The nearest I could get to anything meaningful in the Freudian level was that my tendency to explosive outbursts of emotion (attributable to the withholding of emotion as demonstrated in the acting out of my "two houses" dream) might in some way be connected with anal release originating with the enema trauma. But this was at most a mere intellectual insight, and I had absolutely no idea what to do about my problem. When I applied the Gestalt technique to this dream, however, the results were both illuminating and surprising.

I began by holding a conversation with the "queen," and in the course of it asked her why she was using the rear entrance of Buckingham Palace instead of sweeping majestically up through the main gates at the front as queens normally do. "She" replied in a rather tearful voice,

QUEEN: Oh dear, I know I'm the queen but sometimes I wish I weren't. I admit I enjoy the power and nice clothes, and not having to wash up and all that, but I wish I didn't have to be on my dignity all the time. It's so very tiring. And it's a bore because I never know what's going on in the world. They won't let me mix with people—they say it's improper. That's why I take my car in through the back entrance of the palace—it's a narrow entrance and the car has to slow down. The people crowd up against it, and I can have quite a chat with them, even touch them sometimes. They'd go absolutely mad if they knew. . . .

I interrupted myself to ask exactly who "they" were and the queen told me they were the palace officials, who were frightfully stuffy about protocol. I asked her to confess her misdeed, and the following dialogue took place:

OFFICIAL: Really, your Majesty, this is too bad. How many more times do we have to tell you that familiarity breeds contempt? The people will abuse you if you get too close to them and allow yourself to be seen as a human being. Anyway, you can take our word for it, you have nothing to learn from them—they're dull, insensitive, and diseased. We know because we ourselves once lived among them. But you—you are different, you were born different, and don't you ever forget it. We do our best to protect you from these animals and this is how you repay us. You should be ashamed of yourself.

QUEEN: Oh, dear, oh, dear. What am I to do? Yes, I suppose you're right, but I do need outlets sometimes. I feel so pent up, so cut off from life. I sometimes think I shall go mad with constant polite conversation, cleanliness, and decorum. Won't you give me a day off once in a while?

OFFICIAL: Certainly not, your Majesty. You are here

to serve your country, not to indulge your petty personal needs. You can't have your cake and eat it. Either you remain here and behave yourself or go and join the rabble for good, and we don't think you'd like that.

QUEEN: No, you're dead right, I wouldn't. Oh, all right—don't go on at me. I'll be good and do what you say. (*Thinks*) I'll have to try slipping out in disguise sometimes. That way will be even better because the people won't know who I am and I'll be able to get to know them better.

Here, as with both Joseph's and Peter's dreams, a surprising reversal of roles has taken place when the Gestalt technique is applied, in that the character which at first sight appears humble—slow train, Indian, ragged squaw, and servants—turns out to be topdog. The explanation in my case, as in Peter's, was a complex one which serves to illustrate very well the paradoxical character of the mind's operations. My mother may have been the queen in my life as a child, but this queen was not a simple authority figure. She was herself a deeply divided character, a person who had come from a very poor home and had early on cut herself off from all emotional involvement with her background in a desperate wish to create a family life which was not subject to the dirt and misery of poverty. The authoritarian parent I had introjected, which insisted that I must be correct, clean, calm and well ordered (even to the point of having bowel movements regulated to the clock by an enema), was not my mother's natural self at all, but her own bullying topdog, which meant that the mother image in my mind consisted of a queen who was herself under the rigid control of "palace officials."

This was further reinforced by the fact that my mother's injunctions to me in childhood came over in terms of an expectation that *I myself should always behave like a queen.* I received a fascinating sidelight on this long after I had done my Gestalt work on the dream, when my mother casually told me the story of how, as a child, she had watched the world of the aristocrats go by in their fine clothes and carriages without any feelings of envy. They belonged to a world apart, she said, and she knew she was different. She made a vow, however that her children would belong to "their world," and soon after she was married she bought a fur-lined cape to be worn by her first child. I did not actually arrive until three years later, but the cape was there waiting for me—I had been born to the ermine, and was encouraged to "queen it" over the entire household. Yet, at the same time, I had to obey orders and be ruled by my parents more than most children in order to conform to my mother's strict standards of decorous behavior.

So I inherited my mother's inner division, but whereas her emotional needs were kept rigidly under control because of their association with the unpleasantness of her childhood slum life, mine rebelled in much the same way as the underdog queen rebelled in the Gestalt dialogue. As a child, I was often found talking to street sweepers, dustmen, tramps, and so on, much to my mother's concern, and as soon as I was able, I left home and worked my way around Europe, chuckling to myself as I scrubbed the steps of a French brothel at six o'clock every morning, or earned myself an extra five francs by mopping up the vomit of drunken peasants—for I was the queen among the common people in disguise. After a few years, however, I returned home and settled down in marriage, resuming my proper queenly approach to life, my husband now speaking with the voice of the palace officials whenever I did something he considered out of character.

The voice of my inner topdog, originally taken from my mother, was of course far harsher than that of my real mother or husband. At the time of the dream, my underdog queen was obviously chafing for expression, and some incident in my waking life must have triggered off a hidden train of thought which took my problem right back to the time of its origin. It was probable that my mother, in outwardly obeying her rigid routine of "palace rules" by giving me an enema, had actually allowed herself surreptitiously a degree of intimate contact with me at the physical/emotional level to which something in me at once responded, to the deep confusion of my young mind.

Had I been working with my dream in a group, the

leader would no doubt have made me stand up to the palace officials and say something like this:

I have certain needs which I must fulfill, and one of them is to let myself go occasionally. You are you, and I am I, and I'm not here to live up to your expectations. I'm a big girl now, and I'm going to take responsibility for myself. I'm no longer going around the back door to enjoy myself—I shall do it openly in whatever way I think fit.

The role reversal that took place when I subjected the dream to the Gestalt technique served to link it, as I should never otherwise have done, with another dream I had a couple of years later in which I actually appeared as a queen myself. The dream was set somewhere in Holland, and I was going into a great cathedral for my coronation. As the fanfare sounded, I noticed the people around me smiling in a kindly, almost indulgent fashion. Looking down, I saw that I was wearing an old summer dress and enormous fur boots. I wondered whether I should rush out and change or allow the ceremony to continue. Then suddenly there flooded over me the realization that the officials and the people actually preferred a vulnerable human queen capable of making mistakes to one who was always perfect. For if I were not perfect, I could not demand that they be perfect too.

This dream showed, I think, that I had made some progress in the intervening years. I was taking my place as a queen not by shunning common humanity in favor of decorous propriety, but by bringing fallibility and animal warmth ("furry boots") into my queenliness. It was interesting that I was being crowned in Holland, the "*Nether*-lands" and more specifically, a land reclaimed from the sea, which is a very nice symbol of bringing to conscious awareness something that was formerly submerged.

At the same time, the dream revealed in its conclusion the underlying essence of the self-torture game. If I make demands on myself (as the palace officials did with the queen) then I can make demands on others. If I insist that underdog lives up to the impossible expectations of topdog inside myself, then I can demand that others live up to my impossible expectations in the external world. Some people keep this sort of thing up all their lives, but most are sane enough to realize sooner or later that the rewards of sitting in the seat of the scornful are just not worth the wasteful expenditure of energy required to keep the conflict going.

I am grateful to my dreams for helping me reclaim my humanness and fallibility, not merely because I feel a bigger person with more energy at my disposal, but also because life is more tolerable for those around me. And, in the inner world, the truth is that we not only have to be released from our parents—we also have to learn to release them. As Blake puts it, in terms of his own inner mythology:

> Each man is in his Spectre's power
> Until the arrival of that hour
> When his Humanity awake
> And cast his Spectre into the Lake.

SOMETHING NASTY IN THE CELLAR

Dreams in which people or objects are imprisoned in boxes, basements, or dungeons are particularly suitable for treatment along Gestalt lines, as the prisoners almost invariably represent buried treasure which must be dug up and used to fill the holes they left in our personality when we first banished them into oblivion. One striking dream of this kind occurred in my own life some time ago, and like the queen dream was later followed by further related dreams which helped me to see how the psychic drama was changing as time went on.

The dream, retold in the present tense, was as follows:

I am in a cellar without a door in the company of an old woman who looks like a witch and who is pleading with me to stay with her. I want to go but cannot see any possible exit. She keeps making me cups of tea, knowing full well I want to go, but trying her hardest to keep me with her. Ultimately, she accepts that I intend to go, and as a last resort offers me an apple and asks me to kiss her. I smell danger, but think there can't be any harm in it, and as I bend to bite the apple, I am whisked out of a door that has suddenly appeared, into a ray of white light.

Although I had this dream some time before I took up psychology professionally, I had no difficulty even then in interpreting it by simple association. I immediately identified the woman as my mother, whom I was obviously seeing at the time as a clinging, possessive old witch who would go to any lengths, even poison, to keep me with her. (In the story of Snow White, the wicked queen dresses in black and offers her stepdaughter a poisoned apple.) I interpreted the ray of white light as a religious group I had just joined, and I felt the dream was telling me that I was using it in order to rise above what I felt to be a neurotic attachment. This in itself was a valuable insight, as I was unaware of such motivation at the time.

There were, however, several questions which remained unanswered. Having carefully locked my mother-witch away and blocked all exits to prevent her getting at me, why had I gone to visit her? Why did I intend to bite the apple when I felt it might be dangerous? And why did she want to poison me? To find out, I applied the Gestalt technique many years later, with the following result:

ANN: Why do you want to poison me? I came to see you because I felt sorry for you. I call it most uncivil to play a dirty trick like that on me.

WOMAN: But you don't understand. I'm just a poor old woman who has been locked away in this beastly cellar for twenty years and no one has ever come to see me. There's no light or heating in here, and my rheumatism's getting worse. I don't want to let you go because you might not come again for another twenty years. And, anyway, you misjudge me: the apple isn't poisoned. You're dramatizing the whole situation and confusing

254

me with the wicked stepmother in Snow White. My apple merely contains a harmless drug which would have made you sleepy, so I could have kept you here just a little longer. I don't want to kill you.

At this point, the ray of white light interrupted to say,

RAY: Don't you believe a word of it. Of course she was out to poison you. I've known her a lot longer than you, and believe me the old witch is dangerous. Why else do you think I locked her in the cellar? I know you—you're easily got at and naïve, always willing to believe the best in people. What you'd do without me as your watchdog, I just can't imagine. You'd be lying dead on the floor now, wouldn't you?

ANN: Well, er . . . yes, I suppose so. Thank you. I am grateful for your concern. I just felt sorry for her stuck down here all by herself. I didn't mean any harm.

RAY: Oh, you never do—that's your trouble. You should think more. You don't understand the wickedness of the world as I do. Give people an inch and they'll take a mile. Come along with me now please, and see that it doesn't happen again.

WOMAN: Please don't go and leave me again. Please let me come with you. I promise not to be a nuisance. I don't need much . . .

ANN (to the ray): Yes, let's do that; let's take her upstairs for a bit of comfort.

RAY: Certainly not. It's quite out of the question. She's not to be trusted. And there's no need to feel sorry for the old bag. She brought it on herself. She's never grown up, never learned to stand on her own two feet—always whining and moaning for sympathy. She'll have to learn to be much more self-reliant before I let her out.

ANN: But she'll never learn self-reliance if you keep her locked up . . .

At this point in the drama, I had an image of myself as a small, confused baby cringing on the floor between these two creatures who were wrestling for my soul, not knowing

255

which one to believe. As they are both parts of myself, it is clear that I am torn between the voice of self-reliance, which constantly nags, "You must learn to stand on your own two feet and be independent of other people," and the voice of the clinging old woman, who cries, "I need love and care and warmth." In other words, I have got myself into what R. D. Laing calls a knot, a knot which probably originated in childhood when I both needed my mother and wanted to be free of her. In his book of prose-poems called *Knots*, he describes one that fits this situation precisely:

> Once upon a time, when Jack was little,
> he wanted to be with his mummy all the time
> and was frightened she would go away.
>
> later, when he was a little bigger,
> he wanted to be away from his mummy
> and was frightened that
> she wanted him to be with her all the time....

This shows very neatly how our images of our parents become divided, but I suspect in many cases, and certainly my own, the division in the child's mind hinges on a division that is already there in the parent. My immediate associations to the dream naturally saw the old woman as a symbol of my mother, whose possessive demands I was trying to escape, whereas the acting out indicated that I had become aware, probably at an early date, of two conflicting sides to her personality—the ray of white light, not so dissimilar from the palace officials of the earlier dream, and a rather pathetic person who depended on me for love and affection. As a child, I remember being very confused when she propounded the doctrines of self-reliance and detachment, at the same time berating me for not loving her enough.

My resolution of the conflict had been to resist both my mother's demands for affection and my own feelings of dependency on her, and to identify myself with the ray of white light. I joined a number of religious groups to help me achieve self-reliance (my mother's notions of detachment seemed to have sprung from such sources), reinforcing my endeavor with the words of Jesus: "Unless a man hate his father, mother and brethren, he cannot be my disciple." And of course I had the "secondary gain" of being able to be very tough on any other person in my environment who seemed in the least bit sloppy or dependent.

I am not blaming my mother for my problems: the blaming game leads nowhere except away from the problem, for she could in turn blame her own mother and so on ad infinitum. Parents are never right, whatever they do. They are either too short or too tall, too strict or too permissive, too serious or too gay. As Oscar Wilde says, "Children begin by loving their parents. After a time they judge them. Rarely, if ever, do they forgive them." But until we do forgive them, until we do release them, we conceive of ourselves as children and behave like children. In my case, I should have stood up to the ray of white light (my mother's independence within me) and said, "I'm a big girl now. Stop telling me what to do. If I want to go down to the cellar and see the old woman, I shall, and you won't stop me." In other words, *I* shall choose when to be weak and when to be strong, when to be loving, and when to be detached. Perls says that forgiving and releasing our parents is quite the most difficult part of therapy.

Some time later, I had another dream, which seemed to link directly with this last one. In it, my husband's very smart and efficient secretary, Diana, had left to continue her studies, and he had replaced her with a childish, inefficient, and neurotic woman called Tilly (who had actually been one of his former secretaries). I was furious with him in the dream, because I recalled how she had constantly followed me around the house, complaining about her ailments and trying to get psychological help for her endless problems.

This dream occurred at the time my husband was facing me with the choice between home and career, and it seems clear that my anxiety had resurrected the dependent old witch (Tilly) from her cellar, and had sent the self-reliant, independent ray of white light (Diana) packing. My choice of Diana for this role was probably a condensation of the girl herself and of the Roman goddess Diana, the huntress and protectress of women—goddess of the Women's Liberation Movement? I realized how terrified I was of losing my husband, how much I depended on him emotionally, and how much I feared loneliness, emotions which made me temporarily accede to his request to stay at home. My analyst at this point was the reverse of helpful, because he implied that my "real" self was rising to the surface and that I should now find happiness and fulfillment in my new domestic way of life.

What he failed to explain and what Gestalt therapy taught me later was that the clinging, dependent old woman I had thrust into the cellar was not the "real" me at all, but only a *part of me,* a part moreover that would never have become so repulsive had it not been denied expression for so long. Had I been able to accept my dependency feelings as a child and learned to integrate them into my total psychic system, they would have manifested themselves in behavior as warm, loving feelings toward others, and not as poisonous, self-pitying, possessive emotions which naturally scared the pants off me. So my analyst's attempt to make me recognize and accept the "old witch" side of myself had exactly the opposite effect from the one he hoped for: if that witch is the "real" me, I thought, far better send her straight back to the cellar and put an extra-strong bolt on the door.

So the skeleton in my psyche remained firmly locked away until I became interested in Gestalt therapy and realized that she was merely a monster of my imagination and that if I reintegrated her she would do me no harm. At this point, I had yet another dream, which clarified this point for me very beautifully:

I own a large house and have let two rooms in it. The large, airy, light front room with a marvelous view and central heating is occupied by Tilly, while a small back room, no larger than a cubicle, without windows or heating, is occupied by one of my former, very efficient German au pair's called Regina. Tilly is paying me £3 a week for the large front room and Regina is paying me

£6 for the small back room. I can't understand why Regina doesn't grumble, as she certainly would have done in real life. Instead she tells me she is rarely at home these days on account of a super new job which brings in a lot of money.

As soon as I looked at this dream, I was once again able to recognize Tilly as the old witch of the first dream of this series, who had now left her cellar to occupy the best room of the house upstairs. I had replaced the ray of white light, this time not with Diana but with Regina, another very efficient girl, who in this dream seemed to have better things to do than chase me around and scold me for getting into trouble. When I invited Regina to say how she felt about the new situation, she replied,

REGINA: Well, of course it's unfair to charge me twice as much rent as Tilly, especially as my room has no light or heat. But I'm far too busy to argue about such trivialities at the moment and I haven't time to look for another room. I'll put up with the arrangement for the time being as I'm only here anyway for a couple of nights a week. Tilly lives in hers all the time because she's not well enough to go out yet, so it's better she has the good room. I'll do my bit to help her get better. It's in my own interests anyway becuase she's a bit of a bore the way she is now, isn't she, always complaining about her rheumatism and things. I hope you'll use some of my rent to buy her things she needs. It's only a temporary measure, though; I can't have her sponging off me for ever. When she's better, she can look after herself like everyone else.

It seemed clear that I had moved to a stage where my topdog, although still a little formidable, was much less judging and punitive than she used to be. Moreover, she now saw underdog as a poor sick invalid needing help, rather than as a possessive, dangerous old witch from whom I must be rescued. I interpreted the money she was giving me as psychic energy which was gradually being

259

transferred from the cold, independent, self-reliant side of my personality to the potentially warm, loving nature I banished to the cellar long ago. Regina indicated that this energy was to be used to restore a psychic balance, not to keep Tilly in a helpless state of dependency for the rest of her life. I asked Tilly how she felt about this arrangement, and she replied,

I can't tell you how happy I am to have been released from that damp old cellar. I tried to tell you that the cold was making me ill, but you wouldn't listen, and I was slowly losing the sight of my eyes through being in the dark. It will take me a little time to get well, and I hope you'll bear with me. Just for a little while, all I want to do is sit by the radiator, feeling its warmth soak into me. And I want to gaze and gaze out of the window because I've seen no space or color for so long. I want to make up for all the deprivations I've suffered, and I'd like you to come up and talk to me from time to time. I'm sure I'll get better soon, so I won't be a burden for too long. I'll soon be able to look after myself again.

She does not sound at all dangerous now, and I believe what she says. The ray of light believes her too, or at least is willing to give her the benefit of the doubt. If she fails to live up to her intentions and becomes a drag, then Regina will be around to get her moving and restore balance. After all, self-reliance and a certain amount of detachment are excellent qualities, and I do not want to lose them. But at the same time it will be a great relief to feel that my need for other people is not the shameful thing I believed it to be.

This dream series shows clearly once again how the unconscious mind thinks in opposites with catastrophic expectations and has to be trained to function along a middle path. All the time I disowned my dependency needs and identified with self-reliance, stoicism, and detachment, I fooled those around me into believing me when I insisted that I could manage, cope, and generally look after myself. The old witch, however, like all underdogs, usually made herself felt in mean, underhand, and destructive behavior, such as minor breakdowns and accusations of neglect, whenever I felt I had reached the end of my tether. This puzzled my friends and family because they knew how much I scorned those who were unable to stand on their own feet or who showed any signs of weakness in coping with difficult situations. My game was an obvious and very common one: I expected people to read my innermost thoughts and feelings by something akin to telepathy, but did not want to be bothered to do the same for them. It is difficult to stop playing this game because it is so convenient, but I have decided that the only reasonable answer is to make our needs known openly to others, give them the opportunity of doing the same, and take full responsibility for our resulting decisions.

Professor Peter Beaconsfield, the American surgeon-scientist, wrote recently in *New Scientist,* "To be ignorant that a problem exists is understandable: to ignore it once it is identified is inadmissible." This expresses my feelings about inner conflicts thrown up by our dreams and my whole case rests on dealing with these problems in waking life in order to function more fully and authentically. But long-standing habits are not broken easily, and topdog does not relinquish his power without a struggle. In my own case, just as I thought I had this particular problem licked, I discovered that topdog and underdog were still at each other's throats, continuing their battle in a manner which had escaped my conscious notice.

I am, in fact, writing this in the hospital, where I have been cared for and fussed over by surgeons, nurses, and my family for two weeks following a minor operation on a swollen lymph gland which had grown to enormous proportions because I had not sought medical help in the first instance. I had not recognized the voice of topdog when he whispered, "It's nothing. You're tough. It will be gone by tomorrow. Don't waste the doctor's time." Had I listened more intently, I would also have heard my mother's voice recalling how, as children, she and her sister had been sent out to play in the streets with pneumonia, implying how soft and pampered was the modern generation of children.

How could I then without shame seek medical help for minor symptoms? But underdog wins in the end and is now wallowing in the extra attention he is receiving on account of topdog's ill-advised stoicism.

Still, the last dream of this series, while not indicating inner perfection, offers hope that changes are being made and that in time I shall learn to function more rationally. I found it interesting that the dream chose Regina—whose name means "queen"—to play the role of my topdog, for in the last dream series, the queen was my underdog. Does this mean that my strengths and weaknesses are merging to form some kind of intelligent and discerning integrated unity? Could it be the first step on what Jung calls the road to "individuation," described by him as "the process by which a person becomes a psychological 'in-dividual,' that is, a separate, indivisible unity or 'whole.' " I think Perls would say I was completing a "Gestalt." I hope so.

VISITORS FROM OUTER SPACE

Methinks that dreams from a remoter world visit the soul during sleep.—SHELLEY

By working with my dreams along Gestalt lines, I came to see that all my life I had been repressing or alienating what I quite wrongly considered to be the weaker aspects of my personality. In my "queen" series I was led to reclaim my human fallibility, which resulted in a much more relaxed life-style, and from my "witch" series I eventually learned to establish warm, close relationships without fear of being either rejected or overwhelmed. Both dream series were concerned with the basic problem of weakness, and the following two dreams with which I shall end this chapter add another dimension to this as yet unfinished story. These dreams felt as though they had arisen from some deep level of the psyche and left me with the conviction that something enormously important had happened. Both are very "Jungian" in that they contain a mythological character who had not previously visited me in dreams, but who immediately resonated as my "animus" or inner guiding spirit.

The first dream occurred soon after I had started working along Gestalt lines, and I retell it here in the present tense:

> I have banished Uriel—a primitive man who has a transparent necklace made of crystals—but I have banished him too soon and must get him back. He is wandering the underworld and I know he will have power underground so long as he hangs on to his necklace, which is also a charm. I am conducting a ritual to bring him back to our world, and I start to pronounce an invocation—"Friends, goodfellows . . ."—when I notice a woman who reminds me of the last Lady Macbeth I saw on stage advancing toward me with a smile on her face. She laughingly informs me that I cannot possibly be serious about bringing Uriel back, and when I assure her that I am, she cringes against the wall in a state of absolute terror.

Looking at the dream as a picture, I have no idea who on earth Uriel is or why I should have banished him. But I have learned from my dreams that anyone who is locked up or banished is almost certain to be an alienated part of the personality which must be reclaimed. This is exactly what I seem to be doing in the dream, an operation which greatly upsets Lady Macbeth, who symbolizes for me the qualities of power, ambition, and ruthlessness. It is obvious from her terror that Uriel has some kind of power over her and I have a feeling she is afraid of the necklace, though I have no associations to this. Although I describe Uriel as a "primitive man" in the dream, he sounds more like an angel to me, and I am calling on the friendly nature spirits (Robin Goodfellows) to help me find him.

The dream is a complete mystery and therefore ideal for treatment along Gestalt lines. First of all, I ask Uriel who he is, and he replies,

URIEL: I am your angel and I roam the underworld. I used to watch over you when you were small and you liked me then. I come from the sun—remember, you always loved the sun? And then one day when you were still quite small, you put your hands over your eyes and told me I wasn't real. You said you didn't believe in me anymore and told me to go away. I didn't go away, in fact, but I ceased to exist for you.

ANN: Don't be silly. No one believes in guardian angels these days. You're teasing me. Still, it's true I vaguely sensed something around me when I went off roaming Europe, and more than once I felt I'd been helped to escape from sticky situations. Was that you? No, of course, it wasn't; the whole thing's ridiculous. I'm a scientist and a psychologist, and you just can't be allowed.

URIEL: Yes, it was me. I've been with you all the time. Look, would it help to call me your animus or some other respectable-sounding name? It's all the same, you know.

ANN: Well, yes, I suppose so—and anyway, Uriel you're a lovely thought. But I'm still puzzled about your necklace. Is it a charm?

URIEL: It belonged to you as a child, and the day you banished me I took it with me. I knew one day you'd call me back and the necklace is the link between us.

I am not at all sure what this means, and so I ask the necklace to explain itself. It replies,

NECKLACE: I am a crystal necklace. I am transparent. You can see right through me. I catch the light and reflect it back in many colors. I shine and I am beautiful. I'm not as strong as the diamond or as passionate as the ruby, but I'm pure and innocent. Before me pretension and sophistication vanish, like Dracula before the cross. And I belong to you.

Translated into more prosaic terms, the dream is asking me to reclaim the quality sometimes called innocence—a straightforward, open response to others and to life generally which takes for granted that there is something good in even the toughest, most sophisticated person. This too is an aspect of my character which I have for most of my life tried to disown because it seemed like weakness—"naïveté" is the word my "palace official"/ "ray of white light" used to describe it. Its direct opposite is cynicism, and it is interesting that the figure thrown up by this new dream to represent the tough aspect of my personality was Lady Macbeth, a character in whom realism had passed right over into ruthless, cynical ambition which does not hesitate to "murder" in order to gain power.

Somewhere in my childhood Lady Macbeth had emerged and told me to banish all thought of trusting people or the universe at large. There is probably some fairly standard "explanation" along Freudian lines, probably dating from the time my brother was born and I felt my parents had betrayed me by leading me to believe I was the center of their universe. It was only when I came to act out this dream, however, that I really experienced and understood this conflict as it had subsequently affected my life.

When I allowed Lady Macbeth to speak for herself, it became quite clear that she thoroughly disapproved of my religious attitude toward life, but when she realized that this was something she could not squash, she turned it to her own advantage. She persuaded me that as human beings were fallible and unreliable, I had better turn my back on them and devote my entire loyalty and love to God, who would not let me down. So I found myself using the various religious disciplines to rise above people and the need for involvement in human relationships. But she finally came into her own when I studied psychology and underwent analysis, by joining forces with my tutors and my analyst to convince me that all religious feelings are phony. In my case, she said, I had joined the religious groups simply in order to replace the parents who had betrayed me and to regain my lost sense of identity by becoming important to God. It was at this point in my life that God and Jung became dirty words and I swore (under the influence of Lady Macbeth) never to be taken in by them again.

Just as I despised myself for having been so "naïve," so I scorned all those who persisted in clinging onto their "infantile" religious fantasies, including my first husband. His dream of me as the ex-Mrs. Armstrong-Jones building an ugly church of gray concrete on a desolate piece of wasteland (page 199) could not have pictured my attitude toward life at that time more astutely. Later I was to discover that it mirrored not only *his* feelings about me, but at a deeper, hidden level, my own feelings as well. I became restless, unhappy, and ill, and eventually realized that by banishing Uriel and the necklace I had thrown out the baby with the bathwater. While my *use* of religion had certainly been neurotic, the basic religious feelings themselves were an essential part of my nature and I was doing myself violence by trying to deny them.

At the time of my Uriel dream, Lady Macbeth's topdog position in my life was at last being undermined by my growing willingness to acknowledge and give expression to the "weaker" side of my personality. In particular, my work with dreams was beginning to make me revise my hard, critical "no-nonsense" attitude toward the mysteries of the psyche. Lady Macbeth, of course, was resisting like mad, proclaiming that I must at all costs hold on to scientific respectability by refusing to consider any feelings or aspirations which could not be reduced to thoroughly down-to-earth human problems of work, marriage, divorce, and the like. And, of course, she was not wholly wrong. It is certainly true that people often use high-flown religious or ideological ideas as a means of escaping from life's more prosaic responsibilities, and there is no health in that. What the dream showed, however, was that there is equally no health in putting down altogether the deep concerns that drive people to ask questions about the meaning and purpose of life. In the face of anything as mysterious as the human psyche or as incomprehensible as the universe we live in, it is not naïveté but sheer realism to adopt the childlike attitude which simply accepts that there are far more things in heaven and earth than are dreamed of in the

266

philosophies of most academic psychologists and analysts.

I later discovered that Uriel is indeed an angel (of Hebrew mythology) and on reading Milton's *Paradise Lost* I was staggered to find him described as the "Regent of the Sun" and "sharpest-sighted spirit of all in heaven." Lady Macbeth insists that there must be a perfectly rational explanation for my prior knowledge of him—perhaps I had read *Paradise Lost* at school or had come across him in some Hebrew Scriptures. Maybe, but how fantastic that an image which has lain dormant for so long should suddenly be able to manifest itself in a dream or fantasy with such precision. I decided to take Uriel's own advice and think of him as my "animus" or "soul," which in its positive aspect, writes Jung, "becomes a mediator of the religious experience whereby life acquires new meaning."

I do not know how successful I was in resurrecting Uriel and the necklace, but the following dream, which occurred a few months later, indicated that some real inner change was taking place. In the dream:

I am with a party of people on board a space ship. It lands on some strange territory in outer space, the hatch opens and a man who looks like Prince Arthur in Edward Bond's play *Early Morning* enters and looks us over. He speaks to us in a strange language which I know is a mixture of English and Uri, whatever that may be. I can understand quite a bit of it if I concentrate hard. He picks me out and asks me to follow him. I wonder at what point in time we are, whether we have gone forward or backward. I follow him out of the ship and he tells me that he is going to be my guide and show me around the new world.

Looking at the dream as a picture, I am reminded that the character of Arthur in *Early Morning* represents the "soul" (or so I believe), which in Jungian terminology is another name for the "animus." My companion also spoke in Uri language, which reminds me of my guardian angel/animus, Uriel. So I interpret the dream as a journey through space—an exploration of my own expanded inner psychic space beyond the limited boundary of the ego—to a new world, where I confront and am reunited with my hitherto alienated animus.

I am not sure what this means in terms of my total life-situation or how it will affect my external existence. All I know is that I woke up with a feeling of lightness and joy, as though some internal breakthrough had occurred, and I defy Lady Macbeth to "put down" this experience by explaining it away in terms of wish fulfillment concerning father or brother. Both Jung and Perls would say that there had been an expansion of consciousness through the integration of opposites, and beyond this I feel we cannot go at the moment. Such dreams, which feel as though they have arisen from some deep layer of the psyche, should be accepted for what they are—mysterious and numinous events to be experienced rather than explained. As Jung says:

> What happens within oneself when one integrates previously unconscious contents with the consciousness is something which can scarcely be described in words. It can only be experienced. It is a subjective affair quite beyond discussion; we have a particular feeling about ourselves, about the way we are, and that is a fact which it is neither possible nor meaningful to doubt .... Whether a change has taken place as the result of integration, and what the nature of that change is, remains a matter of subjective conviction. . . . Realistic psychotherapists and psychologists interested in therapy can scarcely afford to overlook facts of this sort.

PART IV

LOOKING FORWARD

CHAPTER 11

DREAM POWER IN SOCIETY

There is a widespread belief among young people that during the past decade mankind has entered a new epoch. They characterize it by using the astrological notion of the age of Aquarius, whose main feature is traditionally supposed to be that the search for spiritual wholeness will cease to be the concern of the few and become the interest of all mankind. It is also supposed to be an age in which people cease to rely on institutions like the church, the family, or the nation and will seek authentic existence as individuals, communicating with each other in a spirit of openness and truth. I have no views on astrology, but I hope they are right about the New Age, because unless people do begin to learn more about the inner springs of their behavior and to seek more authentic self-hood, it seems unlikely that the human race has much hope for any tolerable future at all. I believe this last part of the twentieth century is likely to be marked by all kinds of experiments in new ways of promoting self-understanding and emotional growth, and I am sure that the use of dreams has an enormous part to play in this.

In these concluding chapters, I shall indicate some of the practical contexts in which this may happen, both in the home and in the world outside, and shall end by taking a speculative look at the future, for while I am sure that the use of dreams to illuminate everyday problems of work and human relationships is vital, I also think it is only the beginning of what dream power may eventually come to mean for human life.

The next few years will, I am sure, see a mushroom growth of therapeutic and educational groups of all kinds in which ordinary people come together for the express purpose of promoting self-knowledge and personal growth, and my earlier chapters have indicated how such groups might use dreams. In my view, however, there is absolutely no need for dream work to be restricted to special groups under the guidance of a psychologically trained leader. The kind of techniques I have outlined can be used by anyone, and I believe we shall see them playing an increasing part in family and community life, in religious organizations, and even in the world of business and government.

How shall we find time for all this in a world of increasing rush? The answer is, of course, that if we really want to do something, we *make* time for it, quite apart from the fact that if we continue to allow housework, social life, sermonizing, and moneymaking to take precedence over the deeper issues of modern life, the rush will be nothing more than a headlong plunge to disaster. In fact, it is my belief that much of the frenzied activity of everyday life is merely an escape from facing up to personal problems. The American psychiatrist Eric Berne has done us all a great service by exploring, in his book *Games People Play,* the extent to which we all indulge in what he calls the game of "Harried," taking on quite unnecessary tasks in order to impress those around us (and ourselves) with our devotion to duty, and to gain sympathy, comfort, and approval, as well as being forgiven our sins and failures.

John Wren-Lewis, a British writer who took up Berne's concept and applied it to industrial life in an article called "Games Businessmen Play" in the journal *New Society* in 1970, went so far as to suggest, on the basis of many years' work as a scientist in industry, that far more time is spent on time-wasting activities like this in business life than on really productive work. The American pioneer of the Women's Liberation Movement, Betty Friedan, gives concrete illustrations of Berne's diagnosis as applied to housewives in her book *The Feminine Mystique,* in which she quotes time-motion studies to show that most of the energy spent on housework is superfluous and that housework expands to fill the time available. She concludes, "The time required to do the housework for any given woman varies inversely with the challenge of the other work to which she is committed"; in other words, when a woman has other interests, housework that normally took six hours now gets done in one.

In my own experience this is certainly true, not only with housework, but also with my research work. When I took up meditation several years ago, my teacher insisted that I spend three hours a day on this discipline in the initial stages. When I protested that I could not possibly spare the time, he assured me not only that my work would not suffer but that it would improve in quantity and quality. He was absolutely right, and I have since discovered that this happens when I take time off to explore the night's dreams the following day. When I have arrived at a satisfactory interpretation or a meaningful insight, I experience a state of being which I can only describe as something akin to an awakening—Perls calls it a mini-satori, the Zen Buddhist term for enlightenment—in which energy is liberated throughout the body, bringing increased vigor for everyday pursuits. It is the experience of being more in touch with one's self and senses, so that the world is faced directly and not through a veil of fantasy and projection.

Part of our reluctance to face the inner life probably springs from the widespread myth that it is dangerous to probe too deeply into what goes on below the surface of the mind because we might stir up all kinds of unhealthy forces which could get out of control and send us beserk. I believe psychiatrists and psychoanalysts have to take a good deal of responsibility for spreading this fear, which, in my experience, is exaggerated out of all proportion. While no one denies that there are sick people who are unable to cope with the problems of life and who would be advised not to explore unconscious processes without the help of an expert, there are far, far more "normal," intelligent people with a wide range of psychological knowledge who are perfectly capable of exploring their dreams along the lines suggested in this book. The time is right for the "secret of dreams" to be exposed to the general public and used as an effective method of self-help outside the precincts of the consulting room. I repeat my earlier warning, however, that anyone who does find his dreams worrying, and particularly if he feels himself being overwhelmed by them, should seek professional help.

DREAM POWER IN THE FAMILY

I and my group members have started the campaign for the greater use of dream power in everyday life by encouraging our children to report to us any dreams they may have, so that they come to think of their nocturnal adventures as something important right from the outset of their existence. If my daughter wakes up from a bad dream, instead of dismissing it and sending her back to sleep with the words, "Don't worry, it's only a dream," I ask her why she was telling herself such a frightening story while she was asleep. If she reports a bizarre dream, I ask her why she thought up such funny ideas. And I always encourage her to expand on them by asking her to take the parts of the characters along Gestalt lines. In my experience, children find this great fun.

I believe that if we make children aware of the importance of their dreams from an early age, they will grow up with the idea that dreams are not just things that *happen* to them out of the blue, but fantasies they themselves act out in sleep in order to tell themselves something of importance. If we encourage our children to think of their dreams in this way, I believe we shall be providing them from an early age with an easier and more natural access to the inner life, so that they will learn to accept that side of their nature which we were brought up to hide, with disastrous consequences.

I know of several families who set aside one evening a week for a family group-encounter (the modern equivalent of family prayers?).* During this time, both children and parents air their grievances, resentments, and appreciations about each other and try to arrive at some mutual settlement satisfactory to all parties. If the plan fails to work during the following week, something else is suggested at the next encounter meeting. Dreams are used regularly at these family sessions to bring out into the open feelings which might not otherwise be articulated clearly.

For example, one fifteen-year-old boy reported a dream soon after these family encounter sessions had started in which he watched two men making some kind of business deal. One of them supplied information which the other recorded in a book. As they rose and shook hands, presumably to clinch the deal, the floor suddenly opened and swallowed up the man who had been giving the information. The dreamer realized that the dealer was a fraud, luring clients into his confidence, taking their information, and then calmly bumping them off. The boy's associations led him to identify the dealer as his father, who, he feared, would use the openness and honesty of the encounter sessions not to establish closer and more understanding relationships with his family, but as a way of getting them to reveal weaknesses which he would not hesitate to use against them later. The dream at once rang a bell with the other members of the family, who said they too had felt something of the same fear about their father but had not been able to articulate it; a younger boy said he had privately opted out of the obligation to share confidences because of this fear. When the dream was discussed in the family group, the father promised to watch his behavior for signs of recrimination and moral judg-

* By "encounter" I mean to attempt to express feelings openly and honestly in an atmosphere of acceptance. I am not concerned here with the exercises practiced in organized encounter groups.

ment, and gave the children full permission to point this out to him if they ever felt their openness was being abused again.

The dream often acts as a vehicle which transmits hidden feelings from one individual to another, and I have come across couples who play the "dream game" in much the same way as other people play tennis. One person has a dream, drops it into his partner's court, and awaits the return shot. I call these games "dream duets," a kind of nonverbal communication carried on between two people below the level of waking consciousness, reflecting thoughts, feelings, and fears about each other which might not otherwise become available. I recently received a letter from a man who had attended some of my early dream-study groups with his wife, telling me that such a dream duet has been responsible for their decision to separate. They had been married for seven years when the husband, Sam, started having girlfriends. Lucy, his wife, was very naturally upset, but when it became clear that there was nothing much she could do about it short of breaking the marriage, she opted for an honest relationship in which Sam would keep her informed of his affairs. She also extracted from him the promise not to bring girlfriends to their home when she was away on a job of work (which happened fairly frequently at that time). Sam agreed, as he had no wish for a separation.

At first, the arrangement seemed to work fairly well, with Lucy's becoming increasingly interested in Sam sexually, although she still continued to express hurt and anger when he told her about his affairs. After a while, however, Sam began to lose interest in women and became quiet and morose. Then he had a series of dreams which explained his change of mood. In some of these dreams he would find himself with a woman, looking in vain for somewhere to make love, or being interrupted in the middle of lovemaking, or suddenly finding himself performing sexually in a roomful of people. In one dream a girl led him to a tent, and as they lay down together inside it, he noticed that the canvas was transparent. All these dreams made it quite clear that Sam found his new "public" sex life inhibiting and "castrating," and he blamed Lucy for imposing the rules of honesty upon him, even though her suggestion had seemed reasonable when she first made it. He also realized that he resented the promise not to take his girlfriends home, and admitted to her that he found this an unnecessary restriction as she was away from home a good deal. When the meaning of his dreams became clear to him, he accused Lucy of deliberately trying to thwart his extramarital affairs with her seemingly harmless rules and regulations.

Lucy denied any conscious intention of spoiling things for him, insisting that she really believed an honest relationship was vital to keep the marriage alive under such difficult conditions, much as she disliked hearing about his beastly affairs. Her next dream, however, showed that this was not a true statement of her position. In it, she and several other naked women were chained to a wall of a dungeon and a man stood in front of them running a kind of electrified rod up and down their bodies. This rod dispensed electric shocks which she found extremely painful, but also, against her will, sexually exciting. The dream made it clear that neither she nor Sam were right about her underlying motives for suggesting the honest relationship; the truth, at least in part, lay in the fact that hearing about her husband's affairs excited her sexually and added spice to her rather dull relationship with him.

They decided to continue the honest relationship, feeling that they could not put the clock back, and Sam had another dream in which he and Lucy were running to catch a train to the Vale of Evesham in the west of England. Sam jumped aboard just as the train was about to depart and put out his hand to help Lucy into the compartment. Instead of taking it, she started handing him suitcases and parcels, which he dumped on the seat, at the same time calling to her to leave them and get on the train. He was puzzled in the dream to know where they came from, as they had no luggage when they were running for the train. Lucy took no notice and the train left the station without her. Sam then realized that it was not going to the Vale of Evesham at all, but to "Freebourg."

Looking at the dream as a picture and taking full responsibility for its contents, Sam realized that he had come to the point where he wanted to leave Lucy behind and travel alone. He associated the suitcases and parcels with all the possessions and responsibilities, like mortgages and insurance, which Lucy had saddled him with since the first, early, carefree days of their marriage. Sam recalled how he had often referred to Lucy in those days as Eve, the sexual temptress, which explained why they were going to the Vale of Evesham in the dream: his "Eve" had become a "sham," tempting him into the marriage trap and using him for her own purposes. The train he really wanted to take was to Freebourg, which to Sam meant "freedom," but his dream self realized that even if he succeeded, he would still be landed with all the "suitcases" of responsibility and financial commitments he had accumulated during his years with Lucy.

Naturally, this dream upset Lucy, who responded with her own dream view of the situation, in which she and Sam had taken a sleeper to the Deep South in America. She suddenly realized that they had not paid for this journey and had no tickets. Fearing that the authorities would prosecute them, she said to Sam, "Let's just go back to sleep and see how far we can get before they find out, and then we'll tell them that we overslept our destination." Then she realized they had no tickets for any destination, and as they sped further and further south through Georgia, she became frantic with worry about the price they could not possibly afford to pay at the other end.

Lucy interpreted the journey to the Deep South as the exploration of the psychic depths she and Sam were making by means of dreams—in fact, she associated "Georgia" with the unconscious mind, which, for some reason of her own, she often referred to as "George." The dream was telling her that she had embarked on a journey for which she was not prepared to pay. When she and Sam had first embarked on their dream explorations, she had been convinced that the enterprise would bring them closer together, but when it became clear that it was hurtling them toward separation, she panicked because she felt her emo-

276

tional resources were inadequate to meet this contingency. The price of truth was too high, and she would never have set out on this journey had she known its sad conclusion. Knowing that she could not get off the train, however, she sought to deny the truth by trying to "turn a blind eye" to the realization that she and Sam should have parted long ago—they had indeed "overslept their destination."

A series of further dreams in which she tried to telephone Sam but could get no reply corroborated her intuition that any real communication between them had been severed. The dreams were articulating her feeling that she could not "get through" to him anymore.

In the final dream of the duet before they parted, Sam dreamed that a spacecraft landed, bringing the message that Lucy was dead. He woke up grieving, but he knew enough about dreams to recognize that it was telling him what he already knew but did not want to admit even to himself—that his original feeling for Lucy had ceased to exist. Both of them had been resisting the knowledge that they would survive better apart, and this dream convinced them that they must separate. Sam wrote in his letter to me that although they had both found this difficult at first, they had managed to make the transition amicably and were, in fact, much happier as friends living their own separate lives than they had been as husband and wife, vainly trying to live up to each other's expectations and demands. Like many other couples, their particular combination of qualities served not to promote mutual growth, but to strangle it.

I am not suggesting that people should decide on drastic measures like separation, a new job, or any other reversal of habit purely upon the messages thrown up by their dreams; what I am suggesting is that dreams can make us aware of a problem, and so lead us to tackle it sooner than we might otherwise have done. As I have already said, my own marriage would have been brought to its inevitable conclusion much sooner than it was, with much avoidance of misery and time-wasting recrimination, had I taken sufficient notice of my dreams.

And indeed, dreams can not only help to terminate relationships that are past repair, but can also strengthen those which resentments and dissatisfactions have been undermining below the level of conscious awareness, as I have already described in previous chapters. Very often when these subterranean destructive forces are brought to light and discussed openly, a mutual give-and-take solution can be found. Moreover, such relationships usually recover vitality because the couples find a new authentic way of being with each other.

My final suggestion on the domestic front is that housewives form small groups among themselves to share their dream experiences and the problems they reveal. Many women in our society have been brainwashed into thinking that their life energy must be devoted solely to the home and children, when in fact they could be doing more creative work in the larger world beyond their own front gardens. Time and time again, when housewives act out their dreams along Gestalt lines in the group, we hear the scolding voice of topdog (derived from mother, women's periodicals, and even husband) squashing a feeble underdog who protests weakly that housework, baby minding, and bed are not enough. I am not suggesting that dream power among housewives will immediately result in hordes of dissatisfied and unfulfilled women rushing out to work, though this may often be a highly desirable solution. The point is that dreams often give us clues about the ways in which our repressed energies may best be used, which for many women may still be in or around the home, for example, in reading, writing, painting, teaching, and even running dream-study groups! After all, the age of leisure is approaching fast when even men will be freed from work to "do their own thing," and what could be more constructive than using dreams to discover just what that "thing" is?

DREAM POWER IN THE CHURCHES

Outside the home, the most obvious milieu for the use of dream power is that provided by churches and other religious organizations, for these are society's traditional guardians of the inner life. In my view, the decline in the influence of religious organizations in the Western world over the past century has been the result not so much of theological doubts arising from science, or anything of that sort, as of the organized religions' failure to provide any really practical help to people seeking better understanding of themselves and their problems. It may indeed be significant that during this period the age-old connection between religion and dreams has been scorned by most Western religious organizations.

Today, however, religious leaders everywhere are beginning to wake up to the situation and explore new avenues of activity, particularly along psychological lines. Many have begun to take professional training in the art of psychological counseling alongside their normal training, and in this way have become interested in the Freudian and Jungian approaches to dreams; but I believe dream power might be used much more extensively in the life of the church than has hitherto been contemplated.

In a recent article in the London *Times*, a leading Anglican clergyman, the Reverend Joseph McCulloch, maintained that the clue to the renewal of the churches must be the replacement, or at least supplementation, of formal prayer and worship by dialogue and discussion. He found an enormous interest when he introduced these instead of sermons in the two London churches where he works, and he reported in his article that the discussions almost invariably revolve around questions of "man's inner life, of his integrity, nature, destiny and purpose, of the interior wisdom which enables the individual to understand himself or herself more deeply, and to go more effectively about the problems of living. What is clearly expected of the parson is an inside knowledge of human life, and, because of that an *ars spiritualis*, a skill and technique in diagnosing and coping with the problems of individual personality."

What better way for church leaders to gain at least some of this vast knowledge expected of them by their congregation than through the study of dreams, and I suggest that dream-study groups be conducted along the lines I have described, either in the leader's home or in the church building itself, which all too often remains empty for most of the time. These groups should consist, in the first instance, of the church leader and certain close members of his congregation—but in such groups the priest will have to be a genuine, wholehearted participant, not the aloof interpreter he might be encouraged to be if he approaches the use of dreams along the lines of professional psychoanalytic counseling. In fact, one of the issues that is likely to come up in such dream discussions is the way regular members of the congregation really feel about their priest, which may not always be flattering. At the same time, he too may discover things he did not know about his own feelings for certain members of his flock, and these must be shared with them if authentic communication is to be made. As Joseph McCulloch stresses, the parson must come out into the open and not take refuge behind the structures of doctrinal formulae, or the stock answers of orthodoxy.

How many are prepared to do so? My own feelings on the attitude of the clergy toward new ideas was made clear to me in a dream which I shall share with Dr. John Robinson, former Bishop of Woolwich, for his comments when we next meet. In the dream he and I stood facing each other trying to make contact with our stomachs, but we were somehow out of rhythm so that each time I thrust out my stomach, he drew his back. We managed to bump each other once or twice, but then he started to look very embarrassed, and muttering something about a very interesting exercise, shook hands with me very formally and disappeared.

The dream revealed to me in splendid picture language my feelings of failure at being unable to make contact with the clergy at "gut" level, a type of communication that I feel they fear and that embarrasses them on account of its apparent indignity; the formal "handshake" of cold impersonality is more in their line. I must add that Dr. Robinson is absolved from all personal responsibility in sparking off my dream, for at the time it occurred I had not seen him for many months. He obviously symbolizes for me the group of "new theologians" who seemed to offer the church a new lease of life in their early days, but whose emotional resources I now fear to be inadequate for the task.

I hope my dream is wrong about this and that some clergy at least will take up the challenge to experiment along the lines of dream-study and encounter groups. If they do, they will find that their exhortations to love and forgiveness might become a whole lot more effective than they are at present. In the preceding chapters, I have quoted several examples from my own group members whose lives were in serious trouble because they were trying to be unselfish and forgiving without really knowing what they were doing. Joanna, who believed she had forgiven her husband his affair, dreamed of killing him with a hatchet (page 190) and is probably typical of a great many people who on the surface see the merits of the Christian idea of forgiveness, yet have no idea how to carry it out. Jack, who dreamed of the spider sapping his bodily energies (page 233), and Peter who dreamed of the pagan monarchs burning Christians (page 241), were both suffering in their own ways from the problem of misplaced conscience, which is a very common thing indeed. I myself was led through dreams to a complete reassessment of my former rejection of religion (page 266), and while writing this book I had another dream which seems to me an ideal illustration of the way in which dream power may be used in resurrecting the dry bones of theology to a new life.

It was the last of a series of dreams in which I was always hungry and could not find anything to eat. My associations led to a hidden worry about future lines of research on dreams now that my first ideas about the use of dreams had been formulated and presented; I desperately needed more "food for thought" on this subject, and it was not forthcoming. Then I dreamed that I was attending a party given by Timothy Beaumont, an Anglican clergyman who gave up the professional ministry for politics and later received a peerage for his services to the Liberal Party, thereby becoming Lord Beaumont of Whitley. I was ravenously hungry in the dream and was greatly looking forward to the arrival of some food, but when it appeared hundreds of hands seemed to reach out and clear the plates before I could get anywhere near it. Then, as I stood alone, feeling totally deprived and wondering what to do, Tim himself appeared with an enormous plate of gorgeous food, which he gave to me with a smile. And I woke up smiling because I knew the dream was telling me that "the Lord will provide."

And He did, for there followed a series of remarkable new dreams, which I describe briefly in the next chapter and which provided me with ideas for futher dream power—as a channel through which we may actually receive these influences of creative inspiration which mankind has traditionally associated with the divine.

DREAM POWER IN THE EDUCATIONAL SYSTEM

Religion may well be the most convenient context in which to insert the thin end of the wedge of dream power into the world of education, where the plea of lack of spare time will certainly be encountered if anyone suggests adding anything new to the curriculum nowadays. In Britain, where classes on religion and morning assemblies of a religious character are still a compulsory part of the school curriculum, a great deal of experiment is currently being carried on to make both occasions more meaningful and interesting, in contrast to the dreary formalities they were in my own schooldays. With the world scene becoming increasingly part of every child's background through television, and growing numbers of immigrant children from non-Christian countries, it has become widely accepted that religious-education classes must encompass wider fields than the old-fashioned teaching of the Bible. There is also agreement that discussion should form a major part of such classes, with a strong emphasis on the relevance of religious principles of all kinds to the practical issues of life. Here, the discussion of dreams could be used in much the same way as I have already suggested for the churches.

This is a subject to which John Wren-Lewis has devoted

much space in his recent book *What Shall We Tell the Children*, setting out in detail a scheme for discovering what various religious ideas really mean to teachers and children alike, making particular use of the Gestalt dialogue approach to allow an individual's conscience, or his image of Jesus or God, to "speak for themselves." Dream discussion could fit readily into such a scheme.

School assemblies, whether supposedly religious as in Britain or civic as in many other countries, are notoriously dull occasions, yet there is no doubt that some such event is valuable in focusing the life of the school group. Many schools are currently experimenting with new forms of assembly in which the children themselves are allowed much more participation than the old-fashioned hymn singing, by getting a group of volunteers each day to "do their thing" for the rest of the school—singing songs, reciting their own poems, reading items from the press or books that strike them as significant, and so on. Here again it seems to me that there might be an occasion to introduce dreams, for example by devoting the assembly on certain days to a group discussing and acting out a dream along the lines I have described. Of course, such an event might well lead to some startling revelations of what the pupils (and the teachers) really feel toward school life, but I believe that such a start to the day would be highly therapeutic.

I believe school life is in desperate need of a great deal more emphasis on emotional education, and it is a sign of our distorted social values that anyone should say the curriculum is too overloaded with academic work to allow for it. What does it profit a society to send its children to universities if they have nervous breakdowns when they get there, as more and more students are doing? What is the use of teaching children to think if their whole lives are going to be bedeviled by inability to get in touch with, understand, and cope with their emotions?

In practical terms, I would like to see such experiments as having every class begin each day with an hour's open "class encounter" along the lines of the family group I described earlier, with the teacher and pupils sharing and discussing grievances and appreciations. Dream work could easily be incorporated into this schedule, giving a good start to a day which will almost certainly be primarily devoted to events of the external world. Both teachers and pupils should share their dreams if they are relevant to their mutual relationship, and often the teacher will be able to help a child with a family problem which comes to light in a dream.

In higher education, dream discussions should in my view form a regular part of general studies classes, and here could play an important part in helping students discover their real feelings about possible future careers by articulating their feelings about certain kinds of work.

I believe that if children in schools and students at university were allowed to express themselves freely in encounter or discussion groups with their teachers and professors, many of the destructive student riots—caused mainly by the rigidity of an outmoded power structure at high levels—might be avoided.*

DREAM POWER IN BUSINESS AND GOVERNMENT

If it is a dangerous illusion that education can afford to neglect the emotional side of the personality, it is an even more dangerous illusion that it can be neglected in the workaday world, for here the decisions people make affect not only themselves but often vast numbers of other people. If a production foreman is too preoccupied with personal worries to watch his plant properly, or a soldier too afraid of his superior to tell him some truth that threatens one of his pet theories, whole populations can suffer. Of course, we try to design systems with safeguards against this kind of thing, but ultimately no system can be better than the people who compose it, and accordingly no system can afford to neglect the fact that its employees are not

* School and university teachers interested in these ideas should read *Human Teaching for Human Learning* by George I. Brown (Viking press, 1971).

robots but human beings with feelings and problems. Attention to psychological issues in industrial and government organizations is not just a matter of "staff welfare"; it is an integral part of the proper running of the organization, and we have now reached a stage of industrial development where it will be sheer madness for our society not to recognize this, since the consequences of mistakes can be so catastrophic.

Modern industrial psychology has begun to recognize this to some extent, notably with Douglas McGregor's studies showing that people's motivation in modern industrial life is rarely just the wish to earn more money, but is governed by the whole complex of their personal relationships with the others in the work organization. So far, however, the progress in getting those who manage our governmental or industrial concerns to approach their work and their organization with psychological understanding has been very slow. T-groups and sensitivity methods have begun to establish themselves in management training in some large organizations, but the insights they give are still generally regarded as something of a luxury for the softhearted, apart from the fact that the underlying motive is usually one of trying to adjust the employee to the status quo instead of changing the organization to suit human beings.

I believe it would be highly therapeutic and educational for the whole community if encounter groups involving dream work were to be used in industry and the business world generally on a regular basis. As John Wren-Lewis has pointed out, fantastic amounts of time are wasted in game playing in order to skirt round feelings of jealousy, fear, worry, guilty, ambition, frustration, need for respect, and so on, and it is *this* time which could well be put to more constructive purposes like group work.

One of my own group members, Helen, reported an amusing dream in which a useless piece of office game-playing was exposed. In it, she was sitting at her desk typing in the office when an alarm bell sounded. Immediately, everyone in the office jumped up, including herself, ran blindly around the room waving their arms, bumping into each other and the furniture, opening and closing filing cabinets, milling out into the corridor and back again, and generally giving an impression of total chaos and panic. The commotion ceased just as suddenly as it began, and she found herself sitting quietly at her desk. Then another alarm bell sounded and the same thing happened, except this time she seemed to have more freedom of choice and ventured out of the office, curious to know where the bell was and who was ringing it. After much exploration, she discovered that it came from the sales manager's office and he rang it every time the managing director approached his department.

Helen said the dream articulated for her very clearly the feeling of panic which seemed to pervade the office whenever the sales manager entered and wanted something done, whereupon all work apparently had to cease to deal with it. The truth of the matter was that one person was quite capable of dealing with it quietly and efficiently, but the whole office had learned to carry out this useless ritual of seeming busyness in order to reassure the manager that it was receiving full attention. The dream also revealed Helen's feeling that the manager himself was ruled by fear of his own superior, which, she added, was quite unrealistic as this man often stopped by to chat with his employees about personal things and was in no sense a game player. We asked Helen if she would be willing to share her dream with the sales manager, and after much thought she did. She found the result astonishing, because instead of firing her, which was certainly a possibility, the manager completely opened up and realized that not only was he trying to impress his superior but also subtly reproach him for what he himself considered an irresponsible attitude toward the running of a business organization. Since then, he and Helen have been conducting their own private encounters, including dreams, but have not yet found it possible to extend them further. We all felt it was a good beginning.

My own experience confirms Hall's finding that dreams like these, which actually feature the work situation itself, are relatively rare, but when groups of people work closely

286

together, as a board of directors does, or the officers in a military establishment, their relationships with one another are part of their personal lives as well as matters of business, and are reflected in their dreams. For example, Harry, a businessman in my group, had a dream in which a fellow director, Jones, was going through the office with a hypodermic syringe giving everyone an injection for some unspecified health purpose. When Harry's turn came, the injection made him lose consciousness, and as he grew weaker and weaker until he felt he was dying, he put out his hand for help and felt it grasped by Jones, who said reassuringly, "Don't worry, lad, I'll do my best to pull you around."

This dream articulated for Harry an unease he had felt about Jones for some considerable time without knowing why. Jones was what John Wren-Lewis has so aptly called the "Big Daddy" of the firm, who always encouraged the staff, including his fellow directors, to come to him for help in sorting out all their personal problems and office worries, and had more than once reproached Harry for not doing so. The dream showed clearly Harry's feeling that Jones' benevolence was not wholly genuine and that what Jones was actually doing was knocking people down in order to pick them up, by issuing new regulations which he knew would upset some people, by dropping hints of impending changes, bits of personal gossip, and so on, and then sorting out for his victims the anxieties and insecurities he himself had caused. Harry saw Jones playing what is really a very subtle power game, deliberately designed to make people dependent on him. I do not know in this case how much the dream reflected a genuine perception of Jones' character or how much a purely irrational feeling on Harry's part, but the game is such a common one that I feel there is probably at least a germ of truth in it. Had Harry been able to share his dream with Jones, which he did not, there may have followed an extremely interesting dream duet along the lines I described earlier, leading to a progressive clarification of a relationship which was obviously having a profound effect on the running of a major business.

It seems essential to me for us to find more ways in the future of bringing dream power to bear directly on our work lives, instead of trying to pretend that this part of our existence belongs to some quite separate, impersonal life-scene into which our emotions do not enter. And to consider it a frivolity or luxury is in my view merely another indication of the false priorities in our society. As John Wren-Lewis points out, businessmen or government officials who constantly squash such ideas by declaring, "This is not a charitable institution," are actually playing the game of "Tough Guy" to impress each other. "Industry and commerce," he writes, "would often run more efficiently if it were quite consciously operated as something rather like a charitable institution . . . because the highest productivity comes from people who work together willingly in an atmosphere of mutual trust."

DREAM POWER IN PSYCHOTHERAPY

Dream power is, of course, familiar to every professional psychotherapist, but I believe the new ideas which have been developed over the past decade or so could bring new life into the all-too-often claustrophobic conditions of the consulting room. In particular, Perls' technique of acting out a dream can be of enormous value in putting the patient directly in contact with his feelings. Many Jungians already use the similar technique of "interior dialogue," but I feel that Perls has improved on this by bringing *the body* into the picture and making us aware of posture, gestures, and expressions as we act out a situation. He also, I think, provided us with a rather simpler working model for exposing and integrating opposites into the personality.

In my experience, Freudians are reluctant to use techniques of this sort because they involve active intervention on the part of the therapist, which they feel would destroy the "transference," an unreal relationship in which the analyst tries to remain as impersonal as possible so that the patient will use him as a blank screen and project all his fantasies onto him. In my view, this lack of real emotional contact between the patient and the therapist does more harm than good. In my own case, for example, it set up a vicious circle around which I and my analyst chased for years, with me accusing him of behaving like a bloody brick wall and him reproaching me for treating him like one!

While I do not deny that the transference can be useful for certain kinds of people under certain conditions, I feel that it is very often a game thrust on the patient by the analyst who harbors the catastrophic expectation that his authority will immediately disappear from him the moment he participates in the therapy as a human being. In fact, the opposite is the case, and I am reminded here of the delightful story told by Jung of the time he and Freud were analyzing each others' dreams. Freud recounted one of his dreams to Jung, who said that he could not interpret it without further personal details of Freud's life. Freud refused on the grounds that he could not risk his authority. "At that moment," wrote Jung, "he lost it altogether," and the moral of this story should be borne in mind by all therapists with similar catastrophic expectations.

It is a constant problem in therapy to get the patient really in touch with his feelings. So often he merely talks about his life and problems without *experiencing* any emotion at all, which every therapist knows is useless from the point of view of personal growth and change. It is absolutely no use the therapist interpreting the patient's words from the head of the couch in terms of "You are angry about . . . ," or "You feel your mother didn't love you . . . ," unless the patient actually experiences those feelings himself. As Walter Bonime stresses, "The patient must contact his feelings; he must palpate them, sense them out, feel his feelings with his feelings," for only then does he discover the profound emotions lying beneath his intellectualizing and placid exterior.

Bonime encourages his patients to talk about their feelings *with their feelings* and to use the kind of vocabulary in the consulting room that they would use in everyday life. For example, he notes that patients have a habit of talking about "my behind" when they usually call it "my ass," "defecating" when they normally refer to "taking a crap," and report "having relations with a girl" when what they actually did was "screw." Bonime suggests that the analyst help the patient get himself into focus on the couch by suggesting that he grope openly, forgetting considerations of style, for the first words that occur to him and try to use the language and inflections of his everyday relationships. The Gestalt technique automatically achieves this objective, for when we act out a situation or dream instead of merely talking about it, we cannot help but speak in our normal manner, and feelings rise to the surface with the words, often startling us with their vehemence and strength.

Bonime also talks about the advantages of collecting a personal glossary for each patient, which is a kind of shorthand language for describing personality traits in symbolic form. I have found from my group work that the Gestalt technique of isolating topdog and underdog is particularly useful in providing such a shorthand language. For example, whenever Joseph's wife finds her husband procrastinating over a decision, she asks, "Is it really a difficult decision requiring lots of thought, or is it old 'Slowcoach' up to his tricks again?" Jack, who dreamed of the spiders spoiling his sex life, will sometimes report to the group, "The spiders got at me again," and whenever Clare feels that Peter is neglecting her, she reminds him that she is not a pagan queen but a human being in need of love and attention. In my own case, when I refuse help with some task or criticize people for not standing on their own two feet, I often get asked, "Is that Ann or the ray of white light speaking?," a question which has often brought me to my senses and put me in touch with my real feelings. (All these dreams are described in Chapter 10.) The Gestalt techniques seem to me an invaluable way of arriving at this kind of shorthand language, which is a picturesque and economical method of communication.

In the course of writing and lecturing about dreams, I often quote examples of interpretations we have made in our dream groups. I am rarely allowed to escape a barrage of well-meaning alternative interpretations, especially from analysts and therapists in terms of their own preconceived or idiosyncratic theories. The Freudians on the whole are pretty predictable: "I can't help thinking that your ex-husband's dream of your 'erecting' a modern church on a piece of wasteland referred to castration fears caused by your attempt to substitute a penis for the female genitals," or, "In my experience, I invariably find that being on board ship refers to sexual intercourse"—and so on. The Jungians tend to be more complicated and mystical, and have produced such contributions as, "I feel that Joseph identified with the 'Slowcoach' inside because he didn't want to reach the *King's Cross*," presumably implying some form of symbolic crucifixion.

I always listen carefully to alternative interpretations and welcome constructive suggestions and criticisms, which I put before the dreamer later if he is still a member of my group. But my usual answer is that the dream is the property of the dreamer, a unique production arising out of his own vast network of memories and associations, and, in the end of the day, is meaningful in whatever way he himself finds most useful. If a critic is persistent, I say to him, "That's *your* trip; don't put it onto me," and I often amuse the audience by asking them to interpret the interpretation in terms of the critic's own personality and problems!

I also remind psychotherapists of the book *Dream Interpretation* (from which I have already quoted) by a psychoanalyst, Thomas French, and a psychologist, Erika Fromm, who criticize their professional colleagues for using what they call the "Procrustean bed" technique of dream interpretation, which consists of taking from their patients' dreams the parts that fit nicely into their theory and ignoring the rest. To French and Fromm, an interpretation is not complete until the *whole* dream has been considered (along the lines of Hall's method of looking-at-the-dream-as-a-picture plus associations) and the various parts fitted together like pieces of a jigsaw puzzle. "We try to let our interpretations shape themselves out of the colorful words and vivid analogies which the patient himself uses. Instead of letting our theories influence our interpretations, we hope, rather, to use our interpretive procedure as an ever-renewed check on our theories"—a warning which no psychotherapist can afford to ignore.

I never thrust an interpretation on my students, and this is not just a self-denying ordinance. Often when I thought I had a pretty clear inkling of what the dream might mean before we have actually worked on it, I have had to change my mind before the end. I have constantly to remind myself that any theory I might form is what the dream would mean to *me* and *I* dreamed it, but that it need not mean the same thing to the dreamer. "Don't push the river," wrote Perls, of life generally and one's own effort in particular; "it flows by itself." I have made this the golden rule of dream interpretation, and I believe it is every dreamer's right to insist on it. Psychotherapists above all should live by the old American Indian adage "Respect your brothers' dreams."*

* Since I wrote this chapter, Bill Schutz's remarkable book *Here Comes Everybody* has been published with concrete suggestions for open encounter groups in therapy, education, religion, business, and politics and "scenarios" of possible group sessions that might take place in 1984 involving top people. He even goes so far as to write a scenario for an encounter group between the Presidents of the United States and the Soviet Union. I strongly recommend this entertaining and insightful book, which exemplifies the same principle of self-disclosure in authorship as I have been trying to adopt.

CHAPTER 12

BEYOND THE THIRD STATE

Because it is every dreamer's right to insist on the reality of his own dream experience, and not to allow anyone else to explain it away, I am sure we must take seriously those rare but remarkable dreams which seem to be something more than a reflection of our everyday lives and conflicts. I have tried in this book to be very down-to-earth about dreams, because my own studies have confirmed the general finding of dream research since 1953, that the vast majority of dreams are of this nature, and I have shown that such dreams can perform a very important service for us by bringing us more into touch with ourselves and with the myriad processes that are taking place all the time just below the surface of conscious awareness. My conviction is, however, that precisely in so far as we learn to use our ordinary dreams in this way, the resulting growth of self-awareness is likely to open up other, more mysterious aspects of dream life which have attracted attention in the past because of their rarity. So I believe that as society makes more use of dream power in the coming years along the lines I have described, we shall find that this third state of existence has other kinds of power also, leading beyond itself to the expansion of human consciousness in ways un-dreamed of in most present-day philosophy.

DREAMS OF CREATIVE INSPIRATION

The dream stories which have attracted most attention in the past few centuries have been those in which a great creative inspiration came during sleep or reverie—Coleridge's *Kubla Khan*, Otto Loewe's theory of the chemical transmission of nerve impulses, Kekulé's vision of a snake swallowing its own tail which gave him the clue to the ring structure of benzene, the gynecologist who discovered how to tie a surgical knot deep in the pelvis with his left hand, and similar cases. I believe this phenomenon, at present so rare as to be remarkable, will become much commoner as we learn to clear our minds of the neurotic blocks that sap their energies. Anxiety is the enemy of creativity, and until this is removed, our minds will not be free to deal creatively with all the material that enters it during waking life. As the psychoanalyst Lawrence Kubie has shown in his book *Neurotic Distortion of the Creative Process*, it is a complete misapprehension to suppose that artistic creativity arises from an underlying neurosis; some artists are certainly neurotic, but their creativity functions *in spite of* emotional hang-ups, not because of them.

Most of us may never be destined to write great music or poetry or to produce major inventions or scientific theories, but I am sure we all have great resources of creative talent which at present fust in us unused because we spend so much of our mental energy on unnecessary psychological conflicts and destructive game-playing relationships. My experience suggests that as we learn to use dream power to free ourselves from at least some of these vicious circles, we shall find more and more instances of our dreams' throwing up creative inspirations, even if only relatively minor ones.

Such inspirational dreams do not necessarily imply anything more miraculous about the sleeping mind than some of the mechanisms I have already discussed earlier in the book. Creative inspiration never comes out of the blue; like grace, it comes only to the prepared mind which has already gathered together a whole host of relevant facts, impressions, and ideas.* The moment of inspiration often occurs in waking life, when everything suddenly seems to link together in a new and significant pattern, usually when the mind is relaxed, and it may be that similar inspirations which come to light in dreams are not *products* of the sleeping mind at all, but have already been formed at the back of the mind during the day, only to lie unnoticed beneath the background chatter until sleep intervenes.

On the other hand, there may actually be a process of integration and pattern exploration going on during the dream period itself, but either way, I do not think we need invoke special explanations other than those involved in the very uncanny kind of "unconscious detective-work" about everyday situations described in Chapter 8.

LEARNING TO MANIPULATE DREAMS

A more mysterious kind of dream power, which raises important philosophical and psychological problems about the precise nature of dreaming consciousness, is that in which we can take active steps to manipulate the contents of dreams by processes of deliberate suggestion while awake. I first encountered this possibility some years before I became a psychologist, when I belonged to a religious movement called the Infinite Way, founded by Joel Goldsmith, an American businessman who had become a healer somewhat along the lines of Christian Science. He taught us to deal with physical and psychological problems by "knowing the truth" about them, namely that they had no power over us unless we ourselves allowed it.

At the time, I had no great problems in waking life but

---

* Arthur Koestler's classic book *The Act of Creation* provides massive documentation of this process at work in many different areas of mental life.

often suffered from frightening dreams in which I was pursued by murderous strangers until I woke in terror as they cornered me. It occurred to me that whatever questions I might want to raise about the applicability of Goldsmith's philosophy to waking life, it might work in dreams, so I resolved before going to sleep each night that if my pursuers appeared, I would confront them with the challenge, "You have no power over me." Very rapidly, my dream self responded. Although I did not realize in the dreams that I was dreaming (a phenomenon I shall consider shortly), I found enough courage to turn on my pursuers, at first falteringly, but then with growing confidence as I found they were stopped in their tracks and either melted like Dracula before the cross or became friendly. After a while, these frightening dreams ceased altogether.

Several of my dream-group members have tried this exercise on nightmares with similar results. The mechanism involved is probably akin to that which occurs in the many experiments showing how dream content can be influenced by suggestions implanted by various means before going to sleep. I began to establish in my mind, by imaginative repetition, a program which dictated that when I was pursued by frightening strangers, I should turn on them with the words, "You have no power over me," whereupon this new program became involved with my dream programs that produced the frightening strangers.

There are two puzzling philosophical questions arising out of this experiment: how does the waking mind, which makes this resolve, know that it is *dream* strangers and not real ones I am meant to confront, and what is the relation between the dream self, which carries over the resolve from waking life, and the elements in the dreaming personality which actually produce the strangers? On the psychological plane, if we accept, as I am sure we must, that dream strangers after my blood are symbols of emotional forces in my own mind, what is the significance, in terms of my inner psychological balance, of my learning to confront them as *strangers in sleep* rather than to come to terms in waking life with the emotions producing them?

There seem to be two completely opposite possibilities. On the one hand, it may be that this kind of dream manipulation, however useful as a temporary expedient in dealing with nightmares, is treating the symptom rather than the real problem, postponing still further the day when we come to terms with some emotional conflict that has already been thrust aside in waking life. On the other hand, it may be that the process of suggestion sets in motion some process in the sleeping mind which actually alters the "circuitry" of the brain from which the monster-producing program comes, and that the person who learns to tackle a conflict at the symbolic level during sleep is thereby, without knowing it, actually dealing with the emotional conflict itself. I am sure this is a most important topic for future research, but I do not think we can begin to tackle it until we have become thoroughly versed in the more pedestrian aspects of dream power.

Some important data for research along these lines will come from the famous Senoi tribe of the Malay Peninsula, studied by Kilton Stewart as far back as 1935. This tribe, which has been described as the most democratic group in anthropological literature, and which claims to have had no violent crime or intercommunal conflict for hundreds of years, relies heavily on dream interpretation and manipulation for its psychological health. The Senoi believe that dream images are all part of the personality and consist of psychic forces disguised in external forms (like my dream strangers) and have no doubt that everyone should learn from childhood to master these internal forces. Children are taught that if hostile "spirits" are encountered in dreams, their task is not only to confront but actually to attack them, calling on friendly "dream spirits" (possibly healthy aspects of the personality) for help if they wish, but taking courage to fight alone until they arrive. Their belief is that if the dreamer kills the hostile dream-image, its spirit will always emerge as a servant or ally: dream characters, they say, are bad only as long as we are afraid of and retreat from them.

The Senoi also teach their children not to be afraid of falling dreams, but to let themselves go, whereupon they will find that the falling dream turns into a pleasurable flying dream. I have tried this experiment myself and it works. Kilton Stewart reports that over a period of time, with this kind of dream education, anxiety dreams among the Senoi become dreams of joy, and the effect on waking behavior seems to be very beneficial, since they are a delightfully peaceful people with a rich life of folk poetry, music, and dancing.

Indeed, they actually use their dream-manipulation techniques to stimulate their creative life. The Senoi children are taught that they must always try to return to waking life with some creative idea brought back from the land of the dream spirits. They are told that if they find themselves flying in a dream, they should try to fly *somewhere*, meet the spirits there, and bring back a dance, a poem, or some other creative act or idea. These ideas are shared with the rest of the tribe the following morning, which either accepts and uses them as part of its culture, or rejects them with a gentle admonition to the dreamer, to do better next time! I am sure we have much to learn from these people, and the whole question of dream manipulation is a fascinating subject for future research.

THE "LUCID" DREAM

The "lucid" dream is so called not because it is unusually vivid but because *the dreamer is aware at the time of dreaming that he is dreaming,* and feels himself to be in full possession of what we call normal waking consciousness while knowing himself quite certainly to be asleep in bed. This kind of dream is sometimes called a "dream of knowledge," which, in my view, is a more suitably dramatic title for what is undoubtedly a most dramatic phenomenon.

I have had several lucid dreams over the past few years, and so can testify to the experiential reality of the phenomenon. In one of them, I was chatting quite normally to my grandmother, when I suddenly realized she had been dead for many years. This realization made me aware that I must be dreaming, and I woke up. In another lucid dream, I had been killed by an air raid and found myself

298

with my companions "on the other side." I complained about a pain in my left arm, whereupon one of them rummaged in her bag, produced a bottle of tablets, and said that these would cure the pain. I suddenly burst out laughing, for I realized that I was dead and that pills were not much good for the "astral body," or whatever it may be. This was followed immediately by the thought, "Perhaps I'm not dead but dreaming," and as I pondered this mystery, I woke up.

Dreams like these, a whole host of which are documented in Celia Green's book *Lucid Dreams*, seem to show that at least on some occasions the dreaming mind has experiences which are not in any sense reflections of waking life. What exactly is the nature of this new type of dreaming consciousness, and what is the significance of any actions we might decide to take in the lucid dream once we have become aware that we are dreaming? One thing seems certain, namely that we have the power to change our dream world in ways which in waking life would be termed magical. For example, a member of my dream group reported one in which he found himself walking through a white, frozen landscape, shivering with cold. He thought how nice if it were spring, and in a flash realized he was dreaming and decided he would make it spring. Casting his glance over the snow and ice, he willed it to become green and warm, which it immediately did.

What exactly was he doing? Had the dream of a landscape change like this occurred without being lucid, I should have interpreted it along the lines described in this book, by saying that his hitherto emotionally frozen life was becoming warm, and I knew from his life at the time that this was indeed happening—but did he do anything to help it happen by his act of will in the dream? Or was he waving a magic wand, as it were, to avoid facing the coldness of his nature? Another student reported that whenever he experienced flying dreams, he immediately became aware that he was dreaming and was able to carry out acrobatic feats of great physical enjoyment in his new weightless dream body. Was this a creative or escapist act? Certainly a most interesting experiment would be to allow a dream to continue while remaining fully conscious that one is dreaming but not using this awareness to interfere. This would be rather like employing Jung's method of "active imagination" in the dream itself instead of evoking a fantasy to continue the dream after waking up. For example, if my first student dreamed again of a frozen landscape, it would be interesting if he allowed himself to continue his walk in the snow and ice and see where it led, while the second student might decide, like the Senoi, to fly *somewhere*, instead of merely indulging in acrobatic feats.

The investigation of these possibilities is an important part of the new line of research on which I have now embarked. I mentioned earlier having a series of dreams indicating a worry at the back of my mind that I might have run out of ideas for further research, at the conclusion of which came the dream of Lord Beaumont providing fresh food, which I interpreted as a reassurance from within that "the Lord will provide." What the Lord (or my creative unconscious, according to taste) actually provided was a series of lucid dreams which gave me the opportunity to investigate what effects may follow from deliberately trying to work on Jungian or Gestalt lines *in dreams themselves*. This will have to be the subject of a later book, but the first of these lucid dreams was so remarkable that I will quote it here.

It was sparked off by a conversation with a woman anthropologist friend the previous evening, who had heard one of my broadcasts and said she envied my ability to put over my ideas simply to the lay public; she said she could never bring herself to dilute her own ideas sufficiently to do this. At the time, I detected the implication that my efforts at popularization were not really academically respectable, but my conscious mind brushed this aside as sour grapes on her part. My unconscious, however, was evidently not so happy about it, since that night my dreaming mind confronted me with my own formidable academic topdog. (Professor Macbeth?)

I dreamed I was having dinner with a rather uptight group of psychologists when a woman across the table suddenly started recriminating with me for leaving the world of the academic elite and lowering my standards to those of the Sunday newspapers. I protested that this was an exaggeration, and that I believed the layman was entitled to at least some of our ideas, especially as he was paying for our research. At this, she literally spat across the table that I was bringing the whole profession into disrepute, that we must retain some vestige of authority, and so on. My fury rose to such a pitch that I had an irresistible desire to beat her up, and no sooner had I become aware of this desire than I realized with the utmost clarity that I was dreaming and could do exactly what I wanted because dream bodies cannot get hurt.

So, leaning across the table, I grabbed her by the hair, punched her face, and knocked her front teeth out. This inspired me to further violence and with an exhilaration I have never previously experienced, I dragged her onto the floor and began to beat up her body in the same way. Of course, she fought back, and I can still feel the slashing of her fingernails across my cheek and the kicks of what felt like hobnailed boots on my back. At last I detected the waning of her strength, and the fight was over. Then the scene changed, and I found myself in another room walking toward this woman, who was now transformed and wearing a nurse's uniform. As we approached each other, I reminded myself that I must not magically change the events of my lucid dream but allow them to happen spontaneously and observe the outcome. I noted that she was smiling now and that her front teeth were back in place. She then put out her arms to me in a friendly gesture, and we hugged each other.

I woke up with a great sense of well-being, as if my humanistic underdog had really made its protest against my academic topdog and brought about a Perlsian release of energy through new integration—and I felt it not just in my mind but throughout my whole body in a way that rarely happens in waking Perlsian dialogue, which is mainly a verbal procedure. This discovery of a "dream body" through which *physical* tension can be released without causing harm to anyone seems to be closely related to the ideas of the Senoi, and also echoes the ancient esoteric notion that lucid dreaming can provide a way into a "fourth state of existence" beyond sleep, in which the individual can build up a "psychic body" capable of transcending ordinary life. Here is a most exciting prospect for further exploration, and the first essential step in this particular area must be to see how far we can train ourselves in the capacity for lucid dreaming. This is something we have begun to study in our dream groups concurrently with our more down-to-earth concern with dreams as a means of clearing away life's blocks.

THE "HIGH" DREAM

Several years ago while still a student, I had a dream quite different in kind from any experience I had ever had before either asleep or awake. In it, I was standing on the veranda of my parents' house looking out at the garden, which was in full bloom. Suddenly, the whole garden became filled with a quite new kind of life. The flowers and trees literally pulsated with energy and radiated exotic color, and my own body seemed to join in the dance of nature. The experience seemed to last only a minute or two, and then the garden reverted to its normal very beautiful state, and I woke up. This remained a unique and extraordinary experience for me until much later when I took part in some experimental research on the psychedelic drugs, and realized that in some strange way, for a few moments, my brain must have got itself into a condition similar to that produced by LSD and mescaline, and to a lesser extent by cannabis.

One of the most remarkable effects of these drugs is to make scenes come alive with vibrant intensity which makes even the most beautiful landscape seem lifeless in comparison, and to give the observer a feeling of ecstatic participation in a vibrant life-dance. I had had what Professor Charles Tart in his book *Altered States of Consciousness* (which was not even published then) calls a "high" dream—but whereas he finds that they are usually reported only by people who have experience of the psychedelic

302

drugs in waking life, mine came before I had taken any. This opens up the fascinating possibility of training the mind to achieve this extraordinary ecstatic state without the use of drugs at all.

I had several high dreams during and after the period of my drug research, and the one I remember most vividly still remains somewhat of a mystery to me. In this dream, I found myself on a desert island with some friends when a storm blew up. As we stood and watched the lightning flash across the sky and the waves beating against the rocks, I thought, "I wish I had some acid now." My wish immediately became reality, and I reached a "high" in the dream. For a timeless moment, I danced, flashed, and roared with the storm and seemed to merge with the "being" at the center of it. On regaining normal consciousness in the dream, I turned to my friends and said, "You need acid to see the devil in the storm," and they nodded their comprehension. I woke up feeling exhilarated and joyful beyond belief, a feeling which remained with me for several days. Here again is evidence that the "high" state can be produced without drugs—in this case it was a *mental image* of LSD which succeeded in bringing about the ecstatic dream experience.

Perhaps certain kinds of dream, including the high dream, should not necessarily be valued only in terms of any psychological insight or creative inspiration we might bring back from them to waking life, but also as *experiences in their own right*. For why should not our dream life, like our waking life, contain experiences that are ends in themselves—like looking at beautiful landscapes or pictures, listening to music, talking to people, and making love—rather than merely means to something else? After all, nature has been generous with our dream time, and we can surely—in spite of our Protestant ethic—allow ourselves a little of that time for pure, unadulterated aesthetic pleasure.

The most remarkable dream of this kind I have experienced came my way long after I had completed my drug research, soon after "the Lord" had promised to provide me with new ideas. In it, I seemed to wake up, get out of bed, and wander around the room. Everything seemed perfectly normal, except that there was a large window on the inside wall, and this discrepancy made me aware that I was not really awake at all, but dreaming. Remembering my own advice to go along with such dreams without trying to manipulate things, I told myself to look out of the dream window, which I knew perfectly well did not exist in "reality," and experienced a certain sense of the ridiculous as I did so. To my astonishment, instead of looking through to my daughter's room as I expected, I found myself gazing across a vast green lawn completely covered with white daisies extending as far as the eye could see to what seemed like a bluebell wood beyond.

For a few moments, I was quite disoriented and felt I was standing at the window of one of England's beautiful stately homes set in gentle, green, semicultivated grounds. When at last I tore myself away from the window and turned around, my bedroom was exactly as it always is, and I wondered for a moment whether or not I really might be sleepwalking. Determining to make the most of my lucidity, I pummeled the bed in an attempt to discover whether it felt as substantial as it did in waking life—and it did. I then saw my husband asleep on my side of the bed, and wondered exactly what a human body might feel like in a dream. I shook him awake and found he felt quite normally warm and resilient. By this time, I was seriously wondering whether I was not actually awake and really waking him up, when I found myself curled up in bed alone knowing quite well that he had got up at least an hour before.

And then the most extraordinary feeling came over me. Surges of energy pulsated throughout my body and I entered a "high" in which I was completely transported on the kind of internal journey only those who have experienced psychedelic drugs would understand. I could actually feel my body being moved by this energy although I knew perfectly well that I was asleep. In the distance, I could hear the hammering of the builders in the basement, a dog barking in a neighbor's garden, and the distant sound of traffic. I was filled with an enormous compassion for the whole of mankind for not being able to share my strange and wonderful experience at that moment. Eventually, after what seemed like an eternity, I looked at my watch and discovered that I had fifteen more minutes of this exquisite state before my husband would awaken me with a cup of coffee.

At this moment, he entered the room with the coffee and I really woke up this time, knowing that I had dreamed the whole thing, including looking at my watch and getting a wishful estimate of the time. "The Lord" had provided me with a dream I have never heard described before—an extraordinary experience which I can only call a *lucid high dream*—opening up prospects for further research that are almost literally "out of this world." It seemed to me that history had been made that morning.

But "curiouser and curiouser" (as Alice said), when I reported this experience to my husband, he immediately left the room and returned with a piece of paper on which was written his own dream of the night. It had taken place approximately three hours before mine, and in it I had shaken him awake because he was sleeping on the wrong side of the bed and he noticed a window on the wrong wall. As he pondered this discrepancy, he really woke up and wrote down his dream.

Experiences like this seem to take us out of the ordinary world of comprehensible events to an entirely new realm where, among other things, real extrasensory perception is possible. Can it be that ESP, so elusive in the laboratory, is connected in some way with unusual states of consciousness? And what do these altered states of consciousness tell us about ourselves, the world we live in, and the prospects for more abundant life? My present research is geared toward finding an answer to at least some of these questions—but that, as Alice said, must be another story.

APPENDICES

APPENDIX A

HINTS FOR RECALLING AND RECORDING DREAMS

1. Always keep pen and paper—or better still, a tape recorder—by your bedside.
2. Make sure there is a dim light or flashlight you can switch on from the bed.
3. Suggest to yourself several times before falling asleep, "I shall awaken from a dream tonight," "I shall catch a dream tonight," or whatever suggestion along these lines appeals to you most.
4. Chronic nonawakeners or nonrecallers might like the additional help of the alarm-clock technique. Set the alarm—which must not be too strident—for approximately two hours after your normal falling-asleep time, and thereafter for every two hours during the night. You cannot guarantee awakenings during REM periods, but this way you are likely to get one or even two. If the idea of several awakenings during the night does not appeal to you, set the alarm for a time much later during your sleep period, as REM periods become longer as morning approaches, and in this way you have a very good chance of awakening from one, one hopes with a good dream in mind.
5. If you awaken during the night, either spontaneously or by means of the alarm clock, with a dream in mind, *very gently* sit up in bed and switch on the dim light. It is important not to jolt yourself too strongly into wakefulness, as this tends to obliterate the dream memory. (Some people find it useful to sit up in bed and run through the dream mentally with eyes closed before turning on the light.)
5. Immediately write down, or record into the tape recorder, the dream in as much detail as you can. Make every effort not to doze while doing this or your dream will disappear.

7. Add as many associations as you can—for example, what on first sight you think the dream may mean, events of the previous day which may have helped to spark it off, your feelings both during and immediately after the dream, and anything else you feel is important. It is surprising how useful these are when you come to work on the dream the following day.

8. If you awaken in the morning with a dream in mind, do not immediately leap out of bed thinking you will mull it over while getting ready for work. The odds are that you will lose it. Write down or record the dream while still in bed, and add any relevant associations as described above.

9. As soon as possible after the dream, preferably the following day, work on the dream in the way I have described in this book—first by checking it for objective facts you may have missed in waking life, then by treating it as a looking glass through which you see yourself and your life situation, and finally by acting it out along Gestalt lines in order to expose and integrate conflicting trends in your personality.

10. Keep your dreams plus their interpretations together in a folder or book, all clearly dated, as dream series can be very useful in throwing light on ambiguous dreams and in indicating inner psychological progress.

11. If your dreams still elude you, try the Gestalt method of asking them why they will not come to you, as described on page 152.

12. If this fails, try the waking-fantasy method to catch what is going on below the surface of the conscious mind, as described in Appendix B. If you persevere with this fantasy method, you will find that the stimulation of inner forces will gradually return your lost dreams to you.

APPENDIX B

WAKING FANTASY: A METHOD FOR THOSE WHO FIND IT DIFFICULT TO RECALL DREAMS

Set aside approximately half an hour for the following experiment during waking hours when you are unlikely to be disturbed. Relax on a chair or in bed and allow your mind to wander freely. If you have a tape recorder, speak your thoughts into it. Start with anything at all—a person or a situation of the day—and whenever a vivid image or fantasy arises record or write it down. The first image often turns out to be the most interesting one concerning some current conflict. I quote here an example from one of my dream-study groups.

Liz lies comfortably on the cushions on the floor, and begins,

> I am back in the countryside near my parents' home. The last time I was there, it was a lovely autumn day and I walked through the woods. I remember a tree whose trunk and roots looked so much like a gnarled old man that I almost stopped and talked to it.

I asked Liz to stop now and talk to the tree, and sitting up she said,

LIZ: Poor old tree. You look so perplexed and rather disapproving. Are you reproaching me for something?

TREE (*Moving to opposite cushion*): Well, not you exactly but you represent the people down there. It used to be so quiet and serene in these woods, but nowadays people come and spoil everything. And I notice that many of my old friends—the trees down there—have disappeared. What is happening to the world?

LIZ: There are many more people in the world then there used to be. They are moving out from the towns and encroaching on the country. They are building estates to live on. That's why your old friends have gone. They've been cut down to make room for houses. Maybe you'll be the next to go.

TREE: Oh, dear, oh dear. Whatever shall I do? I don't want to be cut down. I've stood here for hundreds of years. Can't you help me?

LIZ: Well, I don't know. If you weren't so firmly fixed in the earth, I could uproot you and plant you somewhere else because you're rather a nice old thing. But you go too deep. (*Pause.*) That's the trouble with people like you: you put your roots so firmly down in order to be safe, that you forget you'll gradually become immobile, and when danger like this threatens, you can't get up and go. (*Pause.*) You know all the religions of the world have warned against this—putting your values in the things of the earth. Now, if you were like me and had kept your roots *above* the earth, or at least very lightly placed in the earth, you would have been able to move when necessary. It's your own fault really, and I think you should accept your fate like a man.

Topdog is exposed and is lecturing underdog for having become too attached to earthly things. Liz, moving from cushion to cushion, continues:

TREE: But I'm a tree and it's my nature to put my roots firmly in the earth. You forget anyway that I'm in touch with the heavens. I also provide a nesting place for birds and food for insects . . . and I'm beautiful.

LIZ: Yes, yes we know all that. But people are more important than you, and if it came to a choice between housing, clothing, and feeding needy people or allowing you to live, I'm afraid I'd have to sacrifice you.

TREE: But people can't live without me. I convert carbon dioxide into oxygen so that you can continue to breathe. Remember what happened when you cut down the trees in Africa long ago—you got the Sahara Desert.

LIZ: I know, but we're more advanced now. We'll make a machine if necessary to provide oxygen—after all, they'll be doing it on the moon soon and there aren't any trees there. No, you'll have to go; man has to progress. We can't put the clock back.

TREE: I don't want to keep you back and I'd like to help you go forward. I'm sure I must have some place in your life while still remaining a tree. . . .

Underdog is putting up a very poor defense, and I asked Liz if he could not do any better. For instance, how about threatening topdog with something, rather than merely pleading for his existence. Liz thought for a moment, and then said:

I've just had a memory flash back to my first childhood home. My mother, my Aunt Elizabeth, and I are standing in the window overlooking the back garden at the bottom of which stands an enormous, beautiful tree. My aunt says we should cut it down because it spoils the view of the wider countryside behind it. I am filled with horror, because the tree is my best friend; I talk to it, hug it, and share all my secrets with it. I know when it is spring and when it is autumn by the color of its leaves. It is always surrounded by birds around its branches. It's always there when I look out of the window, unlike my friends, who keep moving away.

I rush out to the tree to warn it about my aunt and ask what we are to do, and it replies, "Don't worry, if anyone tries to harm me, I shall call down the whole of nature on his head. They forget that my roots spread wide beneath the earth and are in contact with a whole underworld of animal and insect life. The birds build their homes in my branches; they too will come to my rescue. And if necessary, I shall call upon the sun, wind, and storm to protect me from the ax. I've stood here in contact with the earth and the sky for hundreds of years, and I have hidden resources. If they try to cut me down, they will destroy themselves first."

This seemed to be the great breakthrough. It was interesting to the group that Liz had to go all the way back to childhood to discover the strength of the tree. Somewhere along the line between childhood and adulthood, Liz had lost this and had even reversed roles so far that she was now taking the part of her aunt Elizabeth (after whom she had been named). Liz interpreted her fantasy in terms of a conflict between a joyous, wholehearted participation in nature and physical life, which she had enjoyed in childhood, and her family's strict Christian upbringing, which insisted on the subjugation of body to spirit (yet another case of "flesh versus spirit" conflict caused by the inculcation of religious principles).

Although she had consciously rejected Christianity many years before, she still had doubts about the place of man's animal nature in life. She had subsequently substituted scientific and technological progress for spiritual progress, and continued to insist that man must move forward and not be held back by the demands of the flesh. At the time of the fantasy, it was clear that topdog was very much in charge of the situation and that underdog tree was in grave danger of despatch. The fantasy contained both a warning and an existential message: if Liz severs her contact with the earth, the whole of her "animal" and "elemental" nature will rise up against her and destroy her. But if she roots herself firmly in the earth—in the flesh—not only will she grow strong and beautiful like the tree, but she will also rise above the earth and touch the heavens with her fingertips.

The stimulus for the fantasy, like the stimuli of dreams, lay in an event of the day. That same morning Liz had been reading Alvin Toffler's best-selling book *Future Shock,* in which he draws a picture of mankind growing rapidly into an age of impermanence and transience where neither human relationships nor situations will remain stable for long periods of time. His thesis is that we cannot turn the clock back, that we must go forward with the technological revolution, learn to cope with the new conditions without traditional roots. Liz said he argued the case so well that she had to agree with him, and yet was left with a feeling of unease and loss. The book had obviously triggered off the voice of underdog-tree inside, who felt very threatened by Toffler's vision of the world. The fantasy could not have chosen a more apposite symbol for the strength and stability of the natural life than a tree, and in this respect is very similar to a dream. Of course, the message of the fantasy was to Liz and not to the world, but we all had a feeling that the world would do well to heed it if we are not to plunge to destruction by destroying our natural life in the future.

Other fantasies thrown up by group members who had difficulty in recalling dreams included a traffic warden sticking a fine notice on a car, a row between parents, and a memory of being on a roof and looking down on the house opposite. In the first fantasy, the traffic warden was the topdog, who refused to take responsibility for his punitive action, saying he was merely carrying out the orders of a higher authority. In the second fantasy, topdog-mother berated underdog-father for his weakness and passivity. In the third fantasy, although

the hippie-type young man began by "looking down on" the
comfortable, square, bourgeois family in the house opposite,
it soon became apparent that the family represented topdog in
this particular interest and wondered how many young people
who have rebelled against "straight" society are still struggling
to free themselves from the parents within.

However revealing some fantasies may be, they are still not
as good as dreams for making us aware of hidden feelings and
conflicts. In sleep, the prohibitions of waking consciousness
are relaxed and the mind goes free-wheeling along normally
uncharted pathways, whereas waking fantasy is of necessity
much more structured. Nevertheless, fantasy is a useful
substitute if dreams consistently elude capture and often has a
similar effect on a nonrecaller as an adopted baby has on a
mother who has been hitherto unable to conceive: in some
mysterious way, it stimulates the recall of dreams, probably
on account of the added attention being paid to the inner life.

BIBLIOGRAPHY

Books on Sleep and Dreaming

BONIME, WALTER, *The Clinical Use of Dreams.* New
York, Basic Books, Inc., 1962.

FRENCH, THOMAS, and FROMM, ERIKA, *Dream Interpretation: A New Approach.* New York, Basic Books,
Inc., 1964.

FREUD, SIGMUND, *The Interpretation of Dreams,* new
trans. by James Strachey. London, George Allen & Un-
win, 1954, 1961. New York, Basic Books, Inc., 1955.

FROMM, ERICH, *The Forgotten Language: An Introduction
to the Understanding of Dreams, Fairytales & Myths.*
New York, Holt, Rinehart and Winston, 1951, 1970.

GREEN, CELIA, *Lucid Dreams.* Oxford, Institute of
Psychophysical Research, 1968.

HALL, CALVIN, S., *The Meaning of Dreams.* New York,
McGraw-Hill Book Co., 1953, 1966.

HARTMANN, ERNEST, ed., *Sleep and Dreaming*. Boston, Little, Brown & Co., 1970. London, Churchill, 1970.

KRAMER, MILTON, ed., *Dream Psychology and the New Biology of Dreaming*. Springfield, Ill., Charles C. Thomas, 1969.

LUCE, GAY GAER, and SEGAL, JULIUS, *Sleep*. New York, Coward-McCann, 1966.

MACKENZIE, NORMAN, *Dreams and Dreaming*. London, Aldus Books, 1965.

OSWALD, IAN, *Sleeping and Waking*. New York, Elsevier Publishing Co., 1962.

——, *Sleep*. Harmondsworth, England, Penguin, 1966.

VAN DE CASTLE, ROBERT L., *The Psychology of Dreaming*. New York, General Learning Corporation, 1971.

VON GRUNEBAUM, G. E., and CAILLOIS, ROGER, *The Dream and Human Societies*. Berkeley, University of California Press. 1966.

Books on the Human Potential Movement and related subjects.

BACH, GEORGE R., and WYDEN, PETER, *The Intimate Enemy: How to Fight Fair in Love and Marriage*. London, Souvenir, 1968, 1969. New York, William Morrow & Co., Inc., 1969.

GUSTAITIS, RASA, *Turning On*. London, Weidenfeld & Nicolson, 1969.

HOWARD, JANE, *Please Touch: A Guided Tour of the Human Potential Movement*. New York, McGraw-Hill Book Co., 1970.

JOURARD, SIDNEY M., *Disclosing Man to Himself*. Princeton, D. Van Nostrand Co., Inc., 1968.

——, *The Transparent Self* (rev. ed.), New York, Van Nostrand Reinhold Co., 1971.

——, *Self-Disclosure: An Experimental Analysis of the Transparent Self*. New York, John Wiley & Sons, Inc., 1971.

LOWEN, ALEXANDER, *The Betrayal of the Body*. New York, Crowell Collier Macmillan, 1967.

——, *Pleasure: A Creative Approach to Life*. New York, Coward-McCann, Inc., 1970.

PERLS, FREDERICK S., *Gestalt Therapy Verbatim*. Lafayette, Calif., Real People Press, 1969.

——, *In and Out of the Garbage Pail*. Lafayette, Calif., Real

People Press, 1969.

——; HEFFERLINE, RALPH F.; and GOODMAN, PAUL, *Gestalt Therapy: Excitement and Growth in the Human Personality.* New York, Julian Press, 1969.

PRATHER, HUGH, *Notes to Myself.* Big Sur, Calif., Real People Press, 1970.

ROGERS, CARL, and STEVENS, BARRY, *Person to Person.* Lafayette, Calif., Real People Press, 1967.

SCHUTZ, WILLIAM C., *Joy: Expanding Human Awareness.* New York, Grove Press Inc., 1967.

——, *Here Comes Everybody: Bodymind Encounter Culture.* New York, Harper & Row, 1971.

STEVENS, BARRY, *Don't Push the River.* Lafayette, Calif., Real People Press, 1970.

WREN-LEWIS, JOHN, *What Shall We Tell the Children?* London, Constable, 1971.

Books of General Interest in the Area of Dreams, Therapy, etc.

ASSAGIOLI, ROBERTO, *Psychosynthesis.* Buenos Aires and New York, Hobbs, Dorman & Co., 1965.

JUNG, C. G., ed., *Man and His Symbols.* London, Aldus Books, 1964.

——, *Memories, Dreams, Reflections.* London, Collins and Routledge & Kegan Paul, 1963. New York, Pantheon Books, 1963.

KOESTLER, ARTHUR, *The Act of Creation.* London, Hutchinson Co., Ltd., 1964. New York, Macmillan, 1964.

MARTIN, P. W., *Experiment in Depth.* London, Routledge & Kegan Paul, 1955. New York, Humanities Press, Inc., 1955.

RAWSON, WYATT, *The Way Within.* London, Vincent Stuart Ltd., 1963.

RYCROFT, CHARLES, ed., *Psychoanalysis Observed.* London, Constable, 1966. New York, Coward-McCann, Inc., 1967.

SHEPARD, MARTIN, and LEE, MARJORIE, *Games Analysts Play.* New York, G. P. Putnam's Sons, 1970.

TART, CHARLES, ed., *Altered States of Consciousness.* New York, John Wiley & Sons, Inc., 1969.

INDEX

316